# PAUL BOCUSE IN YOUR KITCHEN

By the same author:

PAUL BOCUSE'S FRENCH COOKING

# PAUL BOCUSE IN YOUR KITCHEN

AN INTRODUCTION TO
CLASSIC FRENCH COOKING

## PAUL BOCUSE

TRANSLATED, ADAPTED,
AND WITH EDITORS' NOTES BY
PHILIP AND MARY HYMAN

PANTHEON BOOKS
NEW YORK

English translation copyright © 1982 by Random House, Inc.
Copyright © 1982 by Flammarion

All rights reserved under International and Pan-American Copyright
Conventions. Published in the United States by Pantheon Books, a divi-
sion of Random House, Inc., New York, and simultaneously in Canada
by Random House of Canada Limited, Toronto. Originally published in
France as *Bocuse dans votre cuisine* by Flammarion et Cie, Paris.

Library of Congress Cataloging in Publication Data

Bocuse, Paul, 1926–
  Paul Bocuse in your kitchen.

  Translation of: Bocuse dans votre cuisine.
  Includes index.
  1. Cookery, French.   I. Title
TX719.B671613   1982         641.5944         82-48010
ISBN 0-394-52853-0                             AACR2

Manufactured in France

First American Edition

Photographs by J. de Nattes

End-paper illustration of open-air market in Lyons by P. Carron, 1982

*To the women I love…*

# TABLE OF CONTENTS

# INTRODUCTION
## by Paul Bocuse

No truffles, no caviar, no foie gras, no lobster — you won't find any such costly ingredients in the recipes I've written for this book. I've wanted to write a book like this for many years — a book for people who love good food but confess that they've never learned to cook properly.

Good cooking doesn't mean complicated recipes or expensive ingredients. The simpler the food the better, in my opinion. When I'm at home with my family, there's nothing I like better than making leek and potato soup and roasting a chicken for dinner. It's this kind of simple food that is the subject of this new book. I wanted to include recipes that everyone, even the most inexperienced cook, could make. Dishes that are often quickly prepared and inexpensive as well — in other words, that could make up *your* family's meals just as they do mine. I've cooked these recipes, not in my restaurant kitchen, but in my home, using standard household appliances and as few utensils as possible. The recipes are written in a clear, direct manner and are as easy to understand as they are to prepare. I hope this book will "demystify" French cooking and show that there's nothing "magical" about preparing a good meal. Cooking should be enjoyable and relaxing; one of the pleasures of life is a nice meal with friends or family — nothing fancy, just good food.

In my first book, there were many more recipes than there are here (over a thousand in all): classics in the great tradition of French cuisine and specialties from my restaurant. Although a variety of people have enjoyed using it, that book was written with an eye to the experienced cook, whether amateur or professional. This time I've limited myself to about 200 recipes — why ? Because I wanted to include only recipes that were simple and could be made without difficulty any day of the week — everyday cooking at its best. I believe that a small and varied group of recipes is better for learning since it allows the beginner to experiment with different techniques and quickly become acquainted with everything from soups to sauces. The list of recipes could have been much longer, and in the future, in fact, I hope to add to it with more recipes in another book.

I've omitted sample menus from this book since I feel that people should construct dinners in the manner that best suits them, but I have included a description of what we in Lyons call a *"machon"* — only translatable as "brunch" in English — it's a custom I like very much.

A word about dinner parties here is not out of order. Personally, I think the ideal number for dinner parties is seven people. I'd suggest that you try to invite no more than eight or ten people at a time: if you have more than that the food might suffer (unless, of course, you make a one-dish dinner like the French Boiled Dinner).

9

Also, don't use your guests as "guinea pigs" and serve them dishes you've never cooked before. Serve dishes which you feel you've mastered and are familiar with — that way, you and everyone else will be more relaxed and enjoy the meal.

Here, as I did in my first book, I can't emphasize too much how important it is that you use top quality fresh ingredients only. Any dish will always be better if it's made with first-rate products.

Lastly, I've included advice on kitchen equipment and organization so that everything will be made as easy for you as possible. In addition, I've seen to it that this book was well illustrated so you can see exactly how the food is served — and to whet your appetite.

I've done all I can, now it's up to you; if you carefully follow the advice you'll find here, good cooking should no longer be a problem. Enjoy yourself and — *Bonne cuisine.*

# GENERAL ADVICE

## THE KITCHEN AND KITCHEN APPLIANCES

The neater and more organized a kitchen is, the easier cooking becomes. Here are some ideas on how to organize your kitchen.

Serving dishes and plates should be stored in cabinets within arm's reach so that they can be gotten to easily. Glasses and coffee cups can be kept higher up (about eye level) in the same cabinet.

Pots and pans, bakings dishes, etc., should be stored in the bottom of the cabinet, and extra supplies like sugar, flour, or oil in the very top.

Cleaning products can be kept under the sink (some products, which should be kept out of the reach of children, should be kept in a locked cabinet).

The two main appliances are the stove and the refrigerator. They should be kept clean.

Defrost the refrigerator once a month, and clean it thoroughly about every three months (remove all the food and wash the walls with a little warm soapy water, rinse, then wipe dry).

Most stoves have self-cleaning ovens these days; nonetheless, it's a good idea to wipe them clean every once in a while using a sponge and soapy water, then rinse and wipe dry. I personally prefer gas stoves to electric ones, but if you are used to them, electric stoves produce equally good results.

A few smaller appliances can also be very useful, especially a heavy-duty blender or food processor. An electric mixer can also come in handy, although I generally prefer using a wire whisk.

## UTENSILS

I'm not one for accumulating lots of "gadgets." What's important is to have high-quality equipement that you really *use* and not lots of bric-a-brac that simply takes up space. A well equipped kitchen should (ideally) contain the following utensils:

**Saucepans:** 4 in a series, ranging in diameter from about 8 inches (20 cm) down to 5 inches (12 cm), with covers. I suggest buying stainless steel ones with thick "sandwich" bottoms.

**Cast iron pots:** 3 pots, either round or oval, for making stews and pot roasts: large — 6 quarts (6 l) ; medium — 4 quarts (4 l) ; and small — 3 quarts (3 l). Either in black or enamelled cast iron.

**Stock pots:** 2 large pots — 8 to 10 quarts (8 to 10 l). For making boiled dinners and stocks.

**High-sided frying pans:** 2 pans, one very large — 11 inches (28 cm) in diameter, the other smaller — 9 1/2 inches (24 cm) in diameter, preferably with tops. Thick-bottomed stainless steel ones are best.

**Frying pans:** 2 pans, large — 11 inches (28 cm) in diameter; and small — 9 1/2 inches (24 cm) in diameter. I like pans made of iron (they should be wiped clean, rather than washed. Put a little coarse salt into them after cooking, rub with a towel to clean, then lightly oil before storing).

**Baking dishes and roasting pans:** 3 dishes, large — 3 quarts (3 l); medium — 2 quarts (2 l); and small — 1 quart (1 l). If made of enameled cast-iron, they can be used as both baking dishes and roasting pans, but if used only as baking dishes, porcelain is fine.

**Egg dishes:** 4 individual dishes about 5 inches (12 cm) in diameter, made of cast iron or porcelain. For baking eggs in the oven.

**Ramekins and soufflé molds:** 8 small ramekins about 3 inches (8 cm) in diameter, 6 individual soufflé molds about 4 inches (10 cm) in diameter, and a large soufflé mold about 7 inches (18 cm) in diameter, made of porcelain or heat-resistant glass.

**Knives:** 1 large kinfe, 1 bread knife, 1 serrated knife (for cutting citrus fruits), 2 medium-sized all purpose knives. Stainless steel knives are the most practical.

**Miscellaneous utensils:**

2 wire whisks, a small one and a large one.

Several wooden spoons, a slotted spoon, ordinary stainless steel spoons, a set of measuring spoons, and a ladle.

A measuring cup or scale.

A colander, a strainer, and a food mill.

A heat diffuser, made of asbestos or metal, to place between the pan and the heat for slow, even, cooking.

A rotisserie (or spit attachment for your oven), a deep fryer, and an ice cream freezer.

A vegetable peeler, can opener, cork screw, and rolling pin.

3 pie pans, 8 inches (20 cm), 9 1/2 inches (24 cm), and 10 inches (26 cm) in diameter.

A pound cake mold, 9 1/2 inches (24 cm) long.


## PROVISIONS AND SHOPPING

Your kitchen cabinets should not be packed with foods bought long in advance; nevertheless there are a certain number of things that store well and should always be on hand: sugar (granulated and confectioner's), flour, oil, vinegar, Dijon mustard, rice, beans, lentils, baking powder, pasta, salt (coarse and fine), jams, chocolate (semi-sweet), peppercorns, nutmeg, vanilla beans, cloves, cinnamon, thyme, and bay leaves.

Try to buy fresh foods only as you need them; too much of even a good thing can lead to monotony, so buy small amounts and vary the meals you prepare.

You should always have butter, heavy cream, milk, and eggs on hand in the refrigerator.

Before you go shopping, check whatever foods you have leftover so that they won't be wasted (leftover meat can be used for stuffings, vegetables for making salads, etc.).

Spring Vegetables.

This brings me to the *mâchon* or *petit mâchon,* a typically Lyonnaise tradition. It's a sort of brunch, served buffet-style, usually on weekends and holidays. Anything and everything can be served at a *mâchon* — including leftovers. This is the perfect place for the Rabbit Pâté (p. 190), Family-Style Braised Beef (p. 206) served cold, the Mixed Raw Vegetable Platter (p. 58), or any number of the salads in this book.

Simple egg or sausage dishes can also be "made to order" on the spot, and there is always a large selection of breads (and plenty of butter), hot and cold drinks, cheese, honeys, jams, and cookies.

## WEIGHTS AND MEASURES

Measurements are given in both the American and French (metric) systems. The metric system is easier and more exact, but since few cooks have scales in the U.S., cup and tablespoon measurements are always given.

Some general rules on measuring, for American cooks, might be appropriate here:

Never sift flour into the measuring cup unless expressly advised to do so; measure it directly from the package or canister. If it must be sifted, sift after measuring.

Never pack ingredients into a cup unless advised to do so.

Teaspoon and tablespoon measurements should *always* be level, unless accompanied by the word "scant" or "generous." "Scant" means that the spoon is almost full, but not quite. "Generous" means that the ingredient forms a gentle mound above the edge of the spoon rather than being level with it.

When applied to cup measurements, "scant" means that the ingredient comes almost up to the line indicating the measurement, but not quite — it should never be more than I fluid ounce (1/8 cup) below the line. "Generous" means that the ingredient should rise slightly above the line indicating the measurement, but never more than I fluid ounce (1/8 cup) above it.

For convenience, butter measurements are given in one of two forms: either tablespoons, for small quantities, or "sticks," for large quantities. Since not all butter is packaged in "sticks," you may find the following information useful : 1 stick = 1/4 pound = 8 tablespoons.

# INGREDIENTS

A Word to American Cooks
by Philip and Mary Hyman

The following is a list of ingredients that occur frequently in the course of these recipes. *Read this section carefully before attempting to make any of the recipes.* A short Dictionary of Cooking Terms and Procedures is also included at the end of the book — consult it whenever you encounter a word, expression, or procedure that is not explained here.

*BOUQUET GARNI:* This aromatic bunch of herbs is made at the last minute, and in France simply consists of tying together a sprig of thyme, a bit of bay leaf, and some parsley (sometimes celery and leek are included in the *bouquet*). The *bouquet garni* is always removed before serving the dish it cooked with. It is never large — often no more than a thumb-sized bundle of herbs — but it subtly flavors liquids in which it cooks. If fresh sprigs of thyme are unavailable, you can make a *bouquet* by placing thyme leaves and a bay leaf inside a little square of muslin or doubled-over cheesecloth, tying it closed, and tying this to the parsley, leek, or celery. It is by far preferable to use this type of *bouquet,* than to simply use a pinch of powdered thyme or bay leaf in the recipes given here.

BUTTER: *Use only unsalted butter in these recipes.* Butter should always be of the highest quality, and no substitutes (such as margarine) should be used if you want an authentic version of these dishes.
Butter is often said to be "softened." This means that it has been left at room temperature for about an hour or until it can easily be broken into soft pieces with your fingers. It's extremely important that butter be sufficiently soft whenever sauces or doughs are being made.

*CREME FRAICHE: Crème fraîche* is a very thick, rich cream. In most cases — and this is indicated in the recipes concerned — heavy cream can be used instead, but even when the choice is given, try to use *crème fraîche* if possible. It is now commercialized on a small scale in the U.S., but you can make an excellent version of it at home using cream and buttermilk. It is important to use cream simply labled "Pasteurized," not "Ultra-pasteurized" : ultra-pasteurized cream gives a very unpleasant metallic taste to the *crème fraîche.*

Mix 1 cup (25 cl) pasteurized heavy (whipping) cream with 2 table-spoons of active culture buttermilk in a saucepan. Heat just until luke-warm to the touch, cover, and allow to stand at a warm room temperature for about 8 hours. A thick layer should have formed on the surface of the cream at the end of this time (it will still be liquid underneath). Stir to make the cream the same consistency throughout, then pour it into a glass jar, cover, and place in the refrigerator overnight before using. The *crème fraîche* will become thick when chilled. It keeps for about 1 week in the refrigerator before turning into (natural) sour cream.

EGGS: Unless otherwise specified, always use 1 3/4 ounce (50 g) eggs — 21 ounces (596 g) per dozen. These are labled Medium on the package. If using much smaller or much larger eggs, compensate by using more or fewer eggs than are called for, as the case might be.

This general rule, by the way, does not apply to the recipes in the chapter on eggs in this book, where you can use any size egg you want.

FLOUR: All purpose flour can be used throughout the book. Do not sift the flour when measuring or when using unless expressly advised to do so.

HERBS: Various fresh herbs, such as tarragon, chervil, and parsley, are frequently called for in these recipes. Whenever possible, try to use the herb in question; otherwise, substitute more available fresh herbs rather than using dried ones or none at all! For instance, fresh chives or parsley, or a little mint or basil, could be used in many recipes that call for chervil...

LEEKS: Leeks are generally sold with their roots intact. To clean them, cut off the roots, then split the leek lengthwise, starting about a third of the way in from the beginning of the white part and drawing the tip of the knife through to the end of the leaves. Wash the leeks carefully under running water, separating the leaves with your fingers to remove any dirt.

OIL: There are basically two kinds of oil; those that support high heat and can be used for frying, and those that cannot. The first type is generally referred to as cooking oil, the second as salad oil. *Choose your oils carefully*. Tasteless oils are preferable for cooking, as well as for some salads; peanut oil and sunflower oil can be used for both, as can corn oil.

Specific oils, especially olive oil, are sometimes called for. Use only the best, cold pressed olive oil — the results are appreciably better than with less expensive oils.

ONIONS: Baby onions are often called for. These are small onions, fresh or dried, that are approximately 1 inch (2.5 cm) in diameter. Generally, onions up to 2 inches (5 cm) in diameter can be used; if only larger onions are available, they can simply be halved or quartered and used instead. Only the appearance will suffer; since the cut onions will not stay together, the dish will look less ''pretty'' than it would with small whole onions.

PEPPER: Use a peppermill and grind your pepper directly onto foods and into sauces. The taste is much better than that of commercially ground pepper. Freshly ground pepper should be understood whenever pepper is called for in these recipes.

WINE: Sometimes specific red or white wines are suggested for cooking. These suggestions are always optional, but if they are followed, the wine in question should be French (i.e., a French burgundy rather than a California one). Otherwise, when cooking, use only a wine that you would consider good enough to drink; it need not be expensive or special, but it should at least be palatable.

# FRENCH WINES:
# HOW TO CHOOSE AND SERVE THEM

## by Georges Dubœuf

## SERVING WINE

Wine and food are inseparable in France. Good food and good wine should be complementary; they should never work against each other.

Wine should be given the same attention as the food at any meal: a well prepared dish deserves a wine that will do it justice.

### In What Order are Wines Served ?

Here are some general rules:
• White wine is served before red. Light wines are served before fuller wines. Chilled wines are served before those that aren't. Dry wines (red or white) are served before sweet wines.
• At a dinner, wines are served in the following order: white Burgundy or white Bordeaux before red bordeaux; red Bordeaux before red Burgundy; red Burgundy before sweet white Bordeaux. In my opinion, champagne is best served as an apéritif before dinner. These are not fixed and invariable rules; I could well imagine serving a light red Burgundy before a powerful Bordeaux from a good year. What's important is to serve young wines before old wines.

### What Not to Serve Wine with

Certain dishes simply don't go well with wine. In those instances, it is best to serve water.
• Red wine should never be served with salads made with an oil and vinegar dressing, or anything else seasoned with vinegar; pickles, artichokes, asparagus, shellfish, cream cheese, sweets, and sweet dishes.
• White wine should never be served with salads made with oil and vinegar dressings, or anything else seasoned with vinegar; pickles, vegetables in cream sauces, extra-rich cream cheeses, roast beef.
• I would advise against serving wine with certain desserts (with which few wines are compatible). They are: ice creams, sherbets, fruit salads, and chocolate mousse.

### White Wine

• Oysters, lobsters, shellfish, hot or cold fish (except those cooked with red wine), vol-au-vent, sweetbreads, roast chicken, boiled hen with rice, baby lamb, ham, galantine, goat cheeses, and low-fat cheeses should be accompanied by white wine.

17

● With oysters and shellfish in general, I recommend serving white wines from the following areas: Mâcon, Chablis, Jurançon, Bordeaux (dry white), Alsace (Riesling or Sylvaner), Touraine (dry white), Muscadet, Sancerre, and Burgundy.

● With shellfish such as crabs, shrimp, etc., I recommend white wines from Sancerre, Pouilly-Fumé, Pouilly-Fuissé, Saumur, Touraine, Chablis, Meursault, Chassagne Montrachet, Mâcon, Graves, Entre-deux-mers, Condrieux, Alsace, Muscadet, and Savoie.

● With broiled lobster, specifically, I would serve the finest whites from Graves or Corton Charlemagne, Puligny-Montrachet, or Château Grillet.

● Snails, frogs' legs and other garlic-flavored dishes should be served with a dry white wine or a rosé.

● Broiled fish can be served with any dry white wine or a rosé from Provence or the Côtes-du-Rhône (e.g., Tavel).

● Smoked fish needs a distinctive wine, one made with the Sauvignon grape or one from Alsace, for example.

● Fish soups, especially bouillabaisse, should be served with a white wine from Provence or Corsica : Cassis, Bandol, or Bellet.

● Foie gras, served at the beginning of a meal, should be accompagnied by the great white wines such as the Montrachets, Meursaults, Rieslings, Gewürztztraminers, or, of course, a chilled Sauterne.

● "Rillettes" from Tours should be served with wines from the region, such as a Sancerre or a Pouilly-Fumé.

● Sauerkraut calls for a wine from Alsace.

● With dessert or fruit, you could serve champagne or a sparkling Vouvray, or else one of the sweet port-like wines from the south, such as Frontignan, Beaumes de Venise, Banyuls, etc. Sauterne and Barsac go well with pastries, dessert creams, sweet fruits, flambéed crêpes, and tarts.

● Sweet wines from Anjou are best with strawberries or raspberries and cream.

## Red Wines

● Lambchops, mutton, beef, poultry, game, starchy vegetables, game pâtés, and cheeses should be accompanied by red wine.

● Sausages and pâtés are always good with young wines from the Beaujolais, Côtes-du-Rhône, Provence, or Loire. With sausages from Lyons, we always drink Beaujolais, of course.

● Boiled pork *(potée),* fricassees, and blanquettes call for light, fruity wines from the Beaujolais, Bourgeuil, or Bordeaux.

● Stews need richer and fuller wines.

● Game, fresh or only slightly aged, demand red wines with lots of character, such as a good Médoc, Pauillac, Pomerol, Côte-Rôtie, Hermitage, Mercurey, Juliénas, or Morgon.

● With venison, which has a very distinctive taste, serve rich, full flavored wines from Burgundy's Côte-de-Nuits, such as Chambertin, Nuits-Saint-Georges, Musigny, or Richebourg.

## Wine and Cheese

In France, cheeses are always served at the end of the meal, just before dessert. This is unquestionably the time to serve a red wine if you really want it to be at its best; but remember, wines have their "favorite" cheeses, and not all wines go well with all cheeses. Here are some suggestions:

● Serve dry white wines or rich red wines with hard cheeses such as gruyère.
● Serve light wines, fruity and dry, either red or rosé, with cheeses like Port-Salut, Tomme, Saint-Nectaire, or Cantal. Light red wines go with the blue cheeses from the Causses or Auvergne.
● Red wines with more body are called for with soft cheeses like Brie, Camembert, and Carrés de l'Est.
● Fresh, unripened cheeses should be served with white wines or rosés.
● Virtually any dry, light wine — either white or red — goes with process cheeses and cheese spreads.
● Serve dry, light, fruity wines and the less well know regional wines with goat cheeses.
● Only a great red wine from a good year, or a sweet white Sauterne or Monbazillac can match the taste of Roquefort.

## Everyday Wines

Finding wines that aren't too expensive to serve as everyday or table wine is always a problem. What should you look for ? It shouldn't be too alcholic, and it should be light, fruity, and easy to drink, without too much tannin. Certain little-known French table wines are excellent value, such as Rhône Valley wines, Côteaux-du-Tricastin, Côtes-du-Ventoux, red wines from Provence or the Minervois, Corbières, the Côteaux-du-Lyonnais, the Côteaux-du-Roannais, or the Côteaux-du-Forest. Some Bordeaux Supérieurs can be drunk young as table wines, as can wines made with the Gamay grape in the Touraine or the Savoie.

## Wine Glasses

The wine you serve and the glass it's served in should be perfectly suited to each other. The glass should be clear to show off the limpidity of the wine. An incident that occurred several years ago is worth relating here apropos of wine and glasses.

I was invited to dinner by some friends; knowing my interest in wines, they had decided to serve a Musigny from an excellent year. They told me before dinner what the wine would be, so it was with great expectations that I went into dining room. There, on the table, I was shocked to see large blue-tinted glasses next to every plate. At the end of the table was the Burgundy in its basket, waiting to be sacrificed. And sacrificed it was. Not a hint of its color was visible through the dark blue crystal of my glass. I took a sip and searched in vain for the dimension the glass hid from me, but tasting could not restore what my eyes couldn't see. The glasses were beautiful in themselves — but what a pity to serve a great wine in them.

You, as a drinker of wine, are the last in a long chain that stretches from the vineyard to your table. Your responsibilities are multiple, and one of them should include serving wine under optimal conditions. The glasses you use are of great importance; they should be suited to the wine you are serving, and they should be perfectly transparent and colorless, so that the beautiful color of a good wine can be appreciated. Any wine drinker who is serious about wine appreciates the way a wine looks and smells as much as how it tastes.

A good wine glass should be sufficiently large, light, well balanced, and plain (not decorated in any way), and the stem of the glass should be plain; any ornamentation is superfluous. The shape of the glass should be appropriate to the wine you serve as well.

- Red wine from Burgundy calls for a big, wide glass, since contact with the air is essential to the development of its bouquet.
- Red Bordeaux are more delicate, fine, and racy; they need less contact with the air, and therefore a narrower glass.
- Never serve Champagne in the wide, shallow glasses that are often used for it — its aroma and elegance can be appreciated only in the tall, narrow "flute" made for it.
- Long-stemmed Alsatian wine glasses should be made of clear glass, even if the stem is colored.
- Anjou wines have their own glass, made with an almost flat base which gives the glass a squarish appearance.

Whatever glass you use, it must have a stem about 2 to 2 1/4 inches (5 to 6 cm) long so that your hand won't touch the bowl of the glass and warm the wine in it, and ideally, the rim should be slightly narrower than the base of the bowl. Fill the glass only halfway when pouring wine, then tip the glass and look at the wine's color. To bring out the bouquet, or aroma, of the wine, gently swirl it in the glass, then smell it for the first time.

## Temperatures for Serving Wine

Before addressing the question of the temperature, here is some general advice about serving wine.

- Wine must always be allowed to rest before being served, so don't buy it at the last minute.
- If you've been on a wine-buying trip to the vineyards, don't open the bottles when you get back, or even the next day. Let the wine rest at least 8 to 10 days if it has been traveling. This is especially important with regard to wines 5 or 10 years old or more, if you want to serve them at their best.

Now to the important question of serving temperatures.

- Beware of people who generalize about temperatures.
- Every wine is unique; it differs from others of the same kind by its maturity and whether it was made in a good or bad year.
- In general, wines should be served cool, rather than warm; the rule of serving wine at room temperature cannot be applied to all wines. Whenever wine is said to be served *chambré,* this means it is served at room tem-

perature. Leaving it for several hours in your dining room will generally mean serving it at 64° to 72°F (18° to 22°C). This is a good temperature for young red wines in general, but light, young red wines from Beaujolais or Bourgueil should be served cool, though not chilled — at about 50° to 54°F (10° to 12°C) — as should light, fruity everyday wines. Better burgundies and Bordeaux should be served at room temperature, as should any red wine, for that matter, 5 years or older.

● White wines need to be chilled, but they should not be too cold. The ideal temperature for serving them is 50°F (10°C). In the summer, without air conditioning, a red wine taken from a cool cellar can be drunk right away, the room temperature having already "warmed" the wine glass. The coolness of the wine in such circumstances is often pleasant. In warm weather, it is best to bring bottles up from the cellar as they are needed, since bottles left in a really warm room too long are not as good as those which are still slightly cool. Whatever you do, don't ever try to speed the process of bringing a wine to room temperature (if you are serving it that way) by heating it, either in hot water or by any other means. Heated wine is not *chambré*.

● Remember, it is better to serve wine cool rather than warm. If need be, you can always slightly warm any wine by simply holding the bowl of the glass in your hand and swirling gently. If, on the contrary, you want to cool wine, simply use an ice bucket; it's the simplest and best way to do it.

● If you refrigerate wine to cool it, leave it for at least an hour or two in the refrigerator before serving, but never leave wines for long periods of time in the refrigerator — overnight, for example — since the cold will damage the taste.

**Uncorking and Decanting Wine**

Taking the cork out of a bottle of wine seems like a very simple operation, but in fact, it can be a delicate one. Don't ever shake the wine before removing the cork; old wines in particular should be handled gently.

The first thing to do is to cut off the seal that covers the cork, just above the little rim on the neck of the bottle. Use a corkscrew that is long enough to go almost through the cork so that you won't tear and break the cork when pulling it out. The corkscrew should not have a tight spiral but rather a wide, open one so as not to bore a big central hole in the cork and damage it.

Young red wines and white wines can be uncorked just before being served. Older reds, and Bordeaux in particular, should be opened at least 30 minutes before being served.

Not all wines need to be decanted. It is rarely done for white wines or for Burgundies. Old red Bordeaux that are going to be decanted should be stood upright for several hours or overnight so that the impurities in the wine will fall to the bottom of the bottle. Decanting is primarily used for such older wines in order to remove this natural deposit (the deposit itself is often a sign of quality in a Bordeaux). To decant the wine, remove the cork, then tip the decanter and the bottle toward each other and gently pour the wine into the decanter. Be careful not to pour any of the deposit into the decanter. Remember that wine should be drunk relatively soon after being decanted. The same holds true for a bottle that has been opened; the wine in it won't keep for a very long time.


## THE WINE CELLAR

I would now like to discuss both the buying and the storing of wine.

### In General

Even someone with a well-stocked cellar is often perplexed as to what wines to serve with an elaborate dinner. You won't always have, even in the best of circumstances, what might be the "ideal" wine. Sometimes, however, you might lack the wine you need because you had not given sufficient thought to the stocking of your cellar: wines bought by impulse rather than because you really wanted them or knew what they were are the kind of purchase you will later regret. Everyone needs advice when purchasing wines for the first time, so try to find a dealer you can place your confidence in.

Wherever you are, beware of "bargains" or "special offers." Look for the names of reputable wine growers and shippers — this is your best guarantee when it comes to purchasing wines. Various "brands" such as the large houses in Champagne, can be depended upon for quality wines.

Ideally, you should buy your wine from the person that produces it; otherwise, purchase it from shippers and dealers who have direct contact with the producers. You can discuss the wine with them and often taste it before buying.

Try to gather as much information about wines that interest you as you can. Take note of the wines that you like when you are in restaurants or with friends. Stop and taste wine whenever you are in a wine growing region. Ask the advice of friends.

Wine magazines often include much useful information and the addresses of good producers or shops you may not be aware of otherwise. Soon enough, you will find that there are a lot of interesting wines to choose from.

### Bottling

When buying inexpensive wine, always have it bottled for you rather than purchasing it in cubitainers and bottling it yourself. This may be a tempting proposition, but often the wine you bottle yourself isn't as good as expected because it wasn't handled properly when bottled. In my opinion, the days of home-bottling are past.

A good wine bottler is hard to find; the profession demands cleanliness, method, and precision of those who practice it. Wine has to be handled with respect when it is being bottled; it is a noble, capricious, and delicate liquid.

22

It has been said of bottling: "Bottling can make a great wine speak or render it dumb forever". Too often, this operation is carelessly performed; wine must be bottled at the proper moment under the proper circumstances. Wine is bottled properly only if you have followed its evolution from the day it was first made, tasted it often, and waited until it was "ripe" for bottling. Wine that is bottled too young is too tannic, strong, and violent. Bottled too late, wine oxidizes, fades, and withers.


## Stocking Your Cellar

The ideal cellar should include a selection of different wines, each with a distinctive character representive of the region from which it comes. Here's how I would stock a small cellar, large enough nonetheless to include the full range of French wines, and capable of supplying different wines for a variety of different occasions, and for different types of food.

To begin with, I would buy a dozen bottles of rosé, either from Tavel (fruity, elegant, and rich), from Provence (lighter, easy to drink), from the Rhône Valley (thicker and warmer), or lastly from Bordeaux.

I would buy wines from the Beaujolais, young new wines that are fruity, light, and pleasant.

I would also buy one of the better "crus" from the Beaujolais, such as Chiroubles or Fleurie — wines with more character, feminine and elegant — as well as a Morgon, Juliénas, or Moulin-à-Vent at least two or three years old (more if possible in better years).

I would, of course, buy Burgundies, but here, selecting them becomes more difficult, since there are so many, and so many good ones. I think you should have wines form the Côte-de-Nuits and the Côte-de-Beaune (in particular Pommard, red Chassagne, and Volnay).

From the Côte-de-Nuits, I would buy Vosne-Romanée, Clos de Vougeot, Chambertin, or Chambolle-Musigny from a good year and two to ten years old.

Among the white Burgundies, I think it would be preferable to own some Chablis, Meursault or Puligny, and Pouilly-Fuissé from a good year.

Bordeaux would not be omitted from my cellar; I would start by buying two dozen relatively inexpensive bottles from a reputable shipper or from a grower in Saint-Emilion or Saint-Estèphe. I would have some very good bottles of great Bordeaux from one of the châteaux: Beyschevelle, Cheval Blanc, Canon, Cos d'Estournel, Laffite, Lascombes, Mouton-Rothschild, Prieuré-Lichine, etc. It's important as well to have some good sweet white wines from Barsac, Sauternes, or Monbazillac, which can go for anything from ten dollars to ten times that for a Château d'Yquem.

I wouldn't forget to buy good wines from Alsace, white wines that are generally drunk young (between two and five years old). I would buy them from reputable shippers in the region or directly from one of the many "cooperatives".

Some Loire Valley wine would be included; among the whites it could be anything from a light fruity Muscadet to a Vouvray. Red Loire Valley wines would also find their place in my cellar. I would suggest a Chinon, which can be drunk between two and ten years old — sometimes older — or a Bourgueil, younger and fruitier.

From the Rhône Valley, I would buy some young (one to two years old) Côtes-du-Rhône reds. Wines from the Rhône that have more character and can be kept from two to ten years, depending on the vintage in question, would be bought from Gigondas or Châteauneuf-du-Pape. A selection of the excellent wines from the northern Rhône valley would not be overlooked: Côte-Rôtie, Hermitage, and Cornas, for example.

Any good cellar should also include a good table wine, which can some from almost anywhere so long as the wine is well made and bought only in good years (a poor year means that the wine will be acid, undeveloped, and often unpleasant, whereas in a good year, the same wine could be fruity and delicious).

Lastly, a good cellar should contain some champagne bought from one of the many good houses there.

## The Wine Cellar

You should be very careful about where you store your wine. Several things should always be kept in mind:
- Wine should be stored in a dark place (light of any kind is bad for it). The cellar should be well ventilated, neither too dry, nor too humid, and be at a temperature varying roughly between 54° and 61°F (12° and 16°C). Ideally, a cellar should be underground and facing north. It should be far from any source of vibration that would prevent the impurities from settling out of the wines as they age.
- A dirt floor, covered with gravel, is preferable to a concrete floor.
- A cellar should be clean, well organized, and aired: too much moisture can affect the corks and, of course, mold will grow on the labels and eventually make them come off. Fruit and vegetables, or any product having a strong odor, should not be kept in a wine cellar.
- If you can't have a real cellar, wine can often be kept in a closet somewhere in the house. So long as the storage place is dark and has a relatively constant temperature (within the limits cited above), you can use it for storing wine. Some companies now make large closet-like units designed specially for storing wine in houses and apartments. These storage units are quite good and keep wine in excellent conditions.
- Wherever the wine is stored, it must be lying down, never standing upright, since it is important for the cork to always be in contact with the wine. Wooden or metal wine racks are perfect for storing wine. Alcohol, like cognac, however, should be stood upright, so a shelf or two should be left for them in the cellar.
- A well-organized cellar should contain a thermometer so that you can monitor the temperature. Wines from the same region should be grouped together, and they should all be clearly labeled. A cellar book, in which you note purchases and observations, should also be kept. It should contain the name of each wine, the year it was made, the amount purchased, the date, the place, and the price. Room should be left on the page so that

on tasting each wine, comments can be added about its evolution, its virtues, and its flaws.

A cellar as I have described it, should contain represenative bottles from all the winegrowing regions of France. It is a collection, like a library, in which personal tastes are reflected, and in which, inevitably, favorites are found. For the owner, each "volume" has its own story to tell.


## The Wine Label

A wine label is the wine's calling card. It is its birth certificate. It tells you where the wine was made, when, by whom, and its shipper, bottler, etc.


## Talking About Wine

I thought it would be useful to include a few words about the vocabulary used to describe wine. This section will deal only briefly with this subject, since it is vast and complex.

A specialized vocabulary is employed by those attempting to describe the taste of wine. As with descriptions of music or painting, these terms are often full of nuances and extremely varied, since the sensations being described are so hard to translate into words.

The first thing one mentions about a wine is its general makeup, its body, its finesse. What I call general makeup here is the result of numerous factors, the most important of which is the quality of the year or vintage in which the wine was made. What follows is a list of terms referring to the qualities a wine can have. Each of these "positive" terms is followed by its "negative" counterpart, that is, the expression used to describe the wine when this quality is absent.

In general, wines can be:
    firm or flat
    clean or rough
    hard or supple
    complete or unresolved
    vigorous or old
    fruity or séché
    noble or dumb
    elegant or stiff
    fine or common
    light or heavy
    full or thin
Wines can look :
    brilliant or cloudy
    purple or tawny
    blackish or brown
    sumptuous or light
    intense or unenticing

Wines can smell :
   lively or sulphury
   fruity or bland
   delicious or passed
   aromatic or faded
The taste of the wine is said to be :
   sweet or dry
   fat or lean
   soft or hard
   big or stiff
   open or closed
   rich or rude
   supple or thin

This list is by no means exhaustive; every wine will solicit a specific reaction on the part of the taster and call up images and words to describe them. All wine lovers eventually develop a vocabulary to describe the sensations perceived.

## CONCLUSION

I have tried here to give you some basic notions about French wines. I could have added chapters about wine-making methods and grape varieties for every region of France, with lists of the specific appelations, but this, I thought, was not the place for such an undertaking. I wanted to limit myself to basic information which would help the reader choose French wines to go with these recipes by Paul Bocuse.

In closing, I would like to remind you to remember all the care that went into making a good wine when you are serving it. A fine dinner depends not only on the cooking, but on the wine you choose to serve with it.

# CHAPTER 1

# SOUPS

It's always nice to have a bowl of hot soup on a cold or rainy day. Here are a few classics.

PUMPKIN SOUP *(Soupe de courge)*

HOME-STYLE VEGETABLE SOUP *(Soupe bonne femme)*

WATERCRESS AND POTATO SOUP *(Soupe cresson-pommes de terre)*

SALT PORK AND CABBAGE SOUP *(Soupe au lard et au chou)*

HERB SOUP *(Soupe aux herbes)*

COUNTRY-STYLE VEGETABLE SOUP *(Soupe paysanne)*

ONION SOUP *(Soupe à l'oignon)*

TAPIOCA SOUP *(Soupe au tapioca)*

COLD CUCUMBER SOUP *(Potage au concombre)*

LEEK AND POTATO SOUP *(Soupe poireaux-pommes de terre)*

POLISH-STYLE SOUP *(Potage polonais)*

CREAM OF ASPARAGUS SOUP *(Velouté d'asperges)*

CREAM OF OYSTER SOUP *(Velouté aux huîtres)*

MINESTRONE

GAZPACHO

# PUMPKIN SOUP
*Soupe de courge*

PREPARATION TIME : 35 minutes

INGREDIENTS FOR 4 SERVINGS :
1 1/2 pound (700 g) pumpkin, peeled, seeded, and cut into cubes
2 medium potatoes, peeled and diced
6 1/3 cups (1 1/2 liter) cold water
1 1/2 teaspoons (10 g) coarse salt
4 tablespoons (60 g) butter
2 medium leeks, cleaned and sliced
Salt, pepper
Butter (for the croutons)
12 slices French bread, or 4 slices ordinary bread cut into quarters
6 tablespoons (10 cl) *crème fraîche* or heavy cream
Nutmeg

Place the pumpkin and potatoes in a large saucepan with the water and salt, and bring to a boil. Meanwhile, melt the butter in a frying pan, add the leeks and cook slowly until they have melted down, then add them to the saucepan. Boil the soup over moderate heat, uncovered, for 20 minutes, then puree it in a blender, food processor, or by using a food mill. The result should be creamy ; add salt and pepper and cook for 5 minutes more over low heat.
Brown the slices of bread in some butter to make croutons, place them on a plate and cover with a clean dish towel to keep them warm.
Pour the cream into a warm soup tureen and stir in the soup little by little.
Add a little nutmeg and serve, with the croutons on the side.

Pumpkin Soup.

# HOME-STYLE VEGETABLE SOUP
*Soupe bonne femme*

PREPARATION TIME : 45 minutes

INGREDIENTS FOR 4 SERVINGS :
6 1/3 cups (1 1/2 liter) water
1 1/2 teaspoons (10 g) coarse salt
5 tablespoons (75 g) butter
1 large onion, peeled, halved, and sliced
1 large or 2 small leeks, cleaned and sliced
About 1/2 pound (250 g) young green cabbage, sliced
2 medium potatoes, peeled and diced
2 cups tightly packed (100 g) sorrel leaves, chopped
Nutmeg
Salt, pepper
2 tablespoons butter (to finish)

Bring the water and coarse salt to a boil in a large saucepan. In another large saucepan, melt the butter ; when it is sizzling hot, add the onions and leeks. Lightly brown the vegetables over moderate heat, then add the cabbage and stir until it has melted down. Pour the boiling water into the pot with the vegetables, add the potatoes, and simmer uncovered for 30 minutes, then add the sorrel and cook for 5 minutes more.
Warm the soup tureen by pouring a little boiling water into it, swirling it around and pouring it out.
Taste the soup, add a little nutmeg, salt, and pepper ; then pour it into the tureen. Stir 2 tablespoons of butter into it and serve.

# WATERCRESS AND POTATO SOUP
*Soupe cresson-pommes de terre*

PREPARATION TIME : 50 minutes

INGREDIENTS FOR 4 SERVINGS :
6 1/3 cups (1 1/2 liter) water
1 1/2 teaspoons (10 g) coarse salt
1 pound (500 g) potatoes, peeled and quartered
1 1/2 cups tightly packed (75 g) watercress leaves (stems removed)
6 tablespoons (10 cl) *crème fraîche* or heavy cream
Salt, pepper

Bring the water and salt to a boil in a large saucepan ; add the potatoes and boil uncovered for 25 minutes. Lift the potatoes out of the water with a slotted spoon and mash or puree them by hand or in a food processor or food mill. Put them back into the water, stir, then add the watercress and boil gently for 10 minutes more. Add the cream, lower the heat, and simmer (do not boil) stirring frequently 5 minutes longer. Add salt and pepper as needed, then pour the soup into a soup tureen and serve.

# SALT PORK AND CABBAGE SOUP
*Soupe au lard et au chou*

PREPARATION TIME : 2 hours (plus 24 hours to desalt the pork)

INGREDIENTS FOR 4 SERVINGS :
1 1/2 pounds (700 g) salt pork
8 1/2 cups (2 liters) water
About 1 pound (500 g) young green cabbage
4 carrots, peeled and cut into julienne strips
2 turnips, peeled and cut into julienne strips
1/2 small celeriac, peeled and cut into julienne strips
4 small onions, peeled and sliced
2 leeks, cleaned and quartered
Pepper
1/2 of an 8-ounce (250 g) loaf of French bread, cut in half lengthwise

Although this is called a soup it is actually a whole meal.

Place the salt pork in a large bowl, cover well with cold water, and leave for 24 hours, changing the water at least 3 times before cooking.

Place the salt pork in a large saucepan, add the water and bring to a boil. Lower the heat and simmer covered for 1 hour. Add the vegetables and a little pepper and cook for 40 minutes more.

Toast the bread under the broiler, then cut it into thick slices ; keep warm in a bowl covered with a clean cloth.

When done, lift out the salt pork and place it on a platter. Pour the soup into a soup tureen and serve everything at once, with the toasted bread and some Dijon mustard on the side.

If there is any pork left over, serve it cold the next day with a salad and some Black Olives (p. 52).

Salt Pork and Cabbage Soup.

# HERB SOUP
## *Soupe aux herbes*

PREPARATION TIME : 35 minutes

INGREDIENTS FOR 4 SERVINGS :
6 1/3 cups (1 1/2 liter) water
1 1/2 teaspoons (10 g) coarse salt
3 tablespoons (40 g) butter
2 small onions, peeled and sliced
About 1/2 pound (250 g) young green cabbage, finely sliced
10 lettuce leaves, finely sliced
20 radish greens, finely sliced
20 sprigs of celery leaves, finely sliced
15 sorrel leaves, finely sliced
2 tablespoons chopped chervil
10 young nettle tips, chopped (optional see *Note*)
Pepper
Nutmeg
2 egg yolks
6 tablespoons *crème fraîche* or heavy cream
2 tablespoons (30 g) butter

Bring the water and salt to a boil in a large saucepan.
In another large saucepan, melt 3 tablespoons (40 g) of butter, add the onions and cook until they begin to color. Add all the other vegetables except the sorrel, chervil, and nettle tips if using. Stir and cook until the vegetables have softened, then add the boiling water, the sorrel, chervil, and nettle tips and cook at a gentle boil for 20 minutes, uncovered.
Add a little pepper and nutmeg, and salt if needed.
Place the egg yolks and cream in a mixing bowl and beat with a whisk to combine. Remove the soup from the heat and whisk 2 ladlefuls into the egg-cream mixture ; then pour back into the saucepan, stirring constantly with a wooden spoon. Stir in 2 tablespoons (30 g) fresh butter, pour the mixture into a warm soup tureen, and serve.

*Note : The young shoots of nettles in the spring (or the tender tips of older nettles) are excellent in soup. Gather them yourself, but wear gloves to pick them. Ed.*

# COUNTRY-STYLE VEGETABLE SOUP
*Soupe paysanne*

PREPARATION TIME : 40 minutes

INGREDIENTS FOR 4 TO 5 SERVINGS :
6 1/3 cups (1 1/2 liter) water
2 teaspoons (15 g) coarse salt
3 tablespoons (40 g) butter
1 onion, peeled and sliced
2 leeks, cleaned and cut into julienne strips
4 carrots, peeled and cut into julienne strips
2 small turnips, peeled and cut into julienne strips
2 stalks celery, sliced
About 1/2 pound (250 g) young green cabbage, sliced
1/4 of an 8-ounce (250 g) loaf of French bread, cut in half lengthwise
2 tablespoons chopped chervil
2 tablespoons (30 g) butter
2 cups (100 g) freshly grated Swiss cheese

Bring the water and salt to a boil in a large saucepan.
In another large saucepan, melt 3 tablespoons (40 g) of butter ; when sizzling hot, add the onions and leeks, lower the heat, and cook to soften but not color. Add the carrots, turnips, celery, and cabbage and cook, stirring frequently, until all the vegetables have softened ; then pour the boiling salted water into the pot and cook covered over low heat for 30 minutes. Toast the bread under the broiler and cut it into thick slices ; then place it in a warm soup tureen, sprinkle with the chervil, and pour in the soup. Stir 2 tablespoons (30 g) of fresh butter into the soup, salt and pepper to taste, and serve with a bowl of freshly grated Swiss cheese on the side.

# ONION SOUP
*Soupe à l'oignon*

PREPARATION TIME : 1 hour
INGREDIENTS FOR 4 SERVINGS :
2 tablespoons (30 g) butter
4 medium onions, peeled and sliced
2 tablespoons (20 g) flour
6 1/3 cups (1 1/2 liter) beef bouillon (see French Boiled Dinner, p. 198)
   or water
1/2 an 8-ounce (250 g) loaf of French bread, cut in half lengthwise
2 cups (100 g) freshly grated Swiss cheese (total)
2 tablespoons (30 g) butter (for layering)
Pepper
3 tablespoons (30 g) breadcrumbs

This soup is a favorite of late night people longing for something to eat after a big night out.

Melt 2 tablespoons (30 g) butter in a large saucepan, add the onions, and brown lightly. Stir in the flour and when it begins to color add the bouillon or water, stirring constantly. Cook over moderate heat uncovered for 15 minutes.

Toast the bread under the broiler, then cut it into thick slices.

Preheat the oven to 400°F (200°C).

In a soup tureen that you can put in the oven, place a third of the bread, sprinkle with a quarter of the cheese, 2 teaspoons of softened butter, and a little pepper. Make three layers in this way, then pour the soup into the tureen, sprinkle with the breadcrumbs and the remaining cheese, and place in the oven for 20 minutes or until the cheese and breadcrumbs have browned. Serve immediately.

VARIATION : A richer soup can be made by beating 3 egg yolks in a bowl with a few spoonfuls of heavy cream, a little port, and a pinch of nutmeg. Whisk in a ladleful of the soup and simmer (do not boil), stirring constantly until the mixture begins to thicken. Pour this mixture into the tureen over the bread and cheese, add the remaining soup, and finish as described above.

Onion Soup

# TAPIOCA SOUP
*Soupe au tapioca*

PREPARATION TIME : 20 minutes

INGREDIENTS FOR 4 SERVINGS :
4 1/4 cups (1 liter) water or beef bouillon (see French Boiled Dinner,
    p. 198)
1 teaspoon (7 g) coarse salt (if using water)
1/3 cup (70 g) tapioca
4 egg yolks
2 tablespoons (30 g) softened butter, broken into pieces
1 1/3 cups (100 g) grated Swiss cheese
Nutmeg
6 tablespoons (10 cl) *crème fraîche* or heavy cream
Pepper

Bring the water and salt or the beef bouillon to a boil in a large saucepan, sprinkle in the tapioca, stirring constantly, and boil for 5 minutes, stirring frequently.

In a bowl, whisk the egg yolks together, then add the softened butter, grated cheese, a little nutmeg, and finally the cream, little by little.

Remove the soup from the heat and add 2 ladlefuls to the egg mixture, whisking constantly, then pour the contents of the bowl into the soup and whisk to combine. Place back over low heat and simmer slowly (do not boil) for 5 minutes, stirring constantly. Add a little pepper and serve.

# COLD CUCUMBER SOUP
*Potage au concombre*

PREPARATION TIME: about 5 hours

INGREDIENTS FOR 4 SERVINGS:
3 cucumbers about 1 1/2 pounds (700 g) total, peeled
Salt
15 walnut meats
2 small cloves garlic, finely chopped
2 tablespoons olive oil
2 cups (1/2 liter) plain yogurt (4 individual yogurts)
3 tablespoons finely chopped chives (total)
Salt, pepper

Cut the cucumbers in half lengthwise and scoop out the seeds with a spoon. Cut the pulp into little cubes, place in a mixing bowl, sprinkle generously with salt, and leave for 45 minutes before making the soup.
Place the salted cucumber in a colander and rinse thoroughly under cold running water, then spread out on a clean towel to dry.
In a soup tureen, mix together the cucumbers, walnuts, garlic, olive oil, yoghurt, and two tablespoons of the chives, and season with salt and pepper. The mixture should be thick and creamy, so stir just long enough to mix everything together. Place the soup in the refrigerator for 3 to 4 hours. Just before serving, sprinkle with the remaining tablespoon of chives.

# LEEK AND POTATO SOUP
*Soupe poireaux-pommes de terre*

PREPARATION TIME : 35 minutes

INGREDIENTS FOR 4 SERVINGS :
6 1/3 cups (1 1/2 liter) water
1 1/2 teaspoons (10 g) coarse salt
2 tablespoons (30 g) butter
4 medium leeks, cleaned and diced
1 pound (500 g) potatoes, peeled and diced
6 tablespoons (10 cl) *crème fraîche* or heavy cream
Pepper

In a large saucepan, bring the water and salt to a boil.
In another large saucepan, melt the butter, add the leeks and simmer until they have softened completely. Pour in the boiling water, add the potatoes, and cook uncovered over moderate heat for 20 minutes, then stir in the cream, add a little pepper, cook 5 minutes more, and serve.

VARIATION : In Lyons we make a version of this soup using a local preparation called *"couennes cuites en paquets"* — you can make something similar by buying large pieces of fresh pork rind and cutting it into strips about 16 inches (40 cm) long and 2 inches (5 cm) wide. Fold each piece in 4, like an accordeon, then tie kitchen string tightly around the middle ; the result will be the size and shape of a bow tie (in fact, in Lyons we call bow ties *"paquets de couennes"*). Add two of these *"paquets"* to the soup 10 minutes before it has finished cooking. Serve them in a separate bowl with a little of the soup to keep them warm, and eat them with Black Olives (p. 52) and mustard (if making the soup this way, don't add the cream).

*Note : The pork rind that can be bought in Lyons is fresh but precooked. Since this will be unavailable in the U.S., use the pork rind that has cooked in the Boiled Pork Dinner (p. 221), or simply place it in cold water, bring just to a boil, and poach for 1 1/2 hours. Allow it to cool, then cut, tie, and cook it in the soup as described above (when tying, be careful not to allow the string to cut the rind). Ed.*

Leek and Potato Soup.

## POLISH-STYLE SOUP
*Potage polonais*

PREPARATION TIME :
   The first day, 2 1/2 hours
   The second day, 45 minutes

INGREDIENTS FOR 4 TO 6 SERVINGS :

1 3/4 pound (800 g) beef shank
1 marrow bone
2 quarts (2 liters) cold water
2 teaspoons (15 g) coarse salt
2 tablespoons (30 g) butter
1 large onion, peeled and
   chopped
2 cloves garlic, peeled and
   chopped
2 shallots, peeled and chopped
4 medium tomatoes, peeled,
   seeded, and chopped
1/2 a small celeriac, or 3 stalks of
   celery, chopped
3 carrots, peeled and cut into
   julienne strips

2 leeks, cleaned and cut into
   julienne strips
About 1/2 pound (250 g) young
   green cabbage, sliced
Pepper
1 clove
4 medium potatoes, peeled and
   diced
1 large cooked beet, peeled and
   diced
4 to 6 tablespoons *crème fraîche*
   or heavy cream
4 to 6 teaspoons red wine vinegar

This soup, which could make a whole meal, is best if the beef and most of
the vegetables are cooked a day in advance.

*A day before serving :* Place the meat and marrow bone in a large pot,
pour in the water and add the salt. Bring to a boil, skimming off any foam
that rises.

In another pot, melt the butter, add the onions, garlic, and shallots, simmer for 5 minutes. Add the tomatoes and cook 1 minute longer. Then add
the celeriac, carrots, leeks, and cabbage, cover, and simmer for 15 minutes. Add the vegetables to the pot with the meat, as well as a little pepper
and the clove. Cook over low heat for 2 hours, then remove from the heat
and allow to cool completely. When cold, the soup may be refrigerated.

*The next day :* Remove the pot from the refrigerator an hour and a half
before dinner. 45 minutes before serving, reheat the soup, add the potatoes and simmer for 35 minutes, then add the beets and cook 10 minutes
more.

To serve, lift the meat and marrow bone out of the soup and serve on a separate platter. Put a tablespoon of cream into each soup bowl as well as a teaspoon of vinegar. Ladle the hot soup into the bowls and serve, with any remaining soup in a tureen, and the platter of meat on the side.

# CREAM OF ASPARAGUS SOUP
*Velouté d'asperges*

PREPARATION TIME : 40 minutes

INGREDIENTS FOR 4 SERVINGS :
1 1/4 pounds (600 g) asparagus
4 1/4 cups (1 liter) water
1 teaspoon (7 g) coarse salt
1 medium onion, peeled (whole)
4 sprigs of parsley (tied in a bunch)
1 tablespoon cornstarch
2 tablespoons water
3 1/2 tablespoons (50 g) softened butter
6 tablespoons (10 cl) *crème fraîche* or heavy cream
Salt, pepper

Take the scales off of green asparagus or peel white asparagus using a vagetable peeler (be careful not to damage the tips). Wash the asparagus in cold water, cut off the tips, and cut the rest of each asparagus into slices. Bring the water and salt to a boil in a large saucepan, add the asparagus, onion, and parsley, and boil gently for 20 minutes. Lift out all the vegetables using a slotted spoon, but reserve only the asparagus.
Lower the heat so that the liquid in the pot just simmers. Mix the cornstarch with 2 tablespoons of cold water and stir into the liquid, then raise the heat and bring the liquid back to a boil, stirring constantly. Lower the heat once more, stir in the butter and cream, put the asparagus back into the pot, and cook for 3 to 4 minutes longer. Taste for salt and pepper and serve.

# CREAM OF OYSTER SOUP
*Velouté aux huîtres*

PREPARATION TIME : 45 minutes

INGREDIENTS FOR 4 SERVINGS :
3 tablespoons (40 g) butter
1 pound (500 g) potatoes, peeled and diced
1 pound (500 g) leeks, cleaned and diced
6 1/3 cups (1 1/2 liter) hot water
16 oysters in their shells
6 tablespoons (10 cl) *crème fraîche* or heavy cream
Salt, pepper
3 tablespoons chopped chervil

Heat the butter in a large saucepan ; when it begins to foam, add the leeks and potatoes, and stir over moderate heat until the leeks have softened. Add the hot water, cover, and simmer for 20 minutes.
Place a sieve over a bowl, line with a doubled-over piece of cheese cloth, and open the oysters over the sieve to strain and catch their liquid. Place the oysters in a small saucepan with their strained liquid and bring just barely to a boil, then remove from the heat, lift the oysters out of the liquid and reserve. Check the oysters to be sure there are no bits of shell caught in them.
Strain the oyster liquid into the soup, then puree the soup in a blender or food processor — this will have to be done in several batches. Blend the cream into the last batch.
Place the blended soup back in the pot, taste for salt and pepper, and heat until very hot but not boiling. Place 4 oysters in each warm soup plate and pour the hot soup over them. Sprinkle with a little pepper and the chervil, and serve.

Cream of Oyster Soup.

# MINESTRONE

PREPARATION TIME : 2 hours

INGREDIENTS FOR 4 TO 6 SERVINGS :

1 cup (185 g) shelled fresh white beans — purchase 1 pound (450 g),
*or* 1/2 cup (90 g) dried white beans

1/4 pound (125 g) salt pork or slab bacon

2 very large tomatoes, peeled and seeded

2 cloves garlic, peeled and finely chopped

12 fresh basil leaves, finely chopped

4 tablespoons (6 cl) olive oil

8 1/2 cups (2 liters) cold water

1 1/2 teaspoons (10 g) salt

2 carrots, peeled and diced

3 leeks, white only, sliced

3 medium potatoes, peeled and diced

2 turnips, peeled and diced

4 stalks celery, diced

1/4 pound (125 g) green beans, cut into small pieces

1 cup (185 g) shelled fresh green peas — purchase 1 pound (450 g)

2/3 cup (100 g) spaghetti, broken into small pieces

Salt, pepper

A bowl of freshly grated parmesan or Swiss cheese

If using dried white beans, soak them over night, then put them in the cold salted water, bring to a boil, and simmer for 45 minutes before adding the other ingredients. (Fresh white beans need simply be added with the other vegetables.)

If using salt pork, soak it in cold water for an hour and a half before making the soup (bacon need not be soaked). Cut the salt pork or bacon into small cubes.

Bring the water and salt to a boil in a large pot, add the (fresh) white beans, carrots, leeks, and salt pork or bacon. Cover and cook for 40 minutes, then add the potatoes, turnips, and celery. 15 minutes later, add the green beans and peas, then cook 15 minutes more.

While the soup is cooking, place the tomatoes in a bowl, crush them with a fork and mix them with the garlic, basil, and olive oil. Reserve.

Spoon a ladleful of soup into the tomato mixture, stir well, then pour back into the soup. Add the spaghetti and finish cooking, uncovered, for 10 minutes. Taste for salt and pepper, then pour the soup into a warm soup tureen and serve, with a bowl of freshly grated parmesan or Swiss cheese on the side.

# GAZPACHO

PREPARATION TIME : 4 hours

INGREDIENTS FOR 4 SERVINGS :
1 3/4 pounds (800 g) tomatoes, peeled, seeded, and chopped
1 large onion, peeled and finely chopped
2 cloves garlic, peeled and finely chopped
1 red bell pepper, seeded and chopped
1 1/2 cucumbers, peeled, seeded and diced (see Cold Cucumber Soup
    p. 39)
2 cups (1/2 liter) cold water
2 tablespoons olive oil
1 tablespoon red wine vinegar
Salt, pepper
10 ice cubes
10 to 12 slices of French bread, or squares of ordinary bread (optional)
2 tablespoons olive oil for browning bread

Place all the vegetables in a large mixing bowl, season generously with salt
and pepper and add the water. Puree in a blender of food processor — this
will have to be done in several batches. Pour each batch of pureed ingredients into a soup tureen. When done, whisk the olive oil and vinegar into
the soup, taste for salt and pepper, and place the tureen in the refrigerator
for 3 to 4 hours to chill before serving.
To serve, coarsely crush the ice cubes by wrapping them in a towel and hit-
ting them with a rolling pin. Add to the soup and serve.
If you like, make croutons by browning the bread in the olive oil, and
serve them on the side.

# CHAPTER 2

# PICKLES AND CONDIMENTS

These are always good when they are homemade.

SWEET AND SOUR PICKLED CHERRIES *(Cerises à l'aigre doux)*

VINEGAR PICKLES *(Cornichons)*

BLACK OLIVES *(Olives noires)*

HOMEMADE VINEGAR *(Vinaigre)*

# SWEET AND SOUR PICKLED CHERRIES
*Cerises à l'aigre-doux*

Photo page 53

PREPARATION TIME : 2 weeks

INGREDIENTS FOR APPROXIMATELY 3 1-QUART (1 LITER) JARS :
4 1/2 pounds (2 kg) fresh cherries
3 tablespoons (40 g) granulated sugar
3 sprigs fresh tarragon (for the cherries) — see *Note*
15 peppercorns (for the cherries)
1 1/4 quarts (1 1/4 liter) crystal (white) vinegar, strength 8 %
1 sprig fresh tarragon (for the vinegar)
5 peppercorns (for the vinegar)

Wash the cherries and dry them on a clean towel. Cut off half of the stem
on each one.
Carefully wash and dry the jars, then place the cherries in them as tightly
as possible without crushing them. Put a tablespoon of sugar, a sprig of
tarragon, and 5 peppercorns in each jar as well.
Boil the vinegar gently for 15 minutes with another branch of tarragon and
5 peppercorns, then strain it and pour enough into each jar to completely
cover the fruit. Leave the jars in a dark place (such as a kitchen cabinet)
until the vinegar has cooled completely, then seal the jars with a lid or a
piece of waxed paper and a rubber band.
The cherries are ready to eat in 2 weeks.

**Serving suggestions :** Serve with cold meats

*Note : If fresh tarragon is unavailable, 1/2 teaspoon dried tarragon may
be added to each jar and to the vinegar instead. Ed.*

# VINEGAR PICKLES
## *Cornichons*

Photo page 53

---

PREPARATION TIME : 6 weeks

INGREDIENTS FOR 5 HALF-PINT (1/4 LITER) JARS :
2 1/4 pounds (1 kg) fresh pickling cucumbers, 2-3 in. (5 cm) long
5 tablespoons (125 g) coarse salt
5 sprigs fresh tarragon (see *Note*)
30 baby onions, peeled
20 peppercorns
1 quart (1 liter) crystal (white) vinegar, strength 8 %

Fresh little gherkins, also called pickling cucumbers or "cornichons," should be shiny and rigid when purchased. Wash them under cold running water and scrub them if necessary to remove any dirt. Place in a large dish and sprinkle the coarse salt over them, then leave them overnight.

Wipe each cucumber with a clean dry towel, then place them one by one on another towel to dry thoroughly in a cool place for 6 hours before placing them into jars. While drying, the cucumbers should be spread out so that they do not touch each other or pile up.

Place the cucumbers in the jars ; do not pack them tightly, but leave as little space between them as possible. Place a sprig of tarragon, 6 baby onions, and 4 peppercorns in each jar as well.

Bring the vinegar to a boil, then pour enough into each jar to completely cover the cucumbers. Leave the jars uncovered until the vinegar has cooled completely, then seal them. Place in a kitchen cabinet (*not* in the refrigerator) ; the pickles are ready to serve in 6 weeks.

*Note : If fresh tarragon is unavailable, 1/4 teaspoon of dried tarragon may be placed in each jar instead.*
*Once opened, store the jars in the refrigerator. Ed.*

---

# BLACK OLIVES
*Olives noires*

PREPARATION TIME : 10 days

INGREDIENTS FOR A 1-QUART (1 LITER) JAR :
1 pound (500 g) black olives
1 clove garlic, peeled and chopped
1 small chili pepper
1 teaspoon thyme leaves
Olive oil

To give a nice flavor to ordinary black olives, try this : Mix the olives, gar-lic, and thyme leaves together in a bowl. Place half of the olives in a stone-ware or glass jar, stand the chili pepper up in the middle, and add the rest of the olives. Pour in enough olive oil to cover and leave for at least 10 days before using.

1. Vinegar Crock. — 2. Green Olives Stuffed with Pimento. — 3. Cracked Olives with Lemon. 4. Pickled Onions. — 5. Vinegar Pickles. 6. Mixed Pickles. — 7. Cracked Olives with Fennel. 8. Baby Olives from Nice. — 9. Sweet and Sour Pickled Cherries. — 10. Black Morrocan Olives 11. Portuguese-style Olives. — 12. Seville-style Green Olives.

# HOMEMADE VINEGAR
*Vinaigre*

PREPARATION TIME : Several months

INGREDIENTS TO START THE VINEGAR :
2 cups (1/2 liter) red wine vinegar
2 cups (1/2 liter) red wine

You can make wine vinegar at home ; it's quite easy, better tasting, and better for you than industrially made vinegars.

You will need a small wooden, stoneware, or dark glass barrel (earthenware is not suited for this). There sould be an opening in the top of the recipient and a spigot at the bottom. Place the barrel in a well-aired, dry place.

Place 2 cups (1/2 liter) of red wine vinegar in the barrel with as much red wine. One week later, add 2 cups more red wine, and continue doing so every week until the barrel is about 2/3 to 3/4 full. Leave the vinegar to mature for at least 6 weeks before using. During this time a film will form on the surface of the liquid : this is called the "vinegar mother". In order not to disturb this film it is best to place a funnel permanently in the barrel, long enough to go down through the "mother" so that the film will not be dispersed when new wine is added.

When you want to withdraw vinegar, two things must be kept in mind : 1) always replace the vinegar you withdraw by an equal amount of wine to keep the level in the barrel up, and 2) don't withdraw vinegar too often. For example, if you had put a total of 5 quarts (5 liters) wine and vinegar into the barrel, you can withdrawn 2 cups (1/2 liter) once every month. Never withdraw more than 1/10 of the total at one time, and it should be noted that the smaller the barrel, the longer you have to wait each time before withdrawing more.

Once a year, you should clean the barrel. Pour the contents through a sieve into a bowl. The "mother", now a somewhat rubbery plaque, will stay in the sieve. Wash the barrel thoroughly with water (no soap), dry, then pour the vinegar back into the barrel. Place a piece of the "mother" back in the barrel, wait two weeks, and continue making vinegar as before.

# CHAPTER 3

# STARTERS AND FIRST COURSES

It's always nicer to start a meal with a small first course than to plunge right into the main dish. Some of the following dishes, however, such as Poached Sausage with Warm Potato Salad, the quiches, or the Chicken Salad, are substantial enough to make a light lunch all by themselves. Also, you might try the French custom of eating the green or mixed green salads, seasoned with simple oil and vinegar dressings, after the main dish (before cheese or dessert) rather than before. It's very refreshing.

BOILED ARTICHOKES *(Artichauts)*

MIXED RAW VEGETABLE PLATTER
  *(Hors-d'œuvres variés)*

ASPARAGUS SALAD *(Asperges)*

CUCUMBER AND CREAM SALAD *(Concombres à
  la crème)*

HAM WITH TOMATO CREAM SAUCE *(Jambon
  chaud)*

GOUGÈRE

CANTALOUPE AND PROSCIUTTO *(Melons et
  jambon de Parme)*

EGGS MIMOSA *(OEufs mimosa)*

QUICHE LORRAINE

SPINACH QUICHE *(Tarte aux épinards)*

FISH DUMPLINGS *(Quenelles aux gratin)*

POACHED SAUSAGE WITH WARM POTATO
  SALAD *(Saucisson chaud, pommes à l'huile)*

MUSHROOM AND GREEN BEAN SALAD
*(Champignons en salade)*

RED AND GREEN CHICORY SALAD *(Chicorée verte et rouge)*

RED CABBAGE SALAD *(Chou rouge en salade)*

BELGIAN ENDIVE SALAD *(Endives)*

CURLY-LEAF ENDIVE SALAD *(Frisée)*

GREEN SALAD *(Laitue)*

LAMB'S LETTUCE AND BEET SALAD *(Mâche à la betterave rouge)*

MY MIXED GREEN SALAD *(Petite salade de mon jardin)*

WARM LENTIL SALAD *(Salade de lentilles)*

DANDELION GREEN AND BACON SALAD *(Pissenlit au lard)*

WARM POTATO SALAD *(Salade de pommes de terre)*

CHICKEN SALAD *(Poulet en salade)*

RICE AND CRABMEAT SALAD *(Salade de riz)*

TABOULI *(Taboulé)*

# BOILED ARTICHOKES
*Artichauts*

PREPARATION TIME : 50 minutes

INGREDIENTS FOR 4 SERVINGS :
4 artichokes
4 quarts (4 liters) water
2 tablespoons coarse salt
1 tablespoon Dijon mustard
3 tablespoons red wine vinegar
9 tablespoons walnut oil
Salt, pepper

Choose only artichokes that are firm and green, not bruised or discolored from shipping. Cook them in an enameled or stainless steel pot to avoid discoloration while they cook.
Bring the water and salt to a boil.
Cut off the stem of each artichoke, then rinse in hot water before placing them in the pot to cook. The artichokes should simmer, not boil, for 40 minutes. When done, lift them out of the pot and place them, leaves down, next to the sink to drain.
Make an oil and vinegar dressing by combining the mustard, vinegar, walnut oil, and a little salt and pepper.
Serve the artichokes warm with the dressing in small individual bowls.

# MIXED RAW VEGETABLE PLATTER
*Hors-d'œuvre variés*

PREPARATION TIME : About 1 hour

INGREDIENTS FOR 6 TO 8 SERVINGS :
1 pound (500 g) new potatoes
Salt, pepper
2 tablespoons olive oil
1/2 pound (250 g) green beans
4 eggs
1 small butterhead (Boston) lettuce
1 bunch radishes
2 small heads celery
1 cucumber
4 medium tomatoes
4 baby artichokes
1 pound (500 g) broad beans
A 7-ounce (200 g) can of tuna packed in oil
A 1-ounce (30 g) can of anchovies packed in oil
1/4 pound (125 g) black olives
Anchovy Paste (p. 112)
3 teaspoons Dijon mustard
3 tablespoons red wine vinegar
9 tablespoons olive oil
Salt, pepper
1 loaf whole wheat or country-style bread
Butter

This vegetable platter takes a little while to make, but it's worth the trouble. It's the perfect thing to serve before (or with) shish kabobs or barbecued pork or lamb. It can also be served alone at lunchtime or as a light late-summer dinner.
Boil the potatoes in their skins for 30 minutes, then peel and slice them. Place in a serving dish, sprinkle with salt and pepper, and spoon 2 tablespoons of olive oil over them. Stir gently and leave to cool.
String the green beans, then drop them into a large pot of lightly salted boiling water and simmer for 10 to 15 minutes. Taste to see if they're done

(they shouldn't be too cooked). Drain the beans in a colander and cool quickly under cold running water ; reserve.

Boil the eggs 15 to 20 minutes, drain and cool under running water, then remove the shells and cut each egg in half lengthwise ; reserve.

Wash the lettuce, remove the rib from the center of each leaf, then place the leaves on a platter or in a bowl ; reserve.

Cut the leaves off the radishes, carefully wash the radishes and reserve.

Wash the celery, place in a serving dish, and reserve.

Peel the cucumber, cut it into thick slices, place in a large bowl, and sprinkle generously with salt. Leave for 20 minutes, then place in a colander and rinse under cold running water. Lay the slices on a paper towel to dry, then put them in a serving dish and reserve.

Wash the tomatoes, cut out the stems, cut the tomatoes into wedges, place them in a serving dish, sprinkle with salt, and reserve.

Cut off the stems of the artichokes and dip the artichokes in a large bowl of cold water mixed with a little lemon juice ; shake them about to wash and remove any dirt, drain, and place on a plate ; reserve.

Shell the broad beans and remove the little skin that surrounds each bean. Place in a bowl and reserve.

Place the tuna in a small serving dish and the anchovies in another ; place the olives in a third bowl.

Place everything in the refrigerator for about 1 hour before serving.

To serve, prepare the Anchovy Paste (p. 112) and an oil and vinegar dressing by mixing together the mustard, vinegar, olive oil, and a little salt and pepper.

Toast 1 or 2 large slices of bread per person, then serve the vegetables, eggs, fish, sauces, and a dish of butter all at once. Place everything on the table and let your guests serve themselves, dipping the vegetables into one of the sauces or simply eating them plain with a little salt and butter.

## ASPARAGUS SALAD
*Asperges*

PREPARATION TIME : About 35 minutes

INGREDIENTS FOR 4 SERVINGS :
2 1/4 pounds (1 kg) asparagus
2 1/2 quarts (2 1/2 liters) water
1 tablespoon salt
1 teaspoon Dijon mustard
1 tablespoon red wine vinegar
3 tablespoons olive oil
Salt, pepper
1/2 egg white

Break off the tough, stringy base of each asparagus ; then, if using large white ones, peel them with a vegetable peeler. Small green asparagus simply need to have the scales along the stem removed.
Wash the asparagus under cold running water and divide them into two or three bunches. Tie each bunch with kitchen string both at the bottom and toward the tip end.
Bring the water and salt to a boil in a large pot. Drop the asparagus into the water, bring back to a boil, then lower the heat and simmer for 18 to 25 minutes, depending on size : the tip of a knife should easily penetrate the stem of the asparagus when done. Lift the asparagus out of the pot and leave them on a clean cloth to drain. Remove the strings.
Serve the asparagus warm with a *vinaigrette mousseline*. Whisk together the mustard, vinegar, and oil, with a little salt and pepper. Beat the egg white until thick and foamy, but not stiff, then gently whisk it into the sauce just before serving.

VARIATION : The asparagus may also be served cold with a simple Oil and Vinegar Dressing (p. 122), or hot as a vegetable with Hollandaise Sauce (p. 117).

Asparagus Salad.

# CUCUMBER AND CREAM SALAD
*Concombres à la crème*

PREPARATION TIME : 40 minutes

INGREDIENTS FOR 4 SERVINGS :
3 cucumbers weighing 1 1/4 to 1 1/2 pounds (600 to 700 g) total
Salt
4 tablespoons *crème fraîche* or heavy cream
1 tablespoon lemon juice
2 tablespoons finely chopped chives
Salt, pepper

Cucumbers are easier to digest if they have been peeled and salted before being used in salads.
Peel the cucumbers and cut them into thin slices. Place them on a large plate, salt, then turn the pieces over and salt again. Leave the cucumbers in the refrigerator for 30 minutes before making the salad.
Remove the cucumbers from the refrigerator, place in a colander, and rinse off under cold running water. Leave them to dry on a paper towel. Make a sauce by stirring together the cream, lemon juice, chives, salt, and pepper. Place the cucumbers on individual plates, spoon the sauce over them, and serve.

# HAM WITH TOMATO CREAM SAUCE
*Jambon chaud*

PREPARATION TIME: About 25 minutes

INGREDIENTS FOR 4 SERVINGS:
4 thick slices — about 1 pound (500 g) — precooked country-style or
  shoulder ham
1 tablespoon granulated sugar
4 tablespoons red wine vinegar
2 tablespoons (30 g) softened butter
1 shallot, peeled and finely chopped
1 tablespoon tomato concentrate
3/4 cups (18 cl) dry white wine
3 tablespoons (5 cl) *crème fraîche* or heavy cream
Salt, pepper

Place the sugar and vinegar in a large frying pan and boil, stirring constantly until the mixture has reduced to nothing but dark bubbles. Stir in the butter and shallot, and cook until the shallot starts to brown ; then add the tomato concentrate aund white wine. Boil the sauce over moderate heat for 2 to 3 minutes, or until reduced by half and beginning to thicken. Place the ham in the pan just long enough to heat through (turn it over once), then place it on a hot serving platter. Add the cream to the sauce, salt and pepper lightly, stir, bring just to a boil, then spoon the sauce over the ham and serve.

**Serving suggestions :** This is very good served as a light lunch with Broccoli (p. 245) or Mixed Vegetables (p. 238).

# GOUGÈRE

PREPARATION TIME : 45 minutes

INGREDIENTS FOR 4 SERVINGS :
4 tablespoons (60 g) butter, for the batter
1/2 cup (12 cl) water
1 scant cup (125 g) flour
3 egg yolks
1 1/3 cup (100 g) grated Swiss cheese
Nutmeg
Butter, for the soufflé dish
3 egg whites

A *gougère* can be served alone as an entree or as an accompaniment to meat, especially roast beef or lamb.
Preheat the oven to 425°F (220°C).
Melt the butter in a saucepan, then pour in the water and bring to a boil. Add the flour all at once, stirring constantly until the batter is smooth, detaches from the sides of the saucepan, and forms a ball around the spoon. Remove the pan from the heat and beat in the egg yolks one by one ; then stir in the grated cheese and a little nutmeg.
Lightly butter a 6-inch (15-cm) soufflé mold or four individual ramekins, and place it (them) in the oven while finishing the batter.
Beat the egg whites until stiff, add a quarter of them to the batter, stirring them in with the whisk ; then add the rest of the egg whites in the same way. Remove the soufflé dish from the oven, pour in the batter, return to the oven, and bake for 25 minutes or until the blade of the knife comes out clean when stuck into the center of the *gougère*. Serve as soon as it comes out of the oven.

Gougère.

# CANTALOUPE AND PROSCIUTTO
*Melons et jambon de Parme*

PREPARATION TIME : 1 hour 15 minutes

INGREDIENTS FOR 4 SERVINGS :
4 small or 2 large cantaloupes
8 very thin slices prosciutto (from Parma)
Crushed ice

Make sure your melons are perfectly ripe. If you keep them in the refrigerator, it is best to first place them in a plastic bag, because a truly ripe melon will impregnate everything with its odor. Othewise, place the uncut melons in a large bowl of ice water and leave for 1 hour before serving. This dish can be served in various ways ; I find the following one particularly attractive. Place some crushed ice on a large serving platter. If using small canteloupes, cut off the very top of each one just below the stem and reserve. Scoop out all the seeds with a spoon, then place 2 slices of ham around the opening of each melon, pleating it so it will look like a fancy collar coming out of the melon. Place the ''top'' with the stem back in place and serve.
If the melons are large, simply cut them in half, scoop out the seeds, place the ham in each half as described above, and serve.

**Serving suggestions :** This is delicious served with a glass of red port.

# EGGS MIMOSA
*OEufs mimosa*

PREPARATION TIME : About 20 minutes

INGREDIENTS FOR 4 SERVINGS :
4 hard-boiled eggs
3 tablespoons finely chopped chives
1 cup (25 cl) mayonnaise (p. 118)
8 black olives
1 butterhead (Boston) lettuce
2 very large tomatoes
Salt
1 lemon, quartered
A 7-ounce can of tuna packed in oil (optional)

Cut the hard-boiled eggs in half lengthwise and separate the yolks from the whites. Put three half-yolks on a plate and reserve ; crush the other yolks with a fork. Place the crushed yolks in a bowl with the chives, then add mayonnaise a spoonful at a time to make a thick smooth paste (there will be mayonnaise left over). Spoon this mixture into the hard-boiled egg whites, and top each half "egg" with a black olive.

Decorate the edge of a round serving platter with some lettuce leaves, then place 4 cupped lettuce leaves in the center. Remove the stem from each tomato, cut them in half, then place half a tomato in each cupped lettuce leaf, cut side up. Lightly salt the tomatoes, then place two half "eggs" on each one.

Crush the remaining egg yolks with a fork or grind them through a food mill, and sprinkle them over the garnished platter.

Serve with the remaining mayonnaise and the lemon wedges, with or without some tuna served in a separate dish.

# QUICHE LORRAINE

PREPARATION TIME : 2 hours 15 minutes

INGREDIENTS FOR 4 SERVINGS :
*For the dough :*
1 generous cup (150 g) flour
1/2 teaspoon (4 g) salt
5 tablespoons (75 g) softened butter
2 tablespoons water
*For the filling :*
1/4 pound (125 g) slab bacon or prosciutto, cut into 1/2-inch (1-cm)
  cubes
2 eggs
6 tablespoons (10 cl) *crème fraîche* or heavy cream
Salt, pepper
Nutmeg

Place the flour and salt in a large mixing bowl. Break the butter into the bowl in little nut-sized pieces, then use your fingers to "pinch" the flour and butter together. Work quickly to make a crumbly mixture, then add the water and quickly form the dough into a ball, working it as little as possible. Cover the ball of dough with a clean cloth and leave for 1 1/2 hours before baking.
Preheat the oven to 450°F (240°C).
Roll out the dough on a well-floured table to make a circle about 1/4-inch (5-mm) thick. Lightly butter an 8-inch (20-cm) pie pan, line with the dough, and prick the bottom with a fork. Place the pieces of bacon evenly over the bottom, gently pushing them into the dough, then place in the oven for 15 minutes.
Whisk the eggs and cream together in a mixing bowl. Add a little salt, pepper, and nutmeg. When the 15 minutes of baking time is up, pour this mixture into the pie pan, lower the over temperature to 350°F (175°C), and bake 20 minutes more. If the quiche colors too much while baking, cover with a piece of aluminium foil.
Serve hot from the oven.

Spinach Quiche *(recipe page 70).*
Quiche Lorraine.

# SPINACH QUICHE
*Tarte aux épinards*

Photo page 69

Photo page 69

PREPARATION TIME : 2 hours 15 minutes

INGREDIENTS FOR 5 TO 6 SERVINGS :
*For the dough :*
1 1/2 cups (200 g) flour
3/4 teaspoon (5 g) salt
6 tablespoons (100 g) softened butter
3 tablespoons water
*For the filling :*
2 1/4 pounds (1 kg) spinach
3 1/2 quarts (3 1/2 liters) water
4 teaspoons (30 g) salt
Salt, pepper
2 eggs
Generous 3/4 cup (20 cl) *crème fraîche* or heavy cream
1 1/3 cups (100 g) grated Swiss cheese
Nutmeg

Make the dough as described in the recipe for Quiche Lorraine (p. 68) but use the measurements given above.
Preheat the oven to 425°F (220°C).
Remove the stem from each leaf of spinach, then wash the spinach carefully in a sink full of cold water. Bring 3 1/2 quarts (3 1/2 liters) of water and the salt to a boil. Drain the spinach and drop it into the boiling water, boil for 5 minutes from the time the water comes back to a boil, then drain in a colander and cool under cold running water. Squeeze all the water out of the spinach, then chop it coarsely with a knife. Season with salt and pepper ; reserve.
Roll out the dough on a well-floured table into a circle about 1/4-inch (5-mm) thick, and line a 9 1/2-inch (24-cm) pie pan with it. Prick the bottom with a fork.
Place the eggs in a large bowl with the cream and grated cheese, and beat to combine. Season generously with salt and pepper, add a little nutmeg, then stir in the cooked spinach. Pour this mixture into the pie pan and bake for 20 minutes, then lower the heat to 400°F (200°C) and continue baking 10 minutes more. Turn off the oven, but leave the quiche inside for 3 minutes more.
Serve hot.

# FISH DUMPLINGS AU GRATIN
*Quenelles au gratin*

PREPARATION TIME : 30 minutes

INGREDIENTS FOR 4 SERVINGS :
2 1/2 quarts (2 1/2 liters) water
4 large fish dumplings (*quenelles,* see *Note*)
3 tablespoons (40 g) butter
1 tablespoon (10 g) flour
6 tablespoons (10 cl) cold milk
6 tablespoons (10 cl) *crème fraîche* or heavy cream
Salt, pepper
Nutmeg
3/4 cup (40 g) grated Swiss cheese

Preheat the oven to 425°F (220°C).
Bring the water to a boil in a large saucepan. Carefully add the dumplings and lower the heat. Simmer for 7 minutes or until the dumplings float ; this is the sign that they are done. Lift them out of the water with a slotted spoon and drain on a clean cloth.
Place the dumplings in a lightly buttered baking dish.
Make a sauce by melting the butter in a saucepan ; when hot, stir in the flour, pour in the cold milk, all at once, stirring constantly, then add the cream. Season with salt, peper, and a little nutmeg, bring to a boil, still stirring, then immediately remove from the heat.
Sprinkle the grated cheese over the dumplings, pour the sauce over them, and bake for 20 minutes, or until they begin to brown.
Serve hot from the oven in the baking dish.

*Note : Quenelles are a sort of delicately seasoned fish dumpling usually made with pike, and sold ready-made in France. If you can buy quenelles or make them, it is best to use them, but any fish dumpling can be used in making this recipe. Ed.*

## POACHED SAUSAGE
## WITH WARM POTATO SALAD
*Saucisson chaud-pommes à l'huile*

PREPARATION TIME : 35 minutes

INGREDIENTS FOR 4 SERVINGS :
1 1/4 pounds (600 g) new potatoes in their skins
1 large or 2 medium pure pork poaching sausages (*saucisson de Lyon* or
    other) weighing 1 3/4 pounds (800 g)
2 quarts (2 liters) water
Salt
3 tablespoons olive oil
1 tablespoon white wine vinegar
1 1/2 tablespoons white wine
Salt, pepper
2 tablespoons finely chopped chives

Wash the potatoes, place them in a large pot with some water and a little salt, and bring to a boil. Cook 30 minutes.
Prick the sausage in several places with a pin or the tip of a knife, then place it in another pot with 2 quarts (2 liters) lightly salted cold water. Bring just to a boil, then immediately lower the heat and simmer for 25 minutes (do not boil).
The potatoes and sausage should finish cooking at about the same time. Keep the sausage warm by covering the pot and removing it from the heat while making the potato salad.
Drain the potatoes, cut them into thick slices, and place them in a salad bowl with the olive oil, vinegar, white wine, salt, pepper, and chives. Toss gently.
Lift the sausage out of the water, cut it into thick slices, and place it on a platter.
Serve with the bowl of warm potato salad on the side.

VARIATION : You may make a mustard dressing to serve with the sausage at the table if you like. Make an Oil and Vinegar Dressing (p. 122), but use lemon juice instead of vinegar, and double the mustard measurement.

Poached Sausage with Warm Potato Salad.

# MUSHROOM AND GREEN BEAN SALAD
*Champignons en salade*

PREPARATION TIME : 20 minutes

INGREDIENTS FOR 4 SERVINGS :
3/4 pound (350 g) green beans, strings and ends removed
2 quarts (2 liters) water
Salt
3/4 pounds (350 g) fresh mushrooms
2 shallots, finely chopped
2 tablespoons red wine vinegar
2 teaspoons Dijon mustard
6 tablespoons salad oil
Salt, pepper

Cook the green beans in 2 quarts (2 liters) lightly salted boiling water for 10 minutes, then drain in a colander and cool under cold running water. Place on a clean towel to dry.
Cut off any dirt on the stem of each muschroom, then wash the mushrooms in cold water and cut into thin slices. Place in a salad bowl with the green beans and shallots.
Make a sauce by whisking together the vinegar, mustard, oil, salt, and pepper. Pour the sauce onto the salad just before serving, toss gently, and serve.

# RED AND GREEN CHICORY SALAD
*Chicorée verte et rouge*

PREPARATION TIME : 10 minutes

INGREDIENTS FOR 4 SERVINGS :
1/4 pound (125 g) green chicory (see *Note*)
1/4 pound (125 g) red *treviso* chicory (see *Note*)
2 stalks celery
1 tablespoon red wine vinegar
1 teaspoon Dijon mustard
3 tablespoons salad oil
Salt, pepper
2 hard-boiled eggs
10 black olives

Cut the base off each little chicory. Wash the leaves carefully and reserve. Remove the stringy filaments from the celery by breaking the base toward the rounded, ridged side and pulling it up toward the leaves. Dice the celery.
In a salad bowl, whisk together the vinegar, mustard, and oil, then season with a little salt and pepper.
Peel the hard-boiled eggs and slice them into the salad bowl. Add the chicory, olives, and celery. Toss gently and serve immediately.

*Note : This kind of chicory forms tiny loose-leafed heads and is either red or green. Its characteristic bitter taste makes substitutions difficult, although other types of chicory and red varieties of lettuce mixed together (2 cups tightly packed (125 g) of each) are worth trying. Ed.*

# RED CABBAGE SALAD
*Chou rouge en salade*

PREPARATION TIME : 15 minutes

INGREDIENTS FOR 4 SERVINGS :
1/2 of a 3-pound (1.4 kg) red cabbage
2 quarts (2 liters) water
Salt
4 tablespoons vinegar, for the cabbage
2 whole juniper berries
3 tablespoons olive oil
2 tablespoons lemon juice
1/2 tablespoon red wine vinegar, for the dressing
Salt, pepper
3 thick slices bacon, diced

Cut the cabbage into julienne strips, then drop into lightly salted boiling water. Once the water comes back to a boil, drain the cabbage in a colander. Pour 4 tablespoons of vinegar onto the cabbage in the colander and toss lightly, then press the water and vinegar out with a wooden spoon. Place the cabbage in a large salad bowl with the juniper berries and leave to cool.
Make an oil and vinegar dressing by beating together the oil, lemon juice, vinegar, salt, and pepper ; reserve.
Cook the bacon in a frying pan until crisp.
When ready to serve, pour the dressing onto the cabbage and toss, season with salt and pepper, then add the bacon, toss again, and serve immediately.

Red Cabbage Salad.

# BELGIAN ENDIVE SALAD
*Endives*

PREPARATION TIME : 10 minutes

INGREDIENTS FOR 4 SERVINGS :
1 pound (500 g) Belgian endives
1/4 cup (50 g) raisins
15 or 20 walnut meats
1 teaspoon Dijon mustard
2 teaspoons sherry vinegar
2 tablespoons walnut oil
Salt, pepper

Wash the Belgian endives and remove the base of each one. Cut each into 4 pieces lengthwise, slicing each section directly into a large salad bowl. Sprinkle in the raisins and nuts. Make a sauce by whisking together the mustard, vinegar, oil, salt, and pepper. Pour this onto the salad just before serving, toss, and serve.

# CURLY-LEAF ENDIVE SALAD
*Frisée*

PREPARATION TIME : 10 minutes

INGREDIENTS FOR 4 SERVINGS :
1 medium head of curly-leaf endive or escarole
8 l-inch (2.5-cm) squares of toasted bread (croutons)
2 cloves garlic, peeled and sliced in half lengthwise
1 teaspoon Dijon mustard
1 tablespoon red wine vinegar
3 tablespoons salad oil
Salt, pepper

Carefully wash, drain, and coarsely chop the endives.
Rub each crouton with garlic.
In a large salad bowl, whisk together the mustard, vinegar, oil, salt, and pepper, then place the croutons in the bowl and stir to coat them with the dressing. Add the endives, toss, and serve immediately.

# GREEN SALAD
*Laitue*

PREPARATION TIME : 10 minutes

INGREDIENTS FOR 4 SERVINGS :
1 medium butterhead (Boston) lettuce
2 hard-boiled eggs
Salt
1 small can anchovies in oil
1 teaspoon Dijon mustard
1 tablespoon red wine vinegar
3 tablespoons salad oil
Salt, pepper

Carefully wash the lettuce. Remove the thick rib from each leaf.
Peel the hard-boiled eggs and cut them in half lenghtwise, sprinkle with salt, and place in a small serving dish.
Roll each anchovy up on itself, then place the little rolls in another small serving dish.
In a bowl, whisk together the mustard, vinegar, oil, salt, and pepper. Place the lettuce in a salad bowl, add the dressing, and toss to mix. Serve immediately, with the eggs and anchovies on the side.

# LAMB'S LETTUCE AND BEET SALAD
*Mâche à la betterave rouge*

PREPARATION TIME : 10 minutes

INGREDIENTS FOR 4 SERVINGS :
1/2 pound (250 g) lamb's lettuce or corn salad (see *Note)*
1 teaspoon Dijon mustard
1 tablespoon red wine vinegar
2 tablespoons walnut oil
Salt, pepper
1 1/4 cups (125 g) diced celery
1 small cooked beet, peeled and diced

Cut off the base of each bunch of lamb's lettuce, then wash carefully and drain thoroughly.
In a salad bowl, whisk together the mustard, vinegar, oil, salt, and pepper. When ready to serve, place the lettuce, celery, and beets in the bowl and toss. Serve immediately.

*Note : Lamb's lettuce is particularly small-leafed and tender ; if it is not available, try using very young spinach leaves with the same seasoning. Ed.*

# MY MIXED GREEN SALAD
*Petite salade de mon jardin*

PREPARATION TIME : 20 minutes

INGREDIENTS FOR 4 SERVINGS :
10 radishes
1/4 small celeriac or 3 stalks celery, cut into julienne strips
2 medium carrots, peeled and cut into julienne strips
1 leafy lettuce
1 1/4 cups tightly packed (65 g) watercress leaves
10 tender pale leaves from a curly-leaf endive
1 small Belgian endives
10 bunches lamb's lettuce corn salad
1 tablespoon red wine vinegar
3 tablespoons olive oil
Salt, pepper

Cut the leaves from the radishes and discard. Place the radishes in a large salad bowl with the celery and carrot strips.
Cut the lettuce into strips and coarsely chop the watercress, curly-leaf endives, Belgian endives, and lamb's lettuce ; place in the salad bowl.
Make a dressing by whisking together the vinegar, oil, salt, and pepper. Just before serving, pour it over the salad, toss, and serve.

VARIATION : This salad can be as large or as small as you like. You can substitute almost any leafy green salad vegetable for the ones I've suggested.

# WARM LENTIL SALAD
*Salade de lentilles*

PREPARATION TIME: 1 1/2 hours

INGREDIENTS FOR 4 SERVINGS:
1 1/2 cups or 10 1/2 ounces (300 g) lentils, preferably dark green or tan
2 quarts (2 liters) cold water
Salt
1 onion, peeled
5 1/4 ounces (150 g) salt pork or slab bacon
1 teaspoon Dijon mustard
1 tablespoon red wine vinegar
3 tablespoons walnut oil
Salt, pepper
3 tablespoons finely chopped chives
1 shallot, finely chopped

Wash the lentils in cold running water, then place in a large saucepan with the water. Salt lightly, add the onion, and bring to a boil. Lower the heat, cover the pan, and simmer for 1 1/2 hours, or until the lentils are tender but not falling apart.
Fifteen minutes before serving, cut the salt pork or bacon into 1/2-inch (1-cm) cubes. Fry until the pieces have browned on all sides, then pour off the fat, remove from the heat, and cover the pan to keep warm.
Make a dressing by whisking together the mustard, vinegar, oil, salt, and pepper.
Once the lentils are done, remove the onion and drain the lentils in a sieve or colander. Place them in a large salad bowl with the chives, shallots, and dressing. Toss gently to season, then place the pieces of bacon on top. Serve warm.

# DANDELION GREEN AND BACON SALAD
*Pissenlit au lard*

PREPARATION TIME : 20 minutes

INGREDIENTS FOR 4 SERVINGS :
3/4 pound (350 g) dandelion greens
1 teaspoon Dijon mustard
1 tablespoon red wine vinegar
3 tablespoons olive oil
Salt, pepper
7 ounces (200 g) salt pork or slab bacon

Carefully wash the dandelion greens, cut each little bunch in half length-wise, then shake them in a bowl of cold water to remove any dirt and drain thoroughly. Place in a large salad bowl and reserve.
In a mixing bowl, whisk together the mustard, vinegar, oil, salt, and pepper ; reserve.
Cut the bacon into 1/2-inch (1-cm) cubes and brown in a frying pan. Pour off all the fat and add the bacon to the dandelion greens. Add the dressing, toss, and serve immediately.

VARIATION : small squares of toasted bread (croutons) may be rubbed with half a clove of garlic and added to the salad just before serving.

*Note : If preferred, the bacon can be cut into 4 slices and each slice cut in half, as shown in the photo. Ed.*

Dandelion Green and Bacon Salad.

# WARM POTATO SALAD
*Salade de pommes de terre*

PREPARATION TIME : 40 minutes

INGREDIENTS FOR 4 SERVINGS :
1 3/4 pounds (800 g) potatoes
1 1/2 quarts (1 1/2 liters) water
Salt
1 teaspoon Dijon mustard
1 tablespoon red wine vinegar
3 tablespoons olive oil
Pepper
1 shallot, finely chopped
3 tablespoons finely chopped chives

Wash the potatoes but don't peel them. Place them in a pot with the water, salt lightly, and bring to a boil. Cook uncovered for 30 minutes or until a knife penetrates them easily. Drain the potatoes in a colander, rinse them rapidly under cold running water to cool them slightly, and peel them while they are still warm (the skins will come off easily).
Cut the potatoes into thick slices and place them in a salad bowl. Make a dressing by whisking together the mustard, vinegar, oil, salt, and pepper. Pour over the potatoes, add the shallot and chives, then toss gently so as not to crush the potatoes. Serve.

# CHICKEN SALAD
*Poulet en salade*

PREPARATION TIME : 25 minutes

INGREDIENTS FOR 4 SERVINGS :
Both breasts from a roast or boiled chicken, cut into strips
1 small butterhead (Boston) lettuce, sliced
Tender pale leaves from a curly-leaf endive, coarsely chopped
3 stalks celery, diced
2 new baby onions, peeled and finely sliced
3/4 cup (100 g) diced Swiss cheese
1 scant cup (100 g) black olives
3 large tomatoes, peeled, seeded, and chopped
1 cup (100 g) walnut meats
1 tablespoon sherry vinegar
3 tablespoons olive oil
Salt, pepper
1 clove garlic, peeled and finely chopped (optional)

This salad could be a meal in itself — it's especially nice on a summer evening.
Place the chicken, lettuce, endives, celery, onion, cheese, olives, tomatoes, and nuts all in a salad bowl and chill until ready to serve.
In a small bowl, whisk together the vinegar, oil, salt, pepper, and garlic (if using). Pour over the salad just before serving, toss, and serve.

# RICE AND CRABMEAT SALAD
*Salade de riz*

PREPARATION TIME : 45 minutes

INGREDIENTS FOR 4 SERVINGS :
3/4 cup (150 g) long-grain rice
3 1/4 cups (75 cl) water
Salt
1 pinch saffron
3/4 cup (125 g) shelled peas — purchase 3/4 pound (350 g)
About 7 ounces (200 g) finest quality crabmeat
About 1/2 to 2/3 cup (12-15 cl) Mayonnaise (p. 118), to taste
20 black olives

Bring the water to a boil in a medium saucepan, salt lightly, add the saffron, and stir. Add the rice and cook at a moderate boil, uncovered, for 15 minutes. Drain thoroughly, then place in a salad bowl.
In another saucepan, boil the peas for 10 to 12 minutes, or until tender, in lightly salted water. Drain, then add to the bowl with the rice.
Separate out the 4 nicest pieces of claw meat from the crab and set aside on a plate. Break up the rest of the meat, removing any pieces of cartilage you find, and set aside on another plate.
When the rice and peas have cooled completely, add the bits of crabmeats. Stir in the Mayonnaise just before serving.
To serve, decorate by placing the reserved claw meat on top of the salad and arrange the olives around it (see photo).

Rice and Crabmeat Salad.

# TABOULI
*Taboulé*

PREPARATION TIME : 1 1/2 hours

INGREDIENTS FOR 4 SERVINGS :
1 1/2 cups (250 g) fine bulghur (cracked wheat)
2/3 cup (100 g) shelled peas — purchase 1/2 pound (250 g)
2 large tomatoes, peeled, seeded, and chopped
2 sprigs fresh mint, finely chopped
4 tablespoons finely chopped chives
6 tablespoons (10 cl) olive oil
Juice of 2 lemons
Salt, pepper

Place the bulghur in a large mixing bowl and add enough lukewarm water to cover by about 1 inch (2.5 cm). Leave to soak for 45 minutes, then drain in a sieve or colander.
While the bulghur is soaking, cook the peas in boiling salted water for 10 to 12 minutes, then drain.
Place the bulghur and peas in a large salad bowl, add the tomatoes, mint, chives, oil, and lemon juice. Salt and pepper generously (this salad can take a lot of salt). Toss the tabouli and refrigerate for at least 30 to 45 minutes before serving.

VARIATION : Other herbs and seasonings can be added to this salad as you like, I'm partial to this simple version.

# EGGS

Use only the freshest possible eggs (grade AA) ; if in doubt, break the eggs into a saucer before using in a recipe (the yolk should be nice and round, the white clear with no unpleasant odor).

Keep eggs away from strong-smelling foods in the refrigerator ; their shells are easily permeated by the odors, which will eventually change the taste of even the freshest eggs.

An hour before cooking eggs, take them out of the refrigerator so they will be at room temperature when you use them.

SOFT-BOILED EGGS *(Œufs à la coque)*

BACON AND EGGS *(Œufs au bacon)*

EGGS WITH VINEGAR *(Œufs sur le plat)*

HAM AND EGGS *(Œufs au jambon)*

CREAMY SCRAMBLED EGGS WITH CHANTERELLES *(Œufs brouillés aux chanterelles)*

CREAMY SCRAMBLED EGGS WITH SALMON *(Œufs brouillés au saumon fumé)*

EGGS POACHED IN BEAUJOLAIS *(Œufs à la beaujolaise)*

POACHED EGGS *(Œufs pochés)*

BAKED EGGS WITH CREAM *(Œufs en cocotte à la crème)*

SCRAMBLED EGGS WITH TOMATO AND BASIL *(Œufs à la tomate)*

WILD MUSHROOM OMELET *(Omelette aux champignons)*

POTATO AND BACON OMELET *(Omelette aux pommes de terre et au lard)*

SOUFFLÉED CHEESE OMELET *(Omelette soufflée au fromage)*

# SOFT-BOILED EGGS
## OEufs à la coque

PREPARATION TIME: 10 minutes

INGREDIENTS FOR 1 SERVING:
1 slice country-style or ordinary bread
Butter
Salt
2 eggs

Bring a small saucepan of water just to a boil.
In the meantime, toast and butter the bread, then cut it into "fingers" about 1/2-inch (1-cm) wide. Sprinkle with a little salt and reserve.
When the water is on the verge of boiling, carefully lower the eggs, one at a time, into the saucepan using a spoon. Simmer for 3 1/2 to 4 minutes, then lift the eggs out of the saucepan, place in egg cups, and serve, surrounded by the pieces of toast.
Excellent for breakfast with tea or coffee.

# BACON AND EGGS
## OEufs au bacon

PREPARATION TIME : 15 minutes

INGREDIENTS FOR 4 SERVINGS :
8 thin slices Canadian bacon or 4 slices ham cut in half
4 tablespoons (60 g) butter (total)
8 eggs
Salt, pepper
4 slices toast

I like to serve eggs and bacon cooked in individual porcelain or enameled cast-iron dishes.
Brown the Canadian bacon or ham in a nonstick frying pan.
Melt 1 tablespoon (15 g) of butter in each of the individual dishes, then place 2 pieces of bacon or ham in each one.
Break the eggs into a small bowl, 2 at a time, then carefully slide them into each dish. Salt and pepper lightly. Cook over low heat for about 3 minutes, or until the white is half-cooked ; then raise the heat and finish cooking for about 3 minutes.
Serve with toast.

# EGGS WITH VINEGAR
*Œufs sur le plat*

PREPARATION TIME : 10 minutes

INGREDIENTS FOR 4 SERVINGS :
4 tablespoons (60 g) butter
8 eggs
Salt, pepper
4 tablespoons vinegar (total)
4 slices toasted country-style or whole wheat bread

Preheat the oven to 350°F (180°C).
Use one small overproof dish per person. Place 1 tablespoon of butter in each one and melt over moderate heat. When the butter starts to foam, break 2 eggs into each dish and continue cooking over low heat for 3 to 4 minutes, or until the white is half-cooked ; then place in the oven to finish cooking for 3 minutes more. Remove from the oven, salt and pepper, and add 1 tablespoon of vinegar to each dish.
Serve with toast.

# HAM AND EGGS
*OEufs au jambon*

PREPARATION TIME : 15 minutes

INGREDIENTS FOR 3 SERVINGS :
3 tablespoons (40 g) butter
3 slices — about 4 to 5 ounces (125-150 g) — precooked country-style
  ham
6 eggs
Salt, pepper
3 slices toasted country-style or whole wheat bread

Preheat the oven to 350°F (180°C).
Melt the butter in a large porcelain or enameled cast iron baking dish, add
the ham, and brown lightly on both sides.
Break the eggs into a small bowl, 2 at a time, and carefully slide them onto
the ham. Continue cooking over very low heat for about 3 minutes, or
until the white is about half-cooked ; then place in the oven to finish cooking for about 3 minutes. Salt and pepper just before serving.
Serve with toast.

Ham and Eggs.

## CREAMY SCRAMBLED EGGS
## WITH CHANTERELLES
*OEufs brouillés aux chanterelles*

PREPARATION TIME : About 25 minutes

INGREDIENTS FOR 4 SERVINGS :
About 5 1/4 ounces (150 g) chanterelles (see *Note*)
2 tablespoons (30 g) butter, for the mushrooms
3 tablespoons (45 g) butter, for the eggs
8 eggs
Salt, pepper
6 tablespoons (10 cl) *crème fraîche* or heavy cream
8 slices toast

Cut off any dirt from the base of each mushroom, then wash them quickly, drain, and dry on a towel.
Melt 2 tablespoons (30 g) of butter in a frying pan over moderate heat and add the mushrooms. At first, they will release some liquid ; as soon as this liquid has evaporated, lower the heat and simmer (the butter absorbed by the mushrooms will now reappear in the pan).
Melt 3 tablespoons (45 g) of butter in the top of a double boiler. Break the eggs into a bowl, add salt and pepper, whisk lightly, then pour into the melted butter. Continue whisking until the eggs are creamy, then stir in the cream with a wooden spoon. Stir constantly as the eggs are cooking so they won't stick to the pan ; when they are thick and creamy and coat the spoon, they are done.
Remove the double boiler from the heat and stir the mushrooms into the eggs.
Serve immediately with buttered toast.

*Note : Although chanterelles are called for, any one of the wild mushrooms that are sometimes commercialized could be used instead (e.g. boletus, Japanese* **shitake** *mushrooms, etc.). About 1/2 cup (15 g) top-quality dried wild mushrooms may also be used. Soak them for about 20 minutes in warm water (or follow the directions on the package), then add them with 6 tablespoons (10 cl) of their water to the melted butter and cook as described for the fresh mushrooms.*
*Eggs scrambled in this way are not stiff but thick and creamy, almost like a sauce, so you may prefer to serve them in bowls and eat them with a spoon. Ed.*

# CREAMY SCRAMBLED EGGS
# WITH SMOKED SALMON
*Œufs brouillés au saumon fumé*

PREPARATION TIME : 10 minutes

INGREDIENTS FOR 4 SERVINGS :
2 thin slices — 4 ounces (115 g) — smoked salmon (total)
2 tablespoons (30 g) butter
8 eggs
Salt, pepper
6 tablespoons (10 cl) *crème fraîche* or heavy cream
8 slices toasted country-style or whole wheat bread

Cut the salmon into thin strips.
Melt the butter in a double boiler. Whisk the eggs just enough to mix, and add the salmon, salt, and pepper. Pour the eggs into the butter and stir with a wooden spoon until very thick and creamy. Add the cream, stir to combine, and remove from the heat. Season with a little more pepper. Serve with buttered toast.

*Note : Eggs scrambled in this way are not stiff but thick and creamy, almost like a sauce, so you may prefer to serve them in bowls and eat them with a spoon. Ed.*

# EGGS POACHED IN BEAUJOLAIS
*OEufs à la beaujolaise*

PREPARATION TIME : 40 minutes

INGREDIENTS FOR 4 SERVINGS :
2 tablespoons (30 g) softened butter, for the *beurre manié*
2 tablespoons (20 g) flour
2 tablespoons (30 g) butter, for the onions
12 baby onions, peeled
1 bottle Beaujolais
1 clove garlic, crushed
*Bouquet garni,* made with 1 sprig thyme, 1/4 bay leaf, 1 stalk celery, and white of 1 leek
Salt, pepper
8 eggs

Make a *beurre manié* by placing 2 tablespoons of softened butter in a small bowl with the flour and mixing the two together with your fingers until smooth. Break the mixture into pea-sized pieces and reserve.
Melt the remaining 2 tablespoons of butter in a high-sided frying pan (preferably not aluminum). Add the onions and cook to color lightly ; then add the wine, garlic, *bouquet garni,* salt, and pepper. Bring to a boil, lower the heat immediately, and simmer uncovered for 20 minutes. Lift the onions out with a slotted spoon and reserve.
Strain the wine through a sieve into a bowl, then pour it back into the pan and heat to simmering. Break an egg into a teacup, then slide it gently into the hot wine (you can poach up to 4 eggs at a time). Poach the eggs for 4 minutes, then lift them out with a slotted spoon. Place them on a plate and cover with aluminum foil to keep warm while poaching the second batch of eggs. Place these eggs on a plate and cover with foil as well. Add the *beurre manié* to the wine and bring to a boil, stirring constantly. Lower the heat once more, place the onions back in the pan to warm up, taste, and add salt and pepper if needed.
Place 2 eggs on each dinner plate, spoon the sauce and onions around them, and serve.
If you like, you can serve the eggs with small squares of bread (croutons) browned in a little butter and rubbed with half a clove of garlic.

Eggs Poached in Beaujolais.

# POACHED EGGS
*Œufs pochés*

PRÉPARATION TIME : 45 minutes

INGREDIENTS FOR 4 SERVINGS :
1 1/2 quarts (1 1/2 liter) water (total)
1 tablespoon white (crystal) vinegar
8 eggs

Absolutely the freshest eggs are essential here (see comments at the beginning of this chapter). You will also need two high-sided frying pans : one to poach the eggs in, and the other to keep the cooked ones warm in while poaching the others.
Bring 2 cups (50 cl) of water to a boil in a small frying pan with 1 tablespoon of vinegar. In a large frying pan, heat 1 quart (1 liter) of water to warm but not boiling.
Break an egg into a teacup, then slide it gently into the boiling water with the vinegar. Lower the heat so the water simmers but does not boil, and poach the egg for 3 1/2 minutes. Lift it out of the water with a slotted spoon and place it in the warm water while poaching the remaining eggs one by one. Be careful not to break the yolks, both when you crack the eggs and when you lift them out of the water. With a little practice, you will be able to poach 2, 3, or even 4 eggs at a time but if you do, increase the amount of water and vinegar in the first pan (2 eggs can be poached in the amounts given) and use a larger frying pan.
Once all the eggs are poached, lift them out of the warm water and leave for a few seconds on a clean towel to drain before serving.

**Serving suggestions :** Serve with the Dandelion Green and Bacon Salad (p. 84) or with Spinach (p. 254).

# BAKED EGGS WITH CREAM
*OEufs en cocotte à la crème*

PREPARATION TIME : About 30 minutes

INGREDIENTS FOR 8 SERVINGS :
2 teaspoons softened butter (total)
16 teaspoons *crème fraîche* or heavy cream (total)
Salt, pepper
8 eggs
4 slices bread, crust removed
8 small celantro (Chinese parsley) leaves

Preheat the oven to 400°F (200°C).
Butter 8 little ramekins ; place 1 teaspoon of cream and a little salt and pepper in each one. One at a time, break the eggs into a teacup, then gently slide each one into a ramekin and top with 1 teaspoon of cream.
Line a large roasting pan with waxed paper, place the ramekins in the pan, and pour in enough hot water to come halfway up the sides of the ramekins (the paper will keep the water from bubbling up too much and spilling into the ramekins later). Heat on top of the stove until the water is simmering but not boiling. Place the pan in the oven and bake for 4 minutes, or until the egg whites are opaque.
Toast the bread, butter it, then cut each slice into "fingers" about 1/2 inch (1 cm) wide.
Remove the roasting pan from the oven, lift the ramekins out, and wipe each one dry. Place two ramekins on a large dinner plate, place a celantro leaf in the center of each one, and surround the ramekins with the pieces of toast.
Serve immediately.

# SCRAMBLED EGGS WITH TOMATO AND BASIL
## OEufs à la tomate et au basilic

PREPARATION TIME : 25 minutes

INGREDIENTS FOR 2 SERVINGS :
5 tomatoes
Salt, pepper
2 tablespoons olive oil
5 eggs
5 basil leaves, chopped

Peel and seed the tomatoes, then cut into halves or quarters. Season with salt and pepper.

Heat 2 tablespoons of oil in a frying pan and add the tomatoes. Cook uncovered over moderate heat for 15 to 20 minutes, or until their water has evaporated, stirring frequently.

Break the eggs into a mixing bowl, season with salt and pepper, and beat lightly with a fork or whisk (the eggs should not be perfectly mixed). Pour them into the pan with the tomatoes and cook over moderate heat for about 2 minutes, stirring to cook the eggs.

Serve, sprinkled with the fresh basil.

Scrambled Eggs with Tomato and Basil.

# WILD MUSHROOM OMELET
*Omelette aux champignons*

PREPARATION TIME: About 30 minutes

INGREDIENTS FOR 4 SERVINGS:
1/2 pound (250 g) fresh wild mushrooms, preferably morels (see *Note*)
3 tablespoons (40 g) butter (total)
Salt, pepper
8 eggs

Cut off any dirt from the stems of the mushrooms, then wash the mushrooms carefully and cut them in half lengthwise or into slices if they are large.
Melt half the butter in a very large frying pan. Add the mushrooms, salt, and pepper, and cook over moderate heat, stirring frequently, until all the liquid from the mushrooms has evaporated (about 10 to 15 minutes).
Break the eggs into a mixing bowl, season with salt and pepper, and beat lightly with a fork. Pour the mushrooms into the bowl with the eggs.
Melt the remaining butter in the pan; when hot, pour in the egg-mushroom mixture and cook for 5 to 10 minutes, or until done. Slide the omelet out of the pan and onto a warm serving platter, giving the pan a gentle flip when the omelet is halfway onto the platter so that it will fold over onto itself. Serve immediately.

*Note: See the note to Creamy Scrambled Eggs with Chanterelles (p. 98) concerning dried mushrooms. In this case, use about 3/4 cup (25 g) dried mushrooms and 1/2 cup (12 cl) of their soaking water.*
*Unless you have a very large frying pan, make two omelets, instead of one, using half the egg-mushroom mixture each time. Keep the first omelet warm in a low oven while making the second one.*
*Be careful not to overcook the omelet; it is done when the surface is set and creamy but not yet dry. Ed.*

# POTATO AND BACON OMELET
*Omelette aux pommes de terre et au lard*

PREPARATION TIME : 15 minutes

INGREDIENTS FOR 4 SERVINGS :
1 cup (100 g) diced slab bacon
3 tablespoons (40 g) butter
2 medium potatoes, boiled and thickly sliced or diced
7 eggs
Salt, pepper
1 tablespoon cold water

Fry the bacon in a very large frying pan. Cook slowly so that the fat will melt and the bacon will brown ; turn the pieces over several times for even browning.
Remove the bacon from the pan and place on a paper towel to drain. Discard the fat. Wipe the frying pan with a clean paper towel, then melt the butter in it. When the butter starts to foam, add the potatoes and brown over moderate heat, turning them over carefully so they do not break.
Break the eggs into a mixing bowl, season with salt and pepper, add 1 tablespoon of cold water, and beat with a fork just enough to break the yolks and mix them slightly with the whites ; they should not be well mixed. Put the pieces of bacon back into the pan, then add the eggs. Cook for 5 to 10 minutes, or until done, then slide the omelet onto a warm serving platter, giving it a gentle flip so that it will fold over onto itself. Serve immediately.

**Serving suggestions :** This omelet is excellent with a Green Salad (p. 80).

*Note : The omelet is done with the surface is set and creamy but not yet dry. Ed.*

# SOUFFLÉED CHEESE OMELET
*Omelette soufflée au fromage*

PREPARATION TIME : 25 minutes

INGREDIENTS FOR 4 SERVINGS :
7 eggs
1 1/3 cups (100 g) grated old Mimolette cheese (see *Note*)
Salt, pepper
Nutmeg
1 1/2 tablespoons (20 g) softened butter, for the dish

Preheat the oven to 400°F (200°C).
Separate the yolks from the whites of the eggs. Place the yolks in a mixing bowl with the grated cheese, a little salt, pepper, and nutmeg. Beat with a spoon to combine.
In a large mixing bowl, beat the whites until stiff, then fold a quarter of them into the yolk-cheese mixture using a wooden spoon or spatula. When smooth, add the remaining whites and fold them in.
Lightly butter a medium-sized baking dish, pour in the batter, and bake for 10 to 12 minutes, or until golden brown on top. Remove from the oven and serve immediately.

*Note : Mimolette is a hard cheese from Holland not generally available in the U.S. Another hard Dutch cheese (preferably an aged one) such as Edam or Gouda, or even a mild cheddar, could be used instead. Ed.*

# CHAPTER 5

# SAUCES

A good sauce should be smooth and creamy; it can be thickened with flour, eggs, or cream. Here are a few sauces that go with recipes in this book as well as with many others.

GARLIC MAYONNAISE *(Ailloli)*

ANCHOVY PASTE *(Anchoyade)*

BEARNAISE SAUCE *(Béarnaise)*

WHITE SAUCE *(Sauce blanche)*

FOAMY BUTTER SAUCE *(Beurre blanc)*

GRIBICHE SAUCE *(Sauce gribiche)*

HOLLANDAISE SAUCE *(Sauce hollandaise)*

MAYONNAISE

MUSTARD SAUCE *(Sauce moutarde)*

TOMATO SAUCE *(Sauce tomate)*

GREEN SAUCE *(Sauce verte aux herbes)*

OIL AND VINEGAR DRESSING *(Vinaigrette)*

# GARLIC MAYONNAISE
*Ailloli*

PREPARATION TIME : 15 minutes

INGREDIENTS FOR 4 SERVINGS :
1 small potato, boiled in its skin
3 cloves garlic, peeled
1 egg yolk
Salt, pepper
1 cup (25 cl) olive oil
2 teaspoons lemon juice
2 teaspoons hot water (optional)

Traditionally, ailloli is made using a wooden or marble mortar and pestle (see *Note* for what to do if you don't have one).
All of the ingredients should be left at room temperature for at least an hour before making the sauce.
Peel the potato and place it in the mortar with the garlic and pound to a paste. Add the egg yolk, salt and pepper, mix well, then add the olive oil little by little, stirring constantly as when making a mayonnaise. Once the oil has been added, stir in the lemon juice and serve.
The finished ailloli should be about the consistency of homemade mayonnaise ; if it seems too thick, stir in a teaspoon or two of hot water.

**Serving suggestions :** Serve with steamed vegetables or poached fish. Garlic mayonnaise can also be spread on toast and served with olives with drinks before dinner.

*Note : Without a mortar, you can mash the potato with a fork and crush the garlic in a garlic press, mix well in an ordinary bowl with a wooden spoon, and finish making the ailloli as described above. Ed.*

# BEARNAISE SAUCE
*Sauce béarnaise*

PREPARATION TIME : 20 minutes

INGREDIENTS FOR 4 TO 6 SERVINGS :
1/4 cup (6 cl) red wine vinegar
3 shallots, peeled and finely chopped
2 tablespoons (total) chopped fresh tarragon
Salt, pepper
2 egg yolks
2 tablespoons cold water
1 1/4 sticks (150 g) softened butter, broken into 10 pieces
2 tablespoons lemon juice
1 tablespoon freshly chopped chervil (*or parsley. Ed.*)

This sauce must be made over very low heat, just before serving. If you make it in a double boiler, you are sure to get good results. Use the top of the double boiler as an ordinary pot for the first stage of making the sauce. Place the vinegar, shallots, half of the tarragon and a little salt and pepper in the top part of the double boiler. Place over high heat and boil until the vinegar has reduced by half. Remove from the heat and leave to cool completely before finishing the sauce (you can speed cooling by holding the pot in a bowl of ice water).
Whisk the egg yolks and 2 tablespoons of cold water into the vinegar mixture. Heat a little water in the bottom of the double boiler and set the top part in place.
Whisk in a piece of the butter, then continue adding the rest of the butter little by little , whisking constantly. The sauce should become foamy at first, then thicken as the butter is added.
Just before serving, add salt and pepper if needed, then whisk in the lemon juice, the remaining tarragon and chervil or parsley.
Serve in a sauceboat.

**Serving suggestions :** This is the perfect sauce for any grilled meat.

# ANCHOVY PASTE
*Anchoyade*

PREPARATION TIME : 20 minutes

INGREDIENTS FOR 4 SERVINGS :
4 ounces (125 g) anchovy filets packed in oil
2 cloves garlic, peeled
1 tablespoon sherry vinegar
1 cup (25 cl) olive oil
Pepper

Place the anchovies and garlic in a mortar and pound to a paste *(or puree them in a blender or food processor. Ed.)* Stir in the sherry vinegar, then add the oil little by little, beating in each addition vigorously with the pestle or a wooden spoon until perfectly smooth. The finished mixture should be the consistency of a mayonnaise. Add pepper *but no salt.*

**Serving suggestions :** Serve in a bowl as an accompaniment to the Mixed Raw Vegetable Platter (p. 58), or simply with celery sticks and toasted slices of whole wheat or country-style bread, or serve with grilled meat for fish.

1. Gribiche Sauce. — 2. Garlic Mayonnaise. — 3. Mayonnaise.
4. Hollandaise Sauce. — 5. Bearnaise Sauce.
6. Foamy Butter Sauce. — 7. Tomato Sauce.

# WHITE SAUCE
*Sauce blanche*

PREPARATION TIME : 15 minutes

INGREDIENTS FOR 4 SERVINGS :
3 1/2 tablespoons (50 g) butter
2 tablespoons (20 g) flour
1 cup (25 cl) cold milk
Generous 3/4 cup (20 cl) *crème fraîche* or heavy cream
Nutmeg
Salt, pepper
1 teaspoon lemon juice (optional)

Melt the butter in a medium-size saucepan (enameled cast iron is excellent). Add the flour and stir until smooth over low heat ; the flour should not brown. Pour in all the cold milk at once, then bring to a boil stirring constantly. Lower the heat and cook at a gentle boil for 8 minutes, stirring occasionally, then add the cream, a little nutmeg, salt, pepper, and the lemon juice if using. Cook and stir for a minute or two more ; the sauce should coat the spoon when done.
Serve immediately, or keep warm in a double boiler for later use.

**Serving suggestions :** Use for making gratinéed vegetables : pour the sauce over cooked vegetables and place in a very hot oven for 15 to 20 minutes to brown.

# FOAMY BUTTER SAUCE
*Beurre blanc*

PREPARATION TIME : 10 minutes

INGREDIENTS FOR 4 TO 5 SERVINGS :
2 shallots, peeled and finely chopped
2 tablespoons red wine vinegar
1 3/4 sticks (200 g) softened butter, broken into 10 -15 pieces
Salt, pepper

A thick-bottomed saucepan that holds the heat is preferable for making this sauce.
Place the shallots and vinegar in a small saucepan and boil until the vinegar has evaporated and the shallots are simply moist in the bottom of the pan. Lift the saucepan off of the heat and begin rapidly stirring in the butter a piece at a time using a wooden spoon. The sauce should become creamy as the butter is added ; it should not become overheated or the butter will oil. Place the pot back onto the burner every so often to keep the sauce warm ; stir constantly, removing the pot from the heat as the butter is being added. Once all the butter has been added, beat the sauce with a whisk to make it foamy.
Season to taste with salt and pepper and serve.

**Serving suggestions :** Serve with poached fish, especially salmon and pike.

# GRIBICHE SAUCE
*Sauce gribiche*

PREPARATION TIME: 10 minutes

INGREDIENTS FOR 4 SERVINGS:
3 Large eggs
2 teaspoons Dijon mustard
Salt, pepper
2 tablespoons red wine vinegar
3/4 cup (18 cl) olive oil
1 tablespoon lemon juice
2 tablespoons finely chopped fresh chives
3 vinegar pickles (cornichons), finely chopped
1 tablespoon capers

Bring a saucepan of water to a boil, carefully add the eggs, and simmer for 8 minutes. Remove from the heat, drain, and place in a bowl of cold water to cool. When cold, carefully peel the eggs and separate the yolks from the whites. Coarsely chop the whites and reserve.
Place the yolks in a mixing bowl and crush with the prongs of a fork. Mix in the mustard, salt, pepper, and vinegar. Stir constantly and add the olive oil little by little as when making a mayonnaise. Once all the oil has been added, stir in the lemon juice, chopped egg whites, chives, pickles, and capers, and serve.

**Serving suggestions:** Serve with Calf's Head (p. 156), Leg of Lamb English Style (p. 214); French Boiled Dinner (p. 198), hard-boiled eggs, raw tomatoes, or celery sticks.

# HOLLANDAISE SAUCE
*Sauce hollandaise*

PREPARATION TIME : 15 minutes

INGREDIENTS FOR 4 SERVINGS :
1 1/2 teaspoons wine vinegar (preferably white wine vinegar)
2 egg yolks
Salt, pepper
1 1/4 sticks (150 g) softened butter, broken into 10 pieces
2 tablespoons lemon juice

As in the Bearnaise Sauce (p. 111), for the surest results, make this sauce in a double boiler.
Heat a little water in the bottom of a double boiler. Place the vinegar and egg yolks in the tops, whisk to combine, and season lightly with salt and pepper. Continue whisking and add the butter a piece at a time. Once all the butter has been added, whisk in the lemon juice (more may be added to taste, if desired). Heat for 10 minutes longer, stirring constantly. Taste for salt and pepper and serve.
It is best to serve this sauce immediately, but it may be kept warm in the double boiler, away from the heat, if need be.
A variation on this sauce, called Mousseline Sauce, can be made by whipping 3 tablespoons of heavy cream until stiff and stirring it into the warm sauce just before serving.
In any case, do not allow to over heat ; especially, *do not boil*.

**Serving suggestions :** Hollandaise is excellent with any poached fish or with boiled vegetables such as asparagus or broccoli.

# MAYONNAISE

PREPARATION TIME : 10 minutes

INGREDIENTS FOR 1 CUP (25 CL) OR 4 SERVINGS :
1 egg yolk
2 generous teaspoons Dijon mustard
1 teaspoon red wine vinegar or lemon juice
1 cup (25 cl) salad oil
Salt, pepper

All of the ingredients should be left at room temperature for at least an hour before making the sauce.
Place the egg yolk in a bowl with the mustard and vinegar or lemon juice and whisk to combine. Whisking constantly, add the oil little by little (no more than a tablespoon at a time at first, then in a very thin stream once the mayonnaise has begun to thicken). When all the oil has been added, stir in a little salt and pepper. Another teaspoon (or more) of vinegar or lemon juice may be added to taste if desired. Il you like a thinner mayonnaise, a little warm water may be added, a teaspoon at a time, until the sauce is the desired consistency.
Mayonnaise should always be made just before you use it ; *never* refrigerate it.

**Serving suggestions :** Serve with cold meat or fish, boiled artichokes or asparagus, grilled or poached lobster.

# MUSTARD SAUCE
*Sauce moutarde*

PREPARATION TIME : 10 minutes (plus time to cool)

INGREDIENTS FOR 3 TO 4 SERVINGS :
3 1/2 tablespoons (50 g) softened butter, broken into 10 pieces
1 1/2 tablespoon lemon juice
2 eggs yolks
Salt, pepper
1 tablespoon cold water
1 generous tablespoon Dijon mustard

It's best to use a double boiler for making this sauce.
Heat a little water in the bottom of the double boiler. Place the butter, lemon juice, egg yolks and a little salt and pepper in the top ; set over the hot water and whisk energetically until the mixture begins to thicken. Whisk in the cold water, remove the sauce from the heat, pour into a clean bowl, and leave to cool completely.
Once the sauce is cold, stir in the mustard and serve.

**Serving suggestions :** A tablespoon of chopped parsley may be added to the sauce just before serving with grilled meats, or a tablespoon of capers to go with grilled fish.

# TOMATO SAUCE
*Sauce tomate*

PREPARATION TIME : 45 minutes

INGREDIENTS FOR 4 TO 6 SERVINGS :
3 1/4 pounds (1.5 kg) ripe tomatoes
6 tablespoons (10 cl) olive oil
1 clove garlic, peeled
1 medium onion, peeled and sliced
1 small *bouquet garni* (parsley, tarragon, thyme, and bay leaf)
1 teaspoon (5 g) granulated sugar
Salt, pepper

The better the tomatoes, the better the sauce, so use perfectly ripe ones. Wash them, cut each one in half, and squeeze gently to remove the seeds. Heat the olive in a large saucepan ; add the garlic, onion, tomatoes, and *bouquet garni.* Cook uncovered over moderate heat at a rapid boil, crushing the tomatoes at first, then stirring occasionally with a wooden spoon for 35 minutes, or until the water in the tomatoes has evaporated and a thick sauce is formed. Stir in the sugar, then grind the sauce through a food mill or puree in a blender or food processor. Taste for salt and pepper. If the sauce seems too thin at this point, you can boil it some more to thicken ; otherwise it is ready to serve.
This sauce keeps well — up to a week refrigerated.

**Serving suggestions :** Serve with pasta, white beans, fish dumplings, or ravioli.

# GREEN SAUCE
*Sauce verte aux herbes*

PREPARATION TIME : 15 minutes

INGREDIENTS FOR 4 SERVINGS :
1 egg yolk
1 cup (25 cl) olive oil
1 tablespoon Dijon mustard
2 tablespoons lemon juice
Salt, pepper
1 tablespoon freshly chopped tarragon
2 tablespoons freshly chopped parsley
1 tablespoon freshly chopped chives
1 tablespoon freshly chopped chervil

All the ingredients should be at room temperature for making this sauce. Place the egg yolk in a mixing bowl with the mustard and stir in the olive oil little by little as when making a mayonnaise. Once all the oil has been added, stir in the lemon juice and season with salt and pepper. Just before serving, stir in the tarragon, parsley, and chives, then sprinkle the chervil over the top and serve.

**Serving suggestions :** This is excellent with any cold meat, hot or cold poached fish, or boiled artichokes, asparagus, or leeks.

# OIL AND VINEGAR DRESSING
*Vinaigrette*

PREPARATION TIME : 5 minutes

INGREDIENTS FOR 2 SERVINGS :
1 teaspoon Dijon mustard
1 tablespoon red wine vinegar
3 tablespoons salad oil
Salt, pepper

Place the mustard and vinegar in a mixing bowl and stir to combine, then add the oil in a steady stream, stirring as it is being added. Season with salt and pepper — the sauce is ready to use.

VARIATIONS : Vary your vinaigrettes by using different oils and different acids : for instance use olive oil or walnut oil, sherry vinegar or lemon juice or a mixture of vinegar and lemon juice.

**Serving suggestions :** Use with any salad greens, or with cold boiled vegetables such as asparagus.

# FISH AND SHELLFISH

The fresher the fish the better : the eyes should be clear and bright, the flesh firm, the gills red to dark red, and the smell pleasant. Shellfish, such as oysters and mussels, are best from September to April and especially good during the winter months. Whenever possible, buy them in their shells.

COURT BOUILLON

COD WITH MELTED BUTTER SAUCE *(Tranches de cabillaud au beurre fondu)*

PORGY PROVENÇALE-STYLE *(Dorade provençale au four)*

BAKED CARP *(Carpe au four)*

SKATE WITH NUT-BROWN BUTTER *(Raie bouclée au beurre « noisette »)*

RED MULLET IN PAPILLOTES *(Rougets en papillotes)*

HAKE WITH CREAM SAUCE *(Colin en tranches)*

MONKFISH *(Lotte)*

ROASTED MONKFISH *(Rôti de lotte)*

MACKEREL MARINATED IN VINEGAR *(Maquereaux au vinaigre de vin blanc)*

FRESH TUNA AND TOMATOES *(Rôti de thon)*

TROUT OR WHITING MEUNIÈRE *(Truites ou merlans meunière)*

SMOKED HADDOCK WITH CREAM SAUCE
   *(Haddock à la crème)*

CARP AND EEL STEWED IN RED WINE
   *(Matelote d'anguille et de carpe)*

SAUTÉED SALT COD AND POTATOES *(Morue
   poêlée)*

SALT COD PORTUGUESE-STYLE *(Morue à la
   portugaise)*

SALT COD LYONNAISE *(Morue sautée lyonnaise)*

FRICASSEE OF SCALLOPS IN CREAM SAUCE
   *(Fricassée de coquilles Saint-Jacques à la crème)*

MUSSELS MARINIÈRE *(Moules marinières)*

MUSSELS IN WHITE WINE SAUCE *(Moules au
   vin blanc)*

TURBOT WITH MIXED VEGETABLES *(Turbotin
   aux légumes)*

# COURT BOUILLON

PREPARATION TIME : 20 minutes

INGREDIENTS FOR ABOUT 2 QUARTS (2 LITERS):
1 leek, split lenghwise
2 stalks celery
2 sprigs tyme
2 sprigs parsley
1/4 bay leaf
Sprig of fennel leaves or a little fresh ginger (optional)
2 carrots, peeled and quartered
1 onion, stuck with a clove
1 cup (25 cl) dry white wine
7 1/2 cups (1 3/4 liters) water
1 tablespoon (7 g) coarse salt
5 peppercorns

A court bouillon is an aromatic liquid used for poaching fish. Any fish can be poached in a court bouillon : pike, salmon, even lobsters or scallops. It can be made well in advance and kept in the refrigerator until you are ready to poach your fish. When the time comes, place the fish in the cold court bouillon, bring to a boil, then immediately lower the heat and poach the fish until it is cooked (cooking times are indicated in specific recipes). Generally, if you intend to eat a fish or large shellfish (lobster, etc.) cold, simply place it in the cold court bouillon, bring to a boil, then remove from the heat and cover the pot (the time it takes for the court bouillon to cool will be long enough to cook the fish).

*To make a court bouillon :* Make a *bouquet garni* by tying together the leek, celery, thyme, parsley, bay leaf, and fennel or ginger if using. Place in a large pot with the carrots, onion, wine, water, salt, and peppercorns. Bring to a boil, boil gently for 15 minutes uncovered, then remove from the heat and leave to cool completely before using.

# COD WITH MELTED BUTTER SAUCE
*Tranches de cabillaud au beurre fondu*

PREPARATION TIME : 15 minutes

INGREDIENTS FOR 4 SERVINGS :
2 quarts (2 liters) court Bouillon (p. 125)
4 slices fresh cod weighing 2 pounds (900 g)
1 tablespoon lemon juice
6 1/2 tablespoons (100 g) softened butter, broken into 10 pieces
Salt, pepper
Finely chopped parsley (optional)
Finely chopped chives (optional)

Several hours or a day in advance, make the Court Bouillon as described on p. 125. Place the slices of fish in the cold liquid, bring to a boil, then immediately lower the heat and simmer for 10 minutes.
When the fish is almost done, place the lemon juice and butter in the top of a double boiler, add a little salt and pepper, and set into place over a little simmering water in the bottom of the double boiler. Melt the butter, stirring constantly. As soon as the butter has melted, the sauce is ready to serve.
Lift the fish out of the Court Bouillon with a slotted spoon and place it on a warm serving platter. If using the freshly chopped herbs, stir into the sauce and serve on the side in a sauceboat.

**Serving suggestions :** This is often served with potatoes that have been peeled and boiled in salted water to which a little olive oil has been added.

# PORGY PROVENÇALE-STYLE
*Dorade provençale au four*

Photo page 129

PREPARATION TIME : 30 minutes

INGREDIENTS FOR 4 SERVINGS :
A 3-pound (1.4 kg) porgy or sea bream, scaled and cleaned
2 tablespoons olive oil
*Bouquet garni,* made with thyme, bay leaf, and parsley
1 small onion, peeled and finely chopped
1 shallot, finely chopped
1/2 pound (250 g) tomatoes, peeled and coarsely chopped
1/2 pound (250 g) fresh mushrooms, sliced
Salt, pepper
1/4 cup (6 cl) dry white wine
1 lemon, quartered

Preheat the oven to 400°F (200°C).
Brush the fish inside and out with a little oil, then place the *bouquet garni* inside it. Pour the remaining oil into a baking dish, add the fish, and surround it with the onion, shallot, tomatoes, and mushrooms. Salt and pepper, then pour in the white wine. Bake for 20 minutes. Turn off the oven, but leave the fish inside for 7 minutes more to finish cooking.
Serve the fish in the dish it cooked in, garnished with lemon wedges.

**Serving suggestions :** Serve with Rice (p. 290) or boiled potatoes.

# BAKED CARP
*Carpe au four*

PREPARATION TIME: 1 hour

INGREDIENTS FOR 4 SERVINGS:
3 1/2 tablespoons (50 g) softened butter
Salt, pepper
A 3 1/4-pound (1.5-kg) carp, scaled and cleaned
4 medium mushrooms, sliced
3 shallots chopped
4 tablespoons finely chopped parsley (total)
1 cup (25 cl) dry white wine

Preheat the oven to 400°F (200°C).
Use the butter to butter a baking dish just large enough to hold the carp comfortably. Salt and pepper the fish inside and out, then place it in the dish. Around the fish arrange the mushrooms, shallots, any roe or milt that was inside the fish, and half the parsley, then sprinkle everything with salt and pepper. Add the wine and bake for 50 minutes, basting occasionally. Five minutes before the fish is done, sprinkle in the remaining parsley.
Serve the fish in the dish it cooked in.

Baked Carp
Porgy Provençale-style *(recipe p. 127).*

# SKATE WITH NUT-BROWN BUTTER
*Raie bouclée au beurre "noisette"*

PREPARATION TIME : 20 minutes

INGREDIENTS FOR 5 TO 6 SERVINGS :
2 quarts (2 liters) water
4 pounds (1.8 kg) skate
1/2 cup (12 cl) white wine vinegar
3 tablespoons coarse salt
4 peppercorns, coarsely crushed
1 sprig thyme
1 small leek, split lengthwise
1 stalk celery
1/4 bay leaf
4 tablespoons Dijon mustard
Salt, pepper
6 tablespoons coarsely chopped parsley
6 tablespoons (60 g) capers
1 tablespoon red wine vinegar
1 1/4 sticks (150 g) butter

In a large, wide pot, bring the water to a boil, then add the skate and boil for 2 minutes, a piece at a time. Drain, place on a cutting board, and use a small knife to remove the skin.
Cut the fish into equal portions, then place the pieces back in the pot. Pour in enough cold water to cover. Add the vinegar, salt, pepper, thyme, leek, celery, and bay leaf. Bring to a boil, then immediately remove the pot from the heat, cover, and leave the skate in the hot water for 10 minutes to cook.
While the skate is cooking, spread the mustard over the bottom of a large porcelaine or earthenware dish. Lift the skate out of its cooking liquid with a slotted spoon or spatula, and place it in the dish with the mustard. Sprinkle with salt, pepper, and parsley, then add the capers and red wine vinegar.
Meanwhile, melt the butter in a frying pan until it begins to color : Don't let it become black and burnt — just a nice, nut-brown color. Pour the butter immediately into the platter with the fish and serve.

**Serving suggestions :** Serve with steamed potatoes.

# RED MULLET IN PAPILLOTES
*Rougets en papillotes*

PREPARATION TIME : 30 minutes

INGREDIENTS FOR 6 SERVINGS :
6 red mullet (goatfish) weighing about 8 ounces (250 g) each (see *Note*)
2 tablespoons olive oil
Fennel seeds
2 tomatoes, peeled and chopped
3 chopped shallots
4 large mushrooms, sliced
Salt, pepper
1 lemon, quartered

Preheat the oven to 400°F (200°C).
Scale the fish and remove the gills, but don't clean otherwise. Brush the fish with oil, then place each one on a piece of aluminum foil or parchment paper about 14 inches (35 cm) square. Use a sharp knife to make several little incisions in the sides of each fish, and insert one or two fennel seeds into each cut. Place a little tomato, shallot, and mushroom over and under each fish, season with salt and pepper, then fold and squeeze the edges of the foil or parchment together to enclose the fish. Don't wrap the fish too tightly ; there should be a pocket of air above each one to allow the steam to circulate while the fish is cooling.
Once all the fish are wrapped up, place them on a baking sheet and bake in the oven for 15 minutes.
Serve in the foil as they come from the oven, with wedges of lemon on the side.

**Serving suggestions :** Serve with Melted Butter Sauce (see Cod with Melted Butter Sauce, p. 126), or Mustard Sauce (p. 119).

*Note : Other fish can be cooked in exactly the same way, but unlike the red mullet, they should be cleaned before cooking. Ed.*

# HAKE WITH CREAM SAUCE
*Colin en tranches*

PREPARATION TIME : 25 minutes

INGREDIENTS FOR 4 SERVINGS :
3 tablespoons (40 g) softened butter (for the dish)
4 slices hake weighing 2 pounds (900 g)
About 2 tablespoons olive oil
Salt, pepper
1/2 cup (12 cl) dry white wine
6 tablespoons (10 cl) *crème fraîche* or heavy cream

Preheat the oven to 450°F (240°C).
Butter a baking dish large enough to hold all the fish flat on the bottom.
Sprinkle in the shallots, arrange the slices of fish on top after brushing
each one on both sides with oil, salt lightly and pepper, and add the white
wine. Bake for 20 minutes.
Remove the fish from the oven, lift out of the dish with a slotted spatula,
and place on a warm serving platter. Pour the cream into the baking dish
and heat on top of the stove until the sauce just comes to a boil, stirring
constantly. Taste for salt and pepper, then spoon the sauce over the fish
and serve immediately.

Hake with Cream Sauce.

# MONKFISH
*Lotte*

PREPARATION TIME : 15 minutes

INGREDIENTS FOR 4 SERVINGS :
4 slices monkfish (anglerfish) weighing 1 3/4 pounds (800 g)
Flour
Salt, pepper
2 tablespoons (30 g) butter
1 clove garlic, whole and unpeeled
1 tablespoon lemon juice
1/2 cup (12 cl) dry white wine


Roll the slices of fish in flour, then shake to remove any excess. Salt and pepper each slice on both sides.

Melt the butter in a large frying pan ; when it begins to foam, place the slices of fish in the pan, add the garlic, and cook over moderate heat for 7 minutes on each side. Remove the fish with a slotted spatula and place on a warm serving platter.

Add the lemon juice and wine to the pan, and boil rapidly, scraping the bottom of the pan with a wooden spoon, for a few secondes. The sauce should thicken slightly. Add a little salt and pepper, then pour the sauce over the fish and serve.

**Serving suggestions :** Serve with Rice (p. 290) or steamed potatoes, with a dish of butter on the side.

# ROASTED MONKFISH
*Rôti de lotte*

PREPARATION TIME : 30 minutes

INGREDIENTS FOR 4 SERVINGS :
A 1 3/4-pound (800 g) piece (preferably toward the tail) of monkfish
   (anglerfish), skinned
1 large clove garlic, peeled and quartered
1/4 cup (6 cl) olive oil
1 tablespoon lemon juice
Salt, pepper

Preheat the oven to 450°F (240°C).
Pat the fish dry with a clean towel, then lard it with garlic by making 4
incisions with a knife and sliding a piece of garlic into each one. Place the
fish in a roasting pan, pour the oil over it, then roll the fish in the oil. Add
the lemon juice, and sprinkle with salt and pepper. Bake in the oven for
20 minutes, basting from time to time.
Serve the fish in the dish it was cooked in.

# MACKEREL MARINATED IN VINEGAR
*Maquereaux au vinaige de vin blanc*

PREPARATION TIME : 20 minutes

INGREDIENTS FOR 4 SERVINGS :
2 cups (50 cl) water
2 carrots, peeled and sliced
2 onions, peeled and sliced
*Bouquet garni,* made with thyme, parsley, and bay leaf
1 whole clove
1 clove garlic, peeled and crushed
8 baby mackerel weighing about 2 pounds (900 g) cleaned (see *Note*)
12 peppercorns
1 teaspoon coarse salt
1 lemon, peeled and sliced
2 cups (50 cl) white wine vinegar

In a medium saucepan bring the water to a boil, then add the carrots, onions, *bouquet garni,* clove, and garlic. Boil over moderate heat for 12 minutes.
Place the mackerel in a deep porcelaine serving dish and sprinkle with the peppercorns and coarse salt. Lay the slices of lemon on top of the fish.
Add the vinegar to the saucepan with the water and vegetables, bring to a rolling boil, and pour immediately over the fish. The fish should be completely covered ; if there is too much liquid, discard any extra, but place all the vegetables and seasonings in with the fish. Leave to cool overnight (the fish will cook while cooling). Serve cold.

*Note : This recipe is for very small fish weighing about 4 ounces (125 g) each. If only large fish are available, fillet them and proceed exactly as described above. Ed.*

# FRESH TUNA AND TOMATOES
*Rôti de thon*

PREPARATION TIME : 40 minutes

INGREDIENTS FOR 4 SERVINGS :
1 3/4 pounds (800 g) fresh tuna, in one piece (see *Note*)
1/4 cup (6 cl) olive oil
2 medium onions, peeled and sliced
3 medium tomatoes, peeled and quartered
1 clove garlic, whole and unpeeled
*Bouquet garni,* made of thyme, bay leaf, and parsley
1/2 cup (12 cl) dry white wine
Salt, pepper
Chopped tarragon (optional)

Red tuna is best. Try to get a slice from the middle of the fish if possible. Heat the oil in a large frying pan, brown the tuna on both sides, add the onion and allow to color lightly ; then add the tomatoes, garlic, and *bouquet garni*. Cook over moderate heat for 15 minutes, turning once, then add the wine, salt, and pepper. Cover the pan and finish cooking over low heat for 15 minutes more. Just before serving, sprinkle with the fresh tarragon if using.

**Serving suggestions :** Serve with rice or steamed potatoes.

*Note : Any large, meaty fish such as swordfish can be cooked in the same way. Ed.*

# TROUT OR WHITING MEUNIÈRE
*Truites ou merlans meunière*

PREPARATION TIME : 20 minutes

INGREDIENTS FOR 4 SERVINGS :
4 trout or whiting weighing about 10 1/2 ounces (300 g) each
Salt, pepper
Flour
2 tablespoons (30 g) butter
1 tablespoon olive oil
2 tablespoons finely chopped parsley
1 lemon, quartered
2 tablespoons (30 g) butter (to finish)

Ask the fish seller to clean the fish by removing the gills and cleaning without opening the stomach.
Salt and pepper the fish, then roll in flour and shake them to remove any excess before cooking.
Heat 2 tablespoons (30 g) butter and the oil in a large frying pan. When it starts to foam, add the fish and garlic. Cook over high heat for about 6 minutes on each side, carefully turning them over once with a spatula (they should be nicely browned on both sides).
Lift the fish out of the pan with a slotted spatula. Place them on a warm serving platter, sprinkle with parsley and garnish with lemon wedges. Add the remaining butter to the frying pan, heat just long enough to melt, and pour over the fish. Serve immediately.

# SMOKED HADDOCK WITH CREAM SAUCE
## *Haddock à la crème*

PREPARATION TIME : 25 minutes (plus 6 hours soaking)

INGREDIENTS FOR 4 SERVINGS :
1 3/4 pound (800 g) smoked haddock, cut into 4 or 8 pieces
Milk
1/2 medium onion, sliced
*Bouquet garni* made of thyme, bay leaf, and parsley
5 1/2 tablespoons (80 g) butter
1 large tomato, peeled and finely chopped
1 clove garlic, peeled and finely chopped
2 small onions, peeled and finely chopped
A pinch of saffron
1 tablespoon flour
1/2 cup (12 cl) dry white wine
6 tablespoons (10 cl) *crème fraîche* or heavy cream
Salt, pepper

Peel off the skin of the haddock if there is any, then place the fish on a platter or in a bowl. Add enough milk to cover, the slices of onion, and the *bouquet garni*. Leave to soak for 6 hours (this will desalt the fish and make it tender).
Drain the haddock and pat it dry with a clean cloth. Melt the butter in a large frying pan. When it foams up, add the fish and cook for 5 minutes on a side over moderate heat, shaking the pan constantly to keep it from sticking (see *Note*). Lift the cooked fish out of the pan with a slotted spatula, place it on a serving platter, cover, and keep warm while making the sauce.
Add the tomato, garlic, and onions to the pan, and simmer for 5 minutes. Sprinkle in the saffron and flour, stir to combine, then add the wine, stirring constantly. Simmer very gently for 8 minutes. Stir in the cream and continue cooking very slowly, over very low heat, for 5 to 6 minutes more. Add pepper, salt if needed, then strain the sauce, stirring and pressing on the vegetables to extract all the liquid. Pour the sauce over the fish and serve.

**Serving suggestions :** Serve with rice or steamed potatoes.

*Note : Unless you have a very large frying pan, it will be necessary to cook the haddock in two batches. In this case, use half of the butter each time. If you prefer, the sauce may be spooned onto the plates and the fish placed on top to serve (see photo). Ed.*

Smoked Haddock with Cream Sauce.

# CARP AND EEL STEWED IN WINE
*Matelote d'anguille et de carpe*

PREPARATION TIME : 45 minutes

INGREDIENTS FOR 5 TO 6 SERVINGS :

*Bouquet garni* made with 1 sprig thyme, 1/4 bay leaf, white of 1 leek, 1 stalk celery, and 4 sprigs parsley, tied together

2 medium onions, peeled and quartered

4 cloves or garlic, peeled

1 carrot, peeled and quartered

2 bottles red wine (preferably from Burgundy)

4 peppercorns, coarsely crushed in a mortar

3 pounds (1.4 kg) eel, skinned, cleaned, and cut into 1-inch (2.5-cm) thick pieces

3 pounds (1.4 kg) carp, scaled, cleaned, and cut into 1-inch (2.5-cm) thick pieces

Salt

3 1/2 tablespoons (50 g) butter

1 tablespoon (10 g) flour

3 tablespoons (5 cl) water

Place the onions, garlic, carrots, and *bouquet garni* in a large saucepan, add the wine and pepper, bring to a boil, and boil slowly for 30 minutes. Stir the water little by little into the flour to make a smooth, thin, mixture. Remove the saucepan from the heat and take out the *bouquet garni*. Whisk in the flour mixture, then blend the wine and vegetables in a blender or food processor (this will have to be done in several batches). Reserve.

While the wine is cooking, remove as many small, hairlike bones from the pieces of fish as possible, using a pair of tweezers.

Melt the butter in a large, high-sided frying pan or pot, add the fish, and cook over low heat for 5 minutes. Add the wine, bring to a boil, then lower the heat and simmer for 10 minutes.

Lift the pieces of fish out of the pan using a slotted spoon and place them in a warm serving dish. Boil the sauce rapidly for a minute or two if it seems too liquid, taste for salt and pepper, then pour over the fish and serve.

**Serving suggestions :** This fish stew is excellent served with Spinach (p. 102), Poached Eggs (p. 254), and small squares of bread (croûtons) fried in a little butter and rubbed with garlic (soft-boiled eggs cooked for 6 minutes and carefully peeled, may be used instead of poached eggs if you find them easier to prepare).

# SAUTEED SALT COD AND POTATOES
*Morue poêlée*

PREPARATION TIME : 1 hour (plus 24 hours to desalt)

INGREDIENTS FOR 4 SERVINGS :

1 1/2 pounds (700 g) dried salt cod with bones and skin, *or* 1 1/4 pounds (600 g) salt cod fillets

1 3/4 pounds (800 g) potatoes, in their skins

Salt

6 tablespoons (10 cl) cooking oil

Pepper

1 whole egg

6 tablespoons (10 cl) *crème fraîche* or heavy cream

1 large clove garlic, peeled and finely chopped

4 tablespoons finely chopped parsley

Salt cod should be purchased in large, flattened and dried pieces on the bone with the skin still attached. If unavailable, fillets may nevertheless be used. In either case, the fish should be cut into large pieces and soaked for 24 hours, before cooking, in the following manner:

Turn a plate upside down in a large bowl or pot so that the fish will not sit directly on the bottom (all the salt falls to the bottom), and place the fish, skin side up, on top of it. Fill the bowl or pot with cold water and add a few ice cubes ; change the water at least 4 times (6 to 8 is preferable) and add a few ice cubes each time. Before cooking, drain the cod and pat it dry with a clean cloth.

Cook the potatoes in a large pot of lightly salted water for 30 minutes, drain, rinse rapidly under running water to cool slightly, then remove their skins while still hot (they will peel very easily). Cut the potatoes into thick slices or large cubes, place in a bowl, cover, and reserve.

While the potatoes are cooking, cook the cod. Place it in a large pot, add cold water to cover, and bring to a boil. As soon as the water boils, cover the pot and remove from the heat. Leave the fish in the water for 20 minutes, then drain, carefully remove the skin and bones, and break the cod into small flaky pieces with your fingers.

Heat the oil in a large frying pan; when hot, add the potatoes and cod, lower the heat, and cook for 10 to 12 minutes, or until very hot, stirring frequently. Generously pepper and taste for salt (it probably won't need any).

When the cod and potatoes are hot, whisk the egg and cream together in a mixing bowl. Remove the frying pan from the heat and quickly stir in the egg-cream mixture. Pour into a hot serving dish, sprinkle with parsley and garlic, and serve immediately.

# SALT COD PORTUGUESE-STYLE
*Morue à la portugaise*

PREPARATION TIME : 1 1/2 hours (plus 24 hours to desalt)

INGREDIENTS FOR 4 SERVINGS :
1 1/2 to 1 3/4 pound (700 to 800 g) dried salt cod with bones and skin,
 *or* 1 1/4 to 1 1/2 pounds (600 to 700 g) salt cod fillets
2 large red bell peppers
About 2 tablespoons olive oil (for the peppers)
6 tablespoons olive oil (for the cod)
1/2 cup olive oil (for the vegetables)
1 fresh chili pepper, seeded and finely chopped
1 large onion, peeled and sliced
1 clove garlic, peeled and crushed
4 tomatoes, peeled and coarsely chopped
1 cup (125 g) black olives
1/2 cup (12 cl) dry white wine
1 pound (500 g) potatoes, peeled

Salt cod should be purchased in large, flattened and dried pieces on the bone with the skin still attached. If unavailable, fillets may nevertheless be used. In either case, the fish should be cut into large pieces and soaked for 24 hours, before cooking, in the following manner:
Turn a plate upside down in a large bowl or pot so that the fish will not sit directly on the bottom (all the salt falls to the bottom), and place the fish, skin side up, on top of it. Fill the bowl or pot with cold water and add a few ice cubes ; change the water at least 4 times (6 to 8 is preferable) and add a few ice cubes each time.
Preheat the oven to 450°F (240°C).
Wash the bell peppers, wipe them dry, cut out the stem, and remove the seeds. Brush each pepper with oil, then place them on a rack in the oven for 15 minutes, turning over once. Remove the peppers from the oven and peel off the skin using your fingers and a paring knife, then cut the peppers into strips and reserve.
Drain the salt cod, pat it dry with a clean cloth, remove the skin and bones, then cut it into pieces about 2 inches (5 cm) on a side. Heat 6 tablespoons (10 cl) of oil in a large, high-sided frying pan, add the cod, and cook over moderate heat 5 minutes on a side. Remove with a slotted spatula and place on a warm serving platter. Cover the platter, turn off the oven, and place the cod inside to warm while cooking the vegetables.
Place the remaining 1/2 cup (12 cl) of oil in a cast iron or earthenware pot.

When hot, add the bell peppers, chili pepper, onion, garlic, tomatoes, and olives. Simmer for 8 minutes. Add the wine, bring to a boil, lower the heat, and simmer slowly for 15 minutes more.

While the vegetables are cooking, boil the potatoes in lightly salted water for 30 minutes.

Add the cod to the pot with the vegetables and simmer together for 8 minutes. Serve in the pot it cooked in, with the potatoes in a serving dish on the side.

# SALT COD LYONNAISE
*Morue sautée lyonnaise*

PREPARATION TIME : 30 minutes (plus 24 hours to desalt)

INGREDIENTS FOR 4 SERVINGS :
1 3/4 pounds (800 g) dried salt cod with skin and bones, *or* 1 1/2
    pounds (700 g) salt cod fillets
2 large tomatoes, peeled and coarsely chopped
*Bouquet garni,* made with thyme, bay leaf, and parsley
2 cloves garlic, peeled and crushed
Salt
2 medium onions, peeled and sliced
1 1/4 sticks (150 g) butter
Flour
1 cup (25 cl) dry white wine
Pepper

Salt cod should be purchased in large, flattened and dried pieces on the
bone with the skin still attached. If unavailable, fillets may nevertheless be
used. In either case, the fish should be cut into large pieces and soaked for
24 hours, before cooking, in the following manner:
Turn a plate upside down in a large bowl or pot so that the fish will not sit
directly on the bottom (all the salt falls to the bottom), and place the fish,
skin side up, on top of it. Fill the bowl or pot with cold water and add a
few ice cubes ; change the water at least 4 times (6 to 8 is preferable) and
add a few ice cubes each time. Drain the cod and pat it dry with a clean
cloth, cut it into pieces about 4 inches (10 cm) square, then remove the skin
and bones from each piece.
Place the tomatoes in a saucepan with the *bouquet garni* and garlic, salt
lightly, and simmer for 15 minutes, or until the water they give out has
evaporated. While the tomatoes are cooking, cook the onions and salt
cod.
Melt the butter in a large frying pan, add the onions, and cook until they
begin to color ; then lift them out with a slotted spoon and reserve. Roll
the pieces of cod in flour and shake to remove any excess. Fry them for
about 5 minutes over moderate heat in the pan the onions cooked in (the
cod should be nicely browned on both sides). If necessary, cook the cod in
two batches. Remove from the pan, place on a serving platter, and keep
warm while finishing the sauce.
Place the onions back in the pan, pour in the wine, and add the cooked
tomatoes (remove the *bouquet garni* and discard). Season the sauce with a

little pepper, boil rapidly for about 2 minutes, or until it has thickened a bit, then pour over the cod and serve immediately.

**Serving suggestions :** Serve with Rice (p. 290) or boiled potatoes.

# FRICASSEE OF SCALLOPS IN CREAM SAUCE
*Fricassée de coquilles Saint-Jacques à la crème*

PREPARATION TIME : 10 minutes

INGREDIENTS FOR 4 SERVINGS :
Salt, pepper
1 pound (500 g) sea scallops or bay scallops
Flour
4 tablespoons (60 g) butter
1 tablespoon lemon juice
1/4 cup (6 cl) white vermouth
Generous 3/4 cup (20 cl) *crème fraîche* or heavy cream

Salt and pepper the scallops, roll them in flour, and shake them lightly to remove any excess.
Heat the butter in a large frying pan. When very hot, add the scallops and cook over moderate heat for 4 to 6 minutes if using sea scallops, half that time if using bay scallops. Shake the pan frequently and turn the scallops over halfway through the cooking time.
Pour the lemon juice over the scallops, stir in the vermouth, then pour over the cream, stirring to scrape any juices from the bottom of the pan into the sauce. Bring the cream just to a boil, add a little salt and pepper, and serve.

**Serving suggestions :** This is delicious with Broccoli (p. 245).

# MUSSELS MARINIÈRE
*Moules marinière*

PREPARATION TIME : 1 1/2 hours

INGREDIENTS FOR 4 SERVINGS :
4 quarts (4 liters) mussels (see *Note*)
5 tablespoons (75 g) butter
4 new onions, sliced
4 tablespoons chopped parsley (total)
2 stalks celery, diced
2 cups (50 cl) dry white wine
Pepper
Juice of half a lemon

Mussels should be tightly closed, or should close tightly when scraped or tapped with the blade of a knife (if they are open) ; if they stay open, it means they are dead and could be dangerous if eaten (don't be afraid, however, if the mussels open and close after being cleaned ; they are simply breathing).
Clean the mussels one by one, scraping off any barnacles or mud, and pulling out the little "beard" that protrudes from the shell. Wash the mussels under cold running water (don't let them sit in water), and place in a large bowl as they are cleaned.
Melt the butter in a large pot, add the onions, half the parsley, and the celery. Cook until the vegetables just begin to brown. Pour in the wine, add a little pepper, and bring to a boil. Cover the pot and remove from the heat. Leave for 5 minutes before cooking the mussels.
Add the mussels and lemon juice to the pot, cover, and return to the stove over high heat. Once all the mussels have opened, remove them with a slotted spoon. Remove one shell from each mussel, then place them in a large serving bowl (discard any mussels that haven't opened).
Line a sieve with a piece of doubled-over cheese cloth and strain the mussels' cooking liquid into the bowl with the mussels. Sprinkle with the remaining parsley and serve immediately.

*Note : 4 quarts of mussels weigh about 6 pounds (2.8 kg); other small shellfish, such as clams, can be prepared in exactly the same way. Ed.*

# MUSSELS IN WHITE WINE SAUCE
*Moules au vin blanc*

PREPARATION TIME : 1 hour 40 minutes

INGREDIENTS FOR 4 SERVINGS :

4 quarts (4 liters) mussels (see *Note* to Mussels Marinière, p. 150)

3 1/2 tablespoons (50 g) butter

4 new onions, coarsely chopped

6 baby carrots, peeled and coarsely chopped

2 shallots, coarsely chopped

2 cups (50 cl) dry white wine (for the vegetables)

1 cup (25 cl) dry white wine (for the mussels)

Pepper

2 tablespoons (25 g) softened butter (for the *beurre manié*)

2 1/2 tablespoons (25 g) flour

Generous 3/4 cup (20 cl) heavy cream

4 tablespoons coarsely chopped parsley

Clean the mussels as described in the recipe for Mussels Marinière (p. 150). Melt 3 1/2 tablespoons (50 g) butter in a large pot. Add the onions, carrots, and shallots, and simmer for 15 minutes. Add the wine, a little pepper, and cook slowly for 7 minutes more.

Place the mussels in a second pot, add the wine, bring to a boil, and cover the pot. When all the mussels are open, lift them out of the pot with a slotted spoon and discard one shell from each one. Place the mussels in a bowl and keep warm while finishing the sauce.

Line a sieve with a piece of doubled-over cheesecloth and strain the mussels' cooking liquid into the pot with the vegetables; taste for seasoning.

Make a *beurre manié* by mixing the softened butter and flour together with your fingers until smooth, then break it into pea-sized pieces.

Whisk the cream into the boiling sauce, then whisk in the pieces of *beurre manié*. When the sauce is creamy, sprinkle the parsley over the mussels, add the sauce, and serve immediately.

# TURBOT WITH MIXED VEGETABLES
*Turbotin aux légumes*

PREPARATION TIME : 30 minutes

INGREDIENTS FOR 4 SERVINGS :
1 turbot (*or other flatfish. Ed.)* weighing 3 1/4 pounds (1.5 kg)
2 carrots, peeled and cut into julienne strips
1/4 celeriac, peeled and cut into julienne strips
1 leek, cleaned and cut into julienne strips
4 tablespoons (60 g) softened butter
Salt, pepper.
*Bouquet garni* made with 2 sprigs thyme, 1/4 bay leaf, and 2 sprigs
  parsley tied together
1 cup (25 cl) dry white wine

Ask the fish seller to cut off the head and fins, and to cut the fish into 4
pieces.
Preheat the oven to 425°F (220°C).
Cook all the vegetables in a pot of lightly salted boiling water for 7 to 8
minutes, drain, cool under running water, and pat dry with a clean cloth.
Butter a baking dish, spread the vegetables over the bottom, and place the
pieces of fish on top. Season with salt and pepper, and place the *bouquet
garni* in the dish. Add the white wine and bake in the oven for 10 minutes.
To serve, remove the *bouquet garni* and serve the fish and vegetables in the
baking dish.

**Serving suggestions :** Serve with Rice (p. 290) or fresh pasta.

# CHAPTER 7

# VARIETY MEATS

Variety meats are not sufficiently appreciated. This is a shame because they are generally inexpensive and delicious if properly prepared. Like any other meat, variety meats should be left at room temperature for an hour before cooking.

BRAISED TONGUE *(Langue de bœuf braisée)*

CALF'S HEAD *(Tête de veau)*

CALF'S LIVER *(Rôti de foie de veau)*

VEAL KIDNEYS IN MUSTARD SAUCE *(Rognons de veau en "cocotte")*

SWEETBREADS WITH VERMOUTH *(Ris de veau au vermouth)*

BRAINS WITH CAPERS *(Cervelles meunières)*

# BRAISED TONGUE
*Langue de bœuf braisée*

PREPARATION TIME : 3 hours

INGREDIENTS FOR 6 TO 8 SERVINGS :
A 4-pound (1.6-kg) beef tongue, roots removed
3 quarts (3 liters) water (for parboiling)
3 teaspoons (20 g) salt
1 3/4 sticks (200 g) butter
4 medium carrots, peeled, quartered, and cut into thick sticks
12 baby onions, peeled
5 ounces (150 g) bacon, cut into 1/2 inch (1 cm) cubes
1 tablespoon (10 g) flour
1 cup (25 cl) dry white wine
3 1/4 cups (75 cl) bouillon (see French Boiled Dinner, p. 198) or hot
    water
2 veal bones
*Bouquet garni,* made of 2 sprigs thyme, 4 sprigs parsley, 1/2 bay leaf,
    and 1 stalk celery tied together
Salt, pepper
1 tablespoon tomato paste

Leave the tongue in a large bowl of cold water for 2 hours; then drain it, place it in a pot, add 3 quarts (3 liters) fresh cold water, the salt, and bring to a boil. Skim off any foam that surfaces and boil the tongue for 10 minutes. Drain in a colander and cool under cold running water until cool enough to handle. Use a paring knife to scrape off the thick skin that surrounds the tongue (a thin white film will be left in most places), then dry it with a clean towel.

Melt the butter in a pot just large enough to comfortably hold the tongue. Add the carrots, onions, and bacon, and cook for about 3 minutes or until the vegetables begin to soften. Place the tongue in the pot and brown on all sides over moderate heat for about 10 minutes. Sprinkle in the flour, stir to combine, then add the wine, stirring constantly. Add the bouillon or hot water, the veal bones and the *bouquet garni;* the tongue should be about half covered by the liquid. Salt and pepper, bring just to a boil, then immediately lower the heat, cover the pot, and simmer slowly for 2 1/2 hours. Turn the tongue over 5 or 6 times while cooking. To test for doneness, pierce it with a long trussing needle after 2 hours; if the needle goes into the tongue with virtually no resistance, it is done.

To serve, remove the tongue from the sauce, stir in the tomato paste, and simmer while slicing the tongue. Place the tongue on a hot platter. To the sauce add any juices that came from it while slicing, spoon a little sauce over the tongue and serve, with a sauceboat of the sauce on the side.

**Serving suggestions:** Serve with Rice (p. 290) or boiled potatoes and butter.

# CALF'S HEAD
*Tête de veau*

PREPARATION TIME : 1 1/2 hours

INGREDIENTS FOR 6 SERVINGS :

1 calf's brain
1 to 2 tablespoons vinegar
1/2 calf's head
1 calf's tongue
1 lemon
2 carrots, peeled and quartered
*Bouquet garni,* made with thyme
    and bay leaf

1 clove garlic, unpeeled
1 large onion stuck with 1 clove
8 peppercorns
1 1/2 teaspoons (10 g) coarse salt
2 cups (50 cl) dry white wine
1 tablespoon (10 g) flour
Water
Gribiche Sauce (p. 116)

Place the calf's brain in a bowl of cold water, add the vinegar, and leave to soak while cooking the head.

Half of a head is plenty for 6 people. It should be boned by the butcher, the tongue placed on it, and the head rolled up around the tongue and tied with string so it looks rather like a large, thick sausage.

Rub the head with half a lemon, then wrap it in doubled-over cheesecloth or some other thin white cloth (such as a dish towel) and tie it at both ends and around the middle. Place the head in a large pot (an oval one is preferable), add the carrots, *bouquet garni,* garlic, onion, peppercorns, salt, and wine. Mix the flour with enough water to form a thin creamy mixture, then pour into the pot as well. Add enough cold water to completely cover the head, bring to a boil, immediately lower the heat, cover the pot by 3/4, and simmer over moderate heat for 1 hour 15 minutes. Skim off any foam that rises to the surface during this time. Test after about 1 hour by piercing the head with a long trussing needle ; it should be tender when done (some people like it more cooked than others, but remember that the ears should be "crunchy" even when completely cooked).

When the head is done, cook the brain. First, hold it under cold running water and use your fingers to remove the membrane that surrounds it. Pat it dry with a clean dish towel. Ladle out about 2 cups (50 cl) of the cooking liquid from the head, place it in a saucepan and poach the brain for about 8 minutes. Remove the saucepan from the heat and cover to keep the brain warm if you don't serve immediately.

Lift the head out of its cooking liquid, remove the cloth around it, and slice it. Place the slices on a hot platter with the brain, carrots, and a little of the cooking liquid. Serve with a sauceboat of Gribiche Sauce on the side.

**Serving suggestions :** Serve with steamed potatoes.

# CALF'S LIVER
*Rôti de foie de veau*

PREPARATION TIME: 45 minutes

INGREDIENTS FOR 4 TO 6 SERVINGS:
A piece of calf's liver weighing 1 3/4 to 2 1/4 pounds (800 g to 1 kg)
Salt, pepper
4 tablespoons (60 g) butter
4 carrots, peeled and quartered
4 onions, peeled and quartered
*Bouquet garni,* made of thyme, bay leaf, and a stalk of celery

Salt and pepper the calf's liver on all sides. In a pot, melt the butter, then add the liver, carrots, onions, and *bouquet garni ;* brown the liver over moderate heat for about 10 minutes, turning frequently. Add the wine and water, heat almost to boiling, then cover the pot and simmer for 20 minutes. Remove the pot from the heat, season with a little salt and pepper, cover the pot again and leave to rest for 15 minutes away from the heat before serving.
To serve, lift the liver out of the pot, slice it on a cutting board, then place the slices on a hot serving platter. Pour any juices that come from the liver back into the pot. Bring to a boil (you can add a little hot water if you feel there won't be enough sauce), then strain over the liver and serve immediately, with the carrots and onions in a dish on the side, or arranged around the liver on the platter.

**Serving suggestions :** Serve with Spinach (p. 254) or Braised Lettuce (p. 267).

# VEAL KIDNEY'S IN MUSTARD SAUCE
*Rognons de veau en cocotte*

PREPARATION TIME : 10 minutes

INGREDIENTS FOR 6 SERVINGS :
3 veal kidneys weighing about 12 ounces (350 g) each
Salt, pepper
4 tablespoons (60 g) butter
3 shallots, peeled and chopped
1/4 cup (6 cl) cognac
6 tablespoons (10 cl) *crème fraîche* or heavy cream
1 tablespoon Dijon mustard

Remove all the fat and gristle from the kidneys. Cut them into thin slices, then sprinkle with salt and pepper.
Melt the butter in a frying pan; when it starts to foam, add the kidneys and sauté over high heat 3 to 4 minutes, shaking the pan frequently so the slices will cook on all sides.
Lift the slices out of the pan with a slotted spoon. Place on a hot platter and keep warm while making the sauce.
Add the shallots to the pan the kidneys cooked in, stir over high heat until soft, then stir in first the cognac, then the cream, scraping the bottom of the pan to dissolve any meat juices, and finally the mustard. Spoon the sauce immediately over the kidneys and serve.

**Serving suggestions :** Serve with Rice (p. 290) or Spinach (p. 254).

# SWEETBREADS WITH VERMOUTH
## *Ris de veau au vermouth*

PREPARATION TIME: About 1 hour 45 minutes (plus soaking overnight)

INGREDIENTS FOR 6 SERVINGS:
2 1/4 pounds (1 kg) veal sweetbreads (whole)
3 quarts (3 liters) water
5 carrots, peeled and sliced
5 onions, peeled and sliced
*Bouquet garni* made with 2 stalks celery, 2 sprigs parsley, 2 sprigs
    thyme and 1 bay leaf tied together
1 tablespoon (25 g) coarse salt
6 peppercorns
2 tablespoons (20 g) flour
4 tablespoons (60 g) butter
1/4 cup (6 cl) white vermouth
Salt, pepper

Place the sweetbreads in a large bowl of cold water and leave in the refrigerator overnight before cooking. Remove from the refrigerator 2 hours before cooking, but leave in the water. Just before cooking, drain the sweetbreads and rinse under cold running water, then leave to drain in a colander.

Pour the water into a large pot, add the carrots, onions, and the *bouquet garni*. Add the salt and peppercorns, then bring to a boil. Add the sweetbreads, lower the heat and simmer for 20 minutes. When the time is up, lift the sweetbreads out with a slotted spoon (save the cooking liquid) and place them in a sieve over a mixing bowl to catch any juices; allow to cool completely.

When the sweetbreads are cool, roll them in the flour. Heat the butter in a highsided frying pan and brown the sweetbreads for about 6 minutes, turning them over to brown evenly on all sides. Add the vermouth and 1 cup (25 cl) of the cooking liquid reserved earlier, as well as any juices that drained from the sweetbreads as they were cooling. Simmer the sweetbreads 30 minutes over very low heat, uncovered. Season with salt and pepper just before they are done, then serve them on a hot platter with the sauce they cooked in.

**Serving suggestions:** Serve with green peas, or Braised Lettuce (p. 267).

160

# BRAINS WITH CAPERS
*Cervelles meunières*

PREPARATION TIME : 40 minutes (plus soaking overnight)

INGREDIENTS FOR 4 SERVINGS :
4 lambs' brains
2 carrots, peeled and quartered
2 medium onions, peeled and halved
*Bouquet garni* made with 2 sprigs parsley, 2 stalks celery, 1 sprig
   thyme, and 1 bay leaf tied together
6 1/3 cups (1 1/2 liters) water
2 tablespoons (20 g) flour
4 tablespoons (60 g) butter
4 tablespoons (40 g) capers
Salt, pepper

Place the brains in a large bowl of cold water overnight in the refrigerator before cooking.

Remove from the refrigerator 2 hours before cooking, but leave in the water. Just before cooking, hold each brain under cold running water and take off the thin membrane that surrounds it. Leave to drain in a colander.

In a large pot, place the carrots, onions, and *bouquet garni ;* add the water and bring to a boil. As soon as the water boils, add the brains, lower the heat, and poach for 10 minutes, then lift the brains out of the pot and place in a strainer above a mixing bowl to cool. Keep any juices that fall into the bowl, measure them, and add enough of the cooking liquid to bring the total to 6 tablespoons (10 cl). Reserve.

When the brains are cold, cut them into thin slices and roll them in the flour, shaking off as much excess flour as possible.

Heat the butter in a large frying pan ; when it starts to foam, add the brains and brown for about 5 minutes (turn each piece over once). When brown, add the capers, sprinkle with salt and pepper, then place the brains on hot dinner plates. Add the reserved cooking liquid to the pan, scraping to dissolve anything stuck to the bottom, then pour over the brains and serve immediately.

**Serving suggestions :** Serve with boiled potatoes or pasta.

# CHAPTER 8

# POULTRY AND GAME

Whenever possible, buy your poultry from a farmer or a very reliable retailer ; the difference in taste between ordinary and top-quality poultry is enormous.

A *stewing hen* is a female chicken that is no longer used for laying eggs. The best generally weigh 3 1/2 to 5 pounds (1.6 to 2.25 kg).

A *broiler* or *fryer* is a tender young chicken weighing 1 1/2 to 3 pounds (700 g to 1.4 kg).

A *roaster* is a larger chicken, weighing from 2 1/2 to 5 pounds (1.15 to 2.25 kg).

A *capon,* a castrated male chicken specially raised and fattened to produce very tender flesh, weighs from 5 to 8 pounds (2.25 to 3.6 kg).

A *cock* or *rooster,* an adult male chicken used generally in stews, weighs from 8 3/4 to 11 pounds (4 to 5 kg).

When buying *turkey,* choose birds with well-developed breast meat (the breast bone should not form a ridge) and fine white skin.

For *squab, pigeon,* or *dove,* choose young birds with large feet and pink flesh on the wings, weighing no more than 1 pound (450 g).

When buying *duck,* choose young ones weighing 3 to 5 1/2 pounds (1.4 to 2.5 kg) with tight white skin and plump breasts.

When buying *rabbit,* look for young animals weighing 2 to 3 1/2 pounds (900 g to 1.6 kg), with meaty thighs and white fat.

*Guinea hen,* although domesticated, is somewhat similar to pheasant. It should have yellow skin and meaty breasts with pale reddish flesh.

Young *pheasants* can be recognized by the small size of the spur on the underside of the foot. Females are generally preferred to the more spectacularly feathered males.

BOILED HEN *(Poule bouillie)*

STUFFED BOILED HEN *(Poularde farcie)*

BOILED MIXED MEAT AND TURKEY DINNER
*(Dindonne au pot)*

POT-ROASTED CHICKEN *(Poulet cocotte)*

CHICKEN IN CREAM SAUCE LOUHANS-STYLE
*(Poulet de Bresse sauté à la crème comme à
Louhans)*

CAPON ROASTED WITH BLACK OLIVES
*(Chapon de Bresse rôti aux olives noires)*

COCK IN RED WINE *(Coq au vin de Julienas)*

DUCK WITH TURNIPS *(Canard aux navets)*

CHICKEN LIVER SOUFFLE *(Gâteau aux foies de
volaille)*

PHEASANT OR GUINEA HEN WITH
CHESTNUTS *(Poule faisane ou faisan, ou
pintadeau, aux marrons)*

GUINEA HEN OR PARTRIDGES WITH
CABBAGE *(Pintade ou perdreaux au chou)*

SQUAB WITH GREEN PEAS *(Pigeons aux petits
pois)*

BREAST OF GUINEA HEN IN CREAM SAUCE
*(Suprêmes de pintadeau de Bresse à la crème)*

RABBIT LYONS-STYLE *(Lapin sauté à la
lyonnaise)*

RABBIT SAUTEED WITH DIJON MUSTARD
*(Lapin à la moutarde)*

HARE STEWED IN RED WINE *(Lapin en civet ou
civet de lièvre)*

RABBIT PATE *(Rillettes de lapin)*

HARE OR VENISON IN MUSTARD SAUCE
*(Râble de lièvre, ou selle de chevreuil, à la
moutarde)*

# BOILED HEN
*Poule bouillie*

PREPARATION TIME : 2 hours

INGREDIENTS FOR 6 SERVINGS :
1 4-pound (1.8 kg) top-quality stewing hen
4 small leeks, cleaned
1/2 head celery, split lengthwise
*Bouquet garni,* made of 1 sprig thyme, 1/4 bay leaf, and 4 sprigs
   parsley tied together
6 medium carrots, peeled and cut in half lengthwise
2 onions, peeled (one stuck with a clove)
3 turnips, peeled and cut in half
1 tomato, peeled
4 teaspoons (30 g) coarse salt
3 peppercorns
6 medium potatoes, peeled

Cut the wing tips and neck off the hen and chop into small pieces; tie the bird as for roasting, and place with the neck and wings in a large pot.
Tie the leeks and celery together with kitchen string. Add these, along with the *bouquet garni,* carrots, onions, turnips, and tomato to the pot. Pour in enough cold water to completely cover, add the salt and peppercorns, then bring to a boil, immediately lower the heat, skim off any foam, and cover the pot. Simmer for 1 hour. Add the potatoes and cook 30 minutes more. To serve, ladle out and strain enough of the bouillon to serve first as a soup, with slices of toasted country-style bread (save any leftover bouillon for use in other recipes). Remove and discard the *bouquet garni,* then lift the hen out of the pot and carve. Place on a hot platter, surround with the vegetables, and serve, with various Dijon mustards (flavored and un-flavored), a bowl of coarse salt (to sprinkle over the meat), and Vinegar Pickles (p. 51) on the side.

# STUFFED BOILED HEN
*Poularde farcie*

PREPARATION TIME : 2 1/2 hours

INGREDIENTS FOR 4 TO 6 SERVINGS :
A 3 1/2-pound (1,6 kg) top-quality stewing hen
1 cup (50 g) fresh breadcrumbs
1/2 cup (12 cl) milk
4 chicken livers, chopped
2 shallots, peeled and finely chopped
1 large clove garlic, peeled and finely chopped
2 tablespoons finely chopped parsley
3 1/2 ounces (100 g) salt pork, chopped
1 egg
1 sprig thyme
1/4 bay leaf
4 peppercorns
1 onion, peeled and stuck with a clove
About 3 1/2 quarts (3 1/2 liters) water
3 1/2 teaspoons (25 g) coarse salt
4 to 6 large leeks, cleaned and tied together
4 to 6 medium carrots, peeled
2 to 3 stalks of celery, strings removed

First make the stuffing. Chop the hen's liver and heart, and reserve in a bowl with the other chopped livers. Place the crumbled bread in another bowl with the milk and leave for about 10 minutes, or until the bread has completely softened. Use the prongs of a fork to crush the bread, then stir in the livers, shallots, garlic, parsley, salt pork, and egg. Season generously with salt and pepper, then stuff the hen and sew it up so that none of the stuffing will escape while cooking.
Place the hen in a large pot with the thyme, bay leaf, peppercorns, and onion. Pour in enough water to completely cover, add the salt, and bring to a boil. Skim off any foam, then lower the heat, cover the pot, and simmer for 1 hour. Add the leeks, carrots, and celery, and cook 1 hour more. To serve, remove the hen from the pot, carve, and serve on a hot platter with the stuffing and vegetables around it, and Dijon mustard and Vinegar Pickles (p. 51) on the side.

166

If you like, the cooking liquid (bouillon) can be served first, as a soup, with slices of toasted country-style bread (any leftover bouillon can be used for other recipes).

# BOILED MIXED MEAT AND TURKEY DINNER
*Dindonne au pot*

PREPARATION TIME : 2 hours

INGREDIENTS FOR 6 TO 8 SERVINGS :
About 4 quarts (4 liters) cold water
*Bouquet garni,* made of 1 leek, 2 stalks celery, 1 sprig thyme, and 1/4
   bay leaf tred together
2 onions, peeled and stuck with 1 clove each
4 carrots, peeled and quartered
4 teaspoons (30 g) coarse salt
4 peppercorns
A 4 1/2-pound (2 kg) turkey (see *Note*)
1 oxtail, cut into pieces
1 veal shank
3/4 cup (18 cl) walnut oil
3 tablespoons red wine vinegar
Salt, pepper
2 tablespoons finely chopped chervil

Fill a very large pot with the cold water, add the *bouquet garni,* onions, carrots, salt, and peppercorns ; then add all the meat and bring to a boil uncovered. Skim off any foam that rises, then immediately lower the heat, cover the pot, and simmer for 1 1/2 hours.
Make a sauce by whisking together the oil, vinegar, and a little salt and pepper. Just before serving sprinkle in the chopped chervil.
First, serve a bowl of the bouillon as a soup, with slices of country-style

bread. Then serve the different meats, sliced and arranged on a hot platter, with the sauce in a sauceboat on the side.

**Serving suggestions :** Thirty minutes before the meat has finished cooking, take some of the cooking liquid out of the pot and use it to make Rice Pilaf (p. 291). Serve at the same time as the meat.

*Note : A very small turkey is called for in this recipe ; if you can't find one, use turkey legs only, or buy a large turkey and use 1 breast and 1 leg, cut apart (the other half of the turkey can be cut into pieces and used to make the Cock in Red Wine (p. 174).*
*Save any leftover bouillon and use it in other recipes. Ed.*

# POT-ROASTED CHICKEN
*Poulet cocotte*

PREPARATION TIME : 1 hour

INGREDIENTS FOR 4 TO 5 SERVINGS :
4 thin slices salt pork or bacon
A 3-pound (1.4 kg) broiling or frying chicken (reserve the liver and
  gizzard)
2 tablespoons (30 g) butter (for the chicken)
Salt, pepper
2 1/4 pounds (1 kg) new baby potatoes, peeled (cut larger potatoes in
  half)
2 tablespoons (30 g) butter (for the vegetables)
1 tablespoon olive oil
16 baby onions, peeled
1/2 teaspoon thyme leaves
4 tablespoons (6 cl) boiling water

Soak salt pork for an hour, then drain and pat dry with a clean cloth
(bacon doesn't need to be soaked). Cover the breasts and thighs of the
chicken with the salt pork or bacon, and tie the slices in place with string or
attach them with toothpicks.
Melt 2 tablespoons butter in a pot slightly larger than the chicken, add the
chicken along with its liver and gizzard, and cook over low heat, turning
frequently for even browning, for 20 minutes. Season with salt and
pepper.
Peel the potatoes, wash in cold water, then drain and pat dry with a cloth
before cooking.
While the chicken is browning, heat 2 tablespoons butter and the oil in a
frying pan. Add the onions, potatoes, and thyme. Cook for 20 minutes,
shaking the pan to brown the vegetables evenly. Season with salt and pepper (the chicken and vegetables should be done at about the same time).
When the cooking time is up, lift the vegetables out of the pan with a slotted spoon, add them to the pot with the chicken, and continue cooking for
15 minutes.
To serve, lift the chicken out of the pot, and carve. Place on a hot platter
and surround with the vegetables. Pour the boiling water into the pot the
chicken cooked in, bring to a boil, stirring constantly, season with salt and
pepper if needed, and serve in a sauceboat on the side.

**Serving suggestions :** Serve with one of the salads (pp. 78-82).

# CHICKEN IN CREAM SAUCE LOUHANS-STYLE
*Poulet sauté à la crème comme à Louhans*

PREPARATION TIME : 1 hour

INGREDIENTS FOR 4 TO 5 SERVINGS :
A 3-pound (1.4-kg) broiling or frying chicken
Salt, pepper
4 tablespoons (60 g) butter
8 baby onions, peeled
3 cloves garlic, whole and unpeeled
1 carrot, peeled and sliced
1 tablespoon (10 g) flour
1 1/2 cups (1/2 bottle) dry white wine (preferably a Mâcon)
2 cups (50 cl) water
*Bouquet garni,* made of thyme, bay leaf, and parsley tied together
3/4 cup (20 cl) *crème fraîche* or heavy cream ; *or* 2 egg yolks,
    6 tablespoons (10 cl) *crème fraîche* or heavy cream, and 1 tablespoon
    lemon juice
Salt, pepper

Cut the chicken into eight pieces (wings and breasts separated, thighs and drumsticks separated), then chop the back and carcass into several pieces as well. Season with salt and pepper.
Melt the butter in a high-sided frying pan just large enough to hold all the pieces of chicken on the bottom. First brown the breast meat and wings ; lift them out and brown the thighs and drumsticks with the onions, garlic, and carrots; lift them out and brown the back and carcass (leave the vegetables in the pan). When the back has browned, place the other pieces of chicken back in the pan, sprinkle in the flour, stirring and turning over the pieces of chicken, then add the wine, water, and *bouquet garni.* Bring to a boil, stirring, and cook over high heat for 20 minutes, or until 2/3 of the liquid has evaporated. Lift out the onions and the chicken, with the exception of the pieces of back and carcass, and keep warm while finishing the sauce. Boil the remaining liquid over high heat to evaporate by half.
The sauce can be finished in one of two ways. In either case, strain it first into a clean saucepan. Then, either simply add 3/4 cup (20 cl) of cream and cook for about 4 minutes, or until thick and creamy. Or, thicken the sauce with egg yolks and cream. In this case, whisk the egg yolks and 6 tablespoons (10 cl) of cream together in a mixing bowl, add a small ladleful of the strained sauce, whisking rapidly, then pour the mixture into the

saucepan, whisking constantly. Heat over low heat until very hot, but do not allow to boil ; then add the lemon juice, and taste for salt and pepper. The chicken and onions can be reheated in the sauce if need be, but stir the sauce constantly in this case and do not allow it to boil or it will curdle. When the sauce is ready, spoon it over the chicken and onions on a hot platter and serve.

**Serving suggestions :** Serve with Spinach (p. 254).

# CAPON ROASTED WITH BLACK OLIVES
*Chapon de Bresse rôti aux olives noires*

PREPARATION TIME : 1 hour 45 minutes

INGREDIENTS FOR 8 SERVINGS :
2 cups (250 g) black olives
A 5 1/2-pound (2 1/2 kg) capon (see *Note*)
3 tablespoons (40 g) butter, for the roasting pan
Salt, pepper
1/2 cup (12 cl) warm water
4 tablespoons (60 g) softened butter, broken into 10 pieces

Preheat the oven to 450°F (240°C).
Rinse the olives in cold running water and drain. Place them inside the capon, then sew up the bird to keep them inside while roasting. Sprinkle the capon with salt and pepper, place it in a generously buttered roasting pan, and roast for 1 1/2 hours (about 17 minutes per pound). Baste after the first 15 minutes and every so often thereafter. Once the cooking time is up, turn off the oven but leave the bird inside for another 10 minutes before serving.
To serve, lift the capon out of the roasting pan and carve ; save any juices that come from it for the sauce. Place the olives in a bowl. Add the warm water and any carving juices to the roasting pan, place over high heat, and add the softened butter. Bring to a boil, whisking constantly ; when all the butter has melded, add salt and pepper, then pour into a sauceboat.
Serve, with the sauce and the olives on the side.

**Serving suggestions :** Serve with Sauteed Potatoes (p. 265) or Green Beans (p. 255).

*Note : If a capon is unavailable, two 3-pound (1.4 kg) chickens may be used instead. Follow the directions given here but roast for only 50 minutes. Ed.*

Capon Roasted with Black Olives

# COCK IN RED WINE
*Coq au vin de Juliénas*

PREPARATION TIME : 1 1/2 to 2 hours

INGREDIENTS FOR 6 SERVINGS :
A 4 3/4 to 6 1/2 pound (2.2 to 3 kg) roasting chicken (see *Note*)
Blood from the bird (see *Note*)
1 clove garlic, peeled and chopped
3 tablespoons (40 g) butter
5 1/4 ounces (150 g) salt pork or slab bacon, cut into cubes
8 baby onions, peeled
1 large tomato, peeled and quartered
1 medium carrot, peeled and quartered
*Bouquet garni* made with 2 sprigs thyme, 1/4 bay leaf, 4 sprigs parsley,
    1 stalk celery, and the white of 1 leek, tied together
8 medium mushrooms, whole and unpeeled
1 generous tablespoon (15 g) flour
3 tablespoons (5 cl) cognac
1 1/2 bottles red wine (preferably Juliénas)
Salt, pepper

If possible, get a freshly killed bird and ask that its blood be saved for making the sauce (see *Note*).
Clean the bird and reserve the liver, heart, and lungs. Cut off the legs and separate the thighs from the drumsticks, cut off the breasts and divide them in half at the wing, then chop the remaining carcass, neck, and back into several large pieces. Sprinkle with salt and reserve.
Chop the liver, heart and lungs to a paste and add to the blood, along with the chopped garlic.
Melt the butter in a large pot, add the chicken, bacon, and onions, and brown, turning frequently, for about 7 minutes, then add the tomato, carrot, *bouquet garni,* and whole garlic. Cook slowly uncovered for 7 minutes more, then sprinkle in the flour and stir to combine. Cook 5 minutes, pour in the cognac and boil for a few seconds, stirring to dissolve the juices stuck to the bottom of the pan. Add the wine, bring just to a boil, then immediately lower the heat and cook at a slow boil, uncovered, for 1 to 1 1/2 hours. Test to see if the chicken is done by piercing a drumstick with the tip of a knife or trussing needle — if it goes in easily the bird is cooked. Remove the pieces of chicken from the pan ; discard the pieces of back and carcass which were just to flavor the sauce. Remove the little onions, bacon, and mushrooms with a slotted spoon and reserve.

Strain the remaining sauce, place back in the pot, and boil for 5 to 10 minutes, then remove from the heat and stir in the blood-liver mixture. Place over low heat and heat just until the sauce thickens ; do not allow to boil. Place the chicken, bacon, onions, and mushrooms back in the pot to warm through, taste for salt and pepper, then serve in the pot it cooked in.

*Note : The blood used to flavor and thicken the sauce need not necessarily come from the bird in question. 6 tablespoons (10 cl) pig's blood may be used instead, but if neither is available, 5 chicken livers (including the one from the chicken you are using) may be used. Sauté them for 1 to 2 minutes in a little butter or oil over high heat, then drain on paper towels and allow to cool. Place in a blender or food processor with 2/3 cup (15 cl) of the sauce and blend until smooth, then whisk this mixture into the sauce. If you would like the sauce to be thicker, add a little* beurre manié *as described in the recipe for Hare Stewed in Red Wine p. 190, using the measurements given there.*

*A true cock is a much larger bird than the one used here, weighing from 8 3/4 to 11 pounds (4 to 5 kg) with tough, but very tasty flesh, not unlike the dark meat on a turkey. It is large enough to feed 8 to 10 people. If you make this recipe with a cock, double all the measurements and the cooking time, and brown the bird in batches. Otherwise follow the recipe exactly as described. Ed.*

# DUCK WITH TURNIPS
*Canard aux navets*

PREPARATION TIME : 1 hour

INGREDIENTS FOR 4 SERVINGS :

A 3-pound (1.4 kg) duck with liver, heart, and lungs

1/4 pound (125 g) salt pork, diced

2 large shallots, peeled and chopped (for the stuffing)

3 duck or chicken livers, chopped to a paste (for the stuffing)

1 pinch powdered thyme

1 pinch powdered bay leaf

2 tablespoons chopped parsley

1 cup (40 g) coarsely crumbled dry or stale toast (or melba toast)

2 egg yolks

1 pinch 4-spice mixture (see *Note*) or allspice

2 pounds (900 g) turnips, peeled (see *Note*)

Butter (for 2 roasting pans)

Generous 3/4 cup (20 cl) *crème fraîche* or heavy cream

Salt, pepper

Nutmeg

1 shallot, peeled and finely chopped (for the sauce)

1 tablespoon cognac

5 teaspoons (25 g) softened butter, broken into 5 pieces

The duck should be cleaned and prepared for roasting ; save the heart, liver, and lungs for the sauce. If you remove the wishbone, which is right where the two breasts meet in the front, the duck will be easier to carve. Preheat the oven to 425°F (220°C).

Mix together the diced salt pork, shallots, the duck or chicken livers for the stuffing, thyme, bay leaf, parsley, crumbled toast, and egg yolks. Season with the 4-spice mixture, then stuff the duck and carefully sew it closed so the stuffing will stay inside.

When the duck is ready to roast, prepare the turnips. Peel and slice them as thinly as possible, drop them into lightly salted boiling water, bring back to a boil, and boil 2 minutes ; then drain and cool under running water. Pat dry with a clean cloth. Lightly butter a baking dish just large enough to hold the turnips and place them so that the slices slightly over-lap; when half of them are in the dish, season with salt, pepper, and nut-meg, then finish filling the dish, spoon over the cream, and season once more with salt, pepper, and nutmeg. Reserve.

Place the duck in a lightly buttered roasting pan, add 4 tablespoons (6 cl) of water, and roast for a total of 50 minutes. After 20 minutes, place the turnips in the oven as well, and continue cooking the final 30 minutes.

*(Continued p. 178)*

Duck with Turnips

Chop the duck's liver, heart, and lungs to a paste. Mix with the shallot, place in a small saucepan with the cognac, season with a little salt and pepper, and cook over very low heat for 1 minute ; remove from the heat.

When the duck is done, remove it from the oven and carve it on a cutting board, being careful to save any juices that come from it. First remove the legs and thighs and place them on a piece of aliminium foil, skin side down ; place them back in the oven to continue cooking while you finish carving the duck and make the sauce.

Place the sliced duck breasts on a hot platter with the stuffing and keep warm. Discard almost all the fat in the roasting pan. Add the carving juices, the cognac-liver mixture, 5 tablespoons (75 cl) warm water, and the softened butter, and heat on top of the stove, stirring, until the butter has melted. Pour into a sauceboat. Remove the legs from the oven, place on the serving platter, and serve, with the turnips and sauce on the side.

*Note : The French 4-spice mixture* (quatre épices) *is a commercial mixture that varies in strength. You can make one version using 10 parts ground pepper, 5 parts ground nutmeg, 3 parts ground cloves, and 2 parts ground ginger.*

*The turnip in the photo is a black variety preferred by Paul Bocuse for its delicate taste. Ed.*

## CHICKEN LIVER SOUFFLE
*Gâteau aux foies de volaille*

PREPARATION TIME : 1 hour

INGREDIENTS FOR 4 SERVINGS :
2 1/4 pounds (1 kg) fresh tomatoes
1 teaspoon olive oil
*Bouquet garni,* made with 1 sprig thyme, 1/4 bay leaf and 1 stalk celery
    tied together
1 teaspoon (5 g) granulated sugar
Salt, pepper
1 tablespoon olive oil (to finish)
3 chicken livers, about 1/4 pound (125 g), finely chopped (see
    Comment)

1 small onion, peeled and sliced
Milk (for the onion)
2 1/4 cups (100 g) stale bread, crumbled
2 cups (50 cl) milk (for the bread)
1 clove garlic, peeled and finely chopped
2 tablespoons parsley leaves
4 egg yolks
1 1/2 tablespoon (20 g) butter (for the mold)
4 egg whites


Fresh tomato sauce is always excellent — this one is a little different from the one in the chapter on Sauces.

Peel the tomatoes, cut them into wedges, and place in a saucepan with a teaspoon of olive oil and the *bouquet garni*. Add the sugar, bring to a boil, then lower the heat and boil gently over moderate heat for about 40 minutes or until thick, stirring frequently. Season with salt and pepper. Just before serving, remove the *bouquet garni* and stir in another tablespoon of fresh olive oil.

Preheat the over to 350°F (180°C).

While the sauce is cooking, you can make the soufflé. If possible, buy livers that are light in color — they are the best. So that the onion will be more digestible, place the slices in a saucepan, add enough cold milk to cover, bring just to a boil, then drain and reserve.

Place the bread in a bowl, add the milk ; once the bread has softened, crush it with the prongs of a fork, then pour off any excess milk. Place the bread on a cutting board with the livers, onions, garlic, and parsley, and chop to a paste. Place in a mixing bowl, stir in the egg yolks, and season with salt and pepper.

Place the butter in a 7-inch (18-cm) soufflé mold and place it in the oven just long enough for the butter to melt. Remove from the oven and turn the dish to coat the sides with the butter.

Beat the egg whites until stiff and fold them into the liver mixture (see Dictionary p. 345), then pour into the soufflé mold. Place in the oven and bake for 45 minutes (check for browning by looking through the window in the oven door, but don't open it until the soufflé is done). Serve the soufflé as it comes from the oven, with the tomato sauce in a sauceboat on the side.

COMMENT : This recipe, which is made in many homes around Lyons, was devised to use leftover chicken livers so they don't go to waste. It can be made with as few as 1 liver, or as many as 6, so if you like chicken livers, don't hesitate to double the measurement given in the list of ingredients.

# PHEASANT OR GUINEA HEN WITH CHESTNUTS
*Poule faisane, ou faisan, ou pintadeau, aux marrons*

PREPARATION TIME : 2 1/2 hours

INGREDIENTS FOR 3 TO 4 SERVINGS :
2 1/4 pounds (1 kg) chestnuts
3 to 4 thin slices salt pork or bacon
A guinea hen or pheasant weighing 2 to 2 1/2 pounds (900 g to 1,15 kg)
    prepared for roasting
2 tablespoons (30 g) butter (for the bird)
Salt, pepper
4 1/2 tablespoons (70 g) butter (for the chestnuts)
4 tablespoons (6 cl) hot water
1 truffle, finely chopped (optional)

Begin by preparing the chestnuts: since peeling them takes quite a while, you might plan to do that the day before cooking.

All chestnuts have two skins, a hard outer one and a thin, furry inner one that clings to the nut. To remove the hard outer one, make a slit in it with a sharp knife, then peel it off (be careful not to cut the chestnut in half when making the slit). Place the peeled chestnuts in a large saucepan, add enough water to cover, a little salt, then cover the pot and bring to a boil. Boil 5 minutes, then remove the pot from the heat but leave the chestnuts in the hot water. With a slotted spoon, remove the chestnuts from the water 3 or 4 at a time, and rub or peel off the inner skin using a clean cloth or dish towel (this must be done while the nuts are very hot). Leave the peeled chestnuts to cool, then place in a container, close tightly, and put them in the refrigerator overnight, or use them right away if peeling them the same day you cook the bird.

Attach the slices of salt pork or bacon to the bird as shown in the photo, using string or toothpicks to hold them in place.

Melt 2 tablespoons (30 g) of butter in a pot large enough to hold the bird comfortably. Salt and pepper the bird, then brown in the butter over moderate heat for 10 minutes, turning frequently to brown evenly (if the butter blackens, pour it off, wipe the pot clean, and replace it with new butter). Butter a piece of parchment paper slightly larger than the pot, place it over the pot buttered side down, then cover the pot and cook about 40 minutes more, turning the bird once or twice.

Just before the bird has finished cooking, melt the remaining 4 1/2 table-

Pheasant or Guinea Hen with Chestnuts

spoons (70 g) butter in a high-sided frying pan and sauté the chestnuts for 10 minutes, gently shaking the pan frequently to roll them around in the butter and brown on all sides. Sprinkle with salt and pepper.

Either serve the bird whole or carve it, and place it on a hot serving platter surrounded by the chestnuts. Add the hot water to the pot the bird cooked in, bring just to a boil, season with salt and pepper, and serve in a sauce-boat on the side.

One truffle, finely chopped, can be added to the sauce just before serving, if you like (but this is strictly optional).

## GUINEA HEN OR PARTRIDGES WITH CABBAGE
*Pintade ou perdrix au chou*

PREPARATION TIME : 2 hours

INGREDIENTS FOR 4 SERVINGS :
1 green Savoy cabbage
3 carrots, peeled and quartered
5 1/4 ounces (150 g) salt pork or bacon, diced
*Bouquet garni,* made of thyme and bay leaf
A 2- to 2 1/2-pound (900-g to 1.15-kg) guinea hen or 2 partridges (see
    *Note)*
2 thin slices fatty bacon or salt pork
Salt, pepper
4 tablespoons (60 g) butter (for the birds)
3 tablespoons (40 g) butter (for the vegetables)
1/2 cup (12 cl) hot water

Preheat the oven to 400°F (200°C).

Cut out the base of the cabbage, then cut it into quarters. Wash it under cold running water, then boil for 15 to 20 minutes in a large pot of lightly salted boiling water with the carrots, diced salt pork or bacon, and the *bouquet garni.* Drain in a colander. Discard the *bouquet garni.*

Place just the cabbage in a roasting pan in the oven to dry out for 10 minutes, then remove from the oven and reserve with the salt pork and carrots.

Clean the bird(s) ; if using freshly killed partridges, pluck them just before cooking. Cover the thighs and breast of each bird with the slices of salt pork or bacon and attach with kitchen string. Sprinkle generously with pepper, but salt lightly because of the pork.

182

Melt 4 tablespoons (60 g) of butter in a pot large enough to comfortably hold the bird(s), and cook for 10 minutes, turning frequently to brown evenly. Cover the pot and finish cooking 20 to 25 minutes for the partridges, or 35 minutes for a guinea hen, turning from time to time. Remove the pot from the heat but leave the bird(s) inside, covered, for 5 minutes more.

Meanwhile, reheat the cabbage, carrots, and diced salt pork by sautéeing them together in a frying pan with 3 tablespoons of butter.

To serve, lift the bird(s) out of the pot, discard the bacon, and carve. Place on a hot platter, surrounded by the vegetables and diced salt pork, and keep warm. Pour any carving juices into the pot, add the hot water, bring to a boil, season with a little pepper, then pour the sauce into a sauceboat and serve.

*Note : Two doves (pigeons) may be used instead or partridges, or a Rock Cornish game hen instead of the guinea hen. Ed.*

# SQUAB WITH GREEN PEAS
*Pigeons aux petits pois*

PREPARATION TIME : 50 minutes

INGREDIENTS FOR 4 SERVINGS :
4 squab, pigeons, or doves weighing about 3/4 to 1 pound (350 to
   450 g) each
4 slices fatty bacon
Pepper
4 tablespoons (60 g) butter (for the birds)
2 cups (50 cl) water
Salt
8 baby onions, peeled
*Bouquet garni,* made of thyme and bay leaf
14 ounces (400 g) shelled fresh peas — purchase 2 1/4 pounds (1 kg)
1 small butterhead (Boston) lettuce, washed and quartered
3 tablespoons (40 g) butter (for the peas)

Prepare the birds as for roasting, then place a slice of bacon across the
breast and thighs of each one and attach with kitchen string. Season with a
little pepper.
In a pot large enough to comfortably hold the birds, melt 4 tablespoons
(60 g) of butter ; when it starts to foam, add the squab and brown, turning
frequently, for 5 to 6 minutes ; then lower the heat, cover the pot, and simmer for 25 minutes, turning from time to time.
About 15 minutes before the squab are done, bring the water to a boil in a
large saucepan, salt lightly, then add the onions, *bouquet garni,* and the
peas. Cook for 7 minutes, then add the lettuce and cook 7 minutes more.
Once the birds and vegetables have finished cooking, remove them from
the heat. Add 3 tablespoons (40 g) of butter to the peas, cover once more,
and leave both the squab and peas to rest for 5 minutes before serving.
To serve, lift the vegetables out of their pot with a slotted spoon and place
them on a hot platter ; arrange the birds on top. Add 6 tablespoons (10 cl)
of the vegetables' cooking liquid to the pot the squab cooked in and bring
to a boil, stirring to detach any juices stuck to the bottom of the pot. Season with salt and pepper if needed, pour into a sauceboat, and serve.

# BREAST OF GUINEA HEN IN CREAM SAUCE
*Suprême de pintadeau à la crème*

PREPARATION TIME: 2 hours

INGREDIENTS FOR 2 SERVINGS:
A 2 3/4-pound (1.25-kg) guinea hen *(or broiling chicken. Ed.)*
2 quarts (2 liters) water
*Bouquet garni* made with 1 small leek, 1 stalk celery, 1 sprig thyme,
   and 1/4 bay leaf tied together
4 carrots, peeled and sliced
1/4 cup (6 cl) dry white wine (preferably Pouilly-Fuissé)
1/4 cup (6 cl) red port
A pinch of salt
5 peppercorns
1/2 pound (250 g) large spinach leaves
Salt, pepper
1 slice pre-cooked country style or shoulder ham — about 3 1/2 ounces
   (100 g) — cut in half
3 tablespoons (40 g) butter
6 tablespoons (10 cl) *crème fraîche* or heavy cream

Only the breast meat from the guinea hen will be used in this recipe. The legs, however, will be cooked in making the stock ; they can be saved and eaten cold with a salad on another occasion.
Begin by cutting off the legs, thighs, and wings. Carefully cut the meat from each breast off in one piece and reserve. Cut the carcass, backbone, and neck of the bird into large pieces and place in a pot with the legs, wings, and cold water. Add the *bouquet garni* to the pot as well as the carrots, white wine, port, salt, and pepper. Bring to a boil, skim, then lower the heat and simmer for 40 minutes, uncovered. Lift out the legs and keep for another meal, then strain the remaining liquid and place it back in the pot.
Wash the spinach leaves, drop them into a pot of lightly salted boiling water, bring back to a boil, and boil slowly for 3 minutes. Lift the leaves out of the water with a slotted spoon and spread them out on a towel to dry, being careful not to tear them.
Split open each piece of breast meat lengthwise, cutting almost through the center so that they will "open", like a book. Season with salt and pepper, then lay half of the ham on each breast and fold it closed inside. Salt and pepper again. Carefully wrap each piece of breast meat in spinach leaves, place half of the butter on each one, wrap each one in a large piece of clear

plastic wrap, going around it several times, then twist the ends once and fold them over to completely enclose the meat inside.

Heat the meat stock prepared earlier, then drop in the breasts and poach for 10 minutes at a gentle boil, turning them over after 5 minutes. Lift out, drain, and reserve.

Boil 1 1/2 cups (35 cl) of the remaining liquid in a frying pan until it is thick and syrupy (draw lines through it with a wooden spoon — when the pan remains visible for a second or two, the liquid it thick enough). Stir in the cream, add salt and pepper if needed, and heat until almost boiling. Remove the plastic wrap from around each breast then place them (still wrapped in the spinach) in the sauce and simmer for 2 minutes (do not boil). Place each breast in the center of a hot dinner plate, pour the sauce around them and serve immediately.

VARIATION : The breasts can simply be wrapped in plastic wrap without being wrapped in spinach, or cabbage leaves, which are much easier to work with, can be used instead of spinach.

# RABBIT LYONS-STYLE
## *Lapin sauté à la lyonnaise*

PREPARATION TIME : 1 hour

INGREDIENTS FOR 4 SERVINGS :
A 3-pound (1.4-kg) rabbit, cut into 10 pieces
Salt, pepper
5 tablespoons (75 g) butter
4 shallots, peeled and chopped
2 cloves garlic, whole and unpeeled
5 1/4 ounces (150 g) salt pork or slab bacon, cut into 1/2 inch (1 cm)
  cubes
*Bouquet garni,* made of thyme, bay leaf, and parsley
1 pound (450 g) tomatoes, peeled and coarsely chopped
2 tablespoons (30 g) butter (for the mushrooms)
1/2 pound (250 g) fresh mushrooms, cleaned and quartered
1/2 cup (12 cl) dry white wine

Salt and pepper the rabbit.
Melt 5 tablespoons (75 g) of butter in a large high-sided frying pan. When
it foams, add the rabbit, shallots, garlic, salt pork, and *bouquet garni* and
cook for 10 minutes, turning frequently, to brown evenly. Add the tomatoes and cook very slowly, uncovered, for 25 minutes, turning 3 to 4 times.
While the rabbit is cooking, melt 2 tablespoons (30 g) of butter in a small
frying pan, add the mushrooms, and sauté until all their moisture has
evaporated and they begin to brown. Lift them out of the pan and add
them ot the rabbit.
When the 25 minutes' cooking time is up for the rabbit, add the white
wine, stirring to detach any meat juices, cover, and cook 8 minutes more
over very low heat. Taste for salt and pepper, then remove the pan from
the heat and leave the rabbit 5 minutes longer in the pan before serving.
Place the rabbit in a hot serving dish, pour over the sauce, and serve.

**Serving suggestions :** Serve with Mashed Potatoes (p. 268) or fresh pasta.

*Note : A chicken the same size as the rabbit can be cut into pieces and
cooked in the same way. Ed.*

# RABBIT SAUTEED WITH DIJON MUSTARD
## Lapin à la moutarde

PREPARATION TIME : 40 minutes

INGREDIENTS FOR 4 SERVINGS :
1 3-pound (1.4-kg) rabbit, cut into 10 pieces
Salt, pepper
1/2 cup (150 g) Dijon mustard
5 tablespoons (75 g) butter
1/4 pound (125 g) salt pork or bacon, diced
1/2 pound (250 g) baby onions, peeled
Bouquet garni, made of thyme, bay leaf, and parsley tied together
3 cloves garlic, whole and unpeeled
1 cup (25 cl) dry white wine
6 medium fresh mushrooms, cleaned and quartered
6 tablespoons (10 cl) heavy cream
1 tablespoon lemon juice

Fresh Dijon mustard is essential for this recipe ; buy a new jar the day you cook the rabbit.

Salt and pepper the pieces of rabbit, then use a spoon to coat them on all sides with the mustard.

Heat the butter in a high-sided frying pan. When it begins to foam, add the rabbit, salt pork, onions, bouquet garni, and garlic. Brown over high heat, turning frequently, for 20 minutes. Add the wine, scraping the bottom of the pan to dissolve any juices stuck to it, and the mushrooms. Cook over moderately low heat for 10 minutes, lower the heat, cover, and simmer very slowly 15 minutes more to finish cooking.

Lift the pieces of rabbit, the onions, and pork out of the pan with a slotted spoon and place them on a hot platter. Discard the bouquet garni. Whisk the cream into the pan juices (if all the wine has evaporated, add 6 tablespoons (10 cl) of water as well), heat until almost boiling, then stir in the lemon juice, remove from the heat, add salt and pepper if needed, spoon over the rabbit, and serve immediately.

**Serving suggestions :** This is excellent with fresh pasta.

*Note : A chicken of the same weight can be cut into pieces and cooked exactly as described above. For a more pronounced mustard taste, save a generous tablespoon of mustard and, just before serving, stir it into the sauce away from the heat. Ed.*

# HARE STEWED IN RED WINE
*Lapin en civet ou civet de lièvre*

PREPARATION TIME : 1 1/2 hours

INGREDIENTS FOR 6 TO 8 SERVINGS :
A 5 1/2- to 6 1/2-pound (2.5- to 3-kg) hare or rabbit
Blood from the animal (see *Note* to recipe for Cock in Red Wine
    p. 174)
1 teaspoon vinegar (if using blood)
Salt, pepper
1 clove garlic, peeled and finely chopped
2 tablespoons finely chopped parsley
3 tablespoons cognac
6 1/2 tablespoons (100 g) butter
1 bottle red wine (preferably Burgundy)
2 tablespoons (20 g) flour
4 tablespoons (6 cl) hot water
*Bouquet garni* made with 2 sprigs parsley, 1 sprig thyme, 1/4 bay leaf,
    1 stalk celery, and the white of 1 leek, tied together
1 clove garlic, peeled but whole
1 1/2 tablespoons (20 g) softened butter (for the *beurre manié)*
2 tablespoons (20 g) flour (for the *beurre manié)*

If possible, use a freshly killed animal and save the blood (mixed with a teaspoon of vinegar) for making the sauce (see *Note* of the Cock with Red Wine recipe, p. 174). Save the liver, heart, and lungs for the sauce as well. Cut the rabbit or hare into 8 to 10 pieces. Season with salt and pepper. Chop the liver, heart and lungs, mix them with the garlic, chopped parsley, and cognac, season with salt and pepper and reserve.
Melt the butter in a pot large enough to comfortably hold the rabbit. When the butter starts to foam, add the pieces of rabbit and cook for 20 minutes, turning frequently to brown on all sides.
In a saucepan, bring the red wine to a boil. Stir the flour into the pot with the rabbit, stir in the hot water to bind the sauce, then pour in the boiling red wine. Add the *bouquet garni* and the whole garlic, bring to a boil, then immediately lower the heat and boil slowly uncovered for 25 minutes ; at the end of this time, place over very low heat (use a heat diffuser if you have one) and simmer very slowly 10 minutes more.
Make a *beurre manié* by mixing together the butter and flour with your fingers. Reserve for thickening the sauce if necessary. Lift the pieces of

rabbit out of the pot and place in a hot serving dish. Keep warm while making the sauce.

Strain the cooking liquid and place back into the pot over moderate heat. Mix the blood with the liver-cognac mixture, stir in a little of the cooking liquid, then pour into the pot, stirring. Heat until the sauce thickens, but do not allow to boil, stirring constantly. If you feel the sauce should be thicker, whisk in the *beurre manié,* broken into small pieces. When smooth, pour the sauce over the rabbit and serve.

**Serving suggestions :** This dish can be made a day in advance and reheated — it's even better. In this case, don't add the blood and liver until just before serving. (If you have some left over, and wish to reheat it with the blood already in it, heat, stirring constantly, and do not allow to boil.) Serve with fresh pasta, a chestnut puree, or celery puree.

# RABBIT PÂTÉ
*Rillettes de lapin*

PREPARATION TIME : About 1 1/2 hour (plus time to marinate and
   chill)

INGREDIENTS FOR 6 TO 8 SERVINGS :
A 2 3/4-pound (1.25 kg) rabbit
1 pound (500 g) pork jowl, cut into 8 to 10 pieces
Salt, pepper
3 carrots, peeled and quartered
*Bouquet garni,* made of 2 celery stalks, 1 sprig thyme, 1/4 bay leaf,
   and 3 sprigs parsley, tied together
5 peppercorns
1 tablespoon olive oil
1 bottle dry white wine
6 1/2 tablespoons (100 g) lard

Cut the rabbit into 6 pieces at the joints in order not to splinter the bones.
Place in a large bowl with the pork, salt, and pepper, then add the carrots,
onions, and the *bouquet garni.* Stir in the peppercorns, oil, and wine, then
leave to marinate for 6 hours or overnight before cooking.

Lift the rabbit and pork out of the marinade and pat dry with a clean
cloth. Heat the lard in a large pot over moderate heat (the pot should be
wide enough for all the meat to sit on the bottom without piling up). Cook
the rabbit and pork for 10 minutes to brown lightly, turning frequently,
then pour all the marinade ingredients into the pot (the liquid should
barely cover the meat). Bring to a boil, then lower the heat and cook at a
slow boil, uncovered, for about 1 1/2 hours. Measure the liquid in the pot
occasionally by straining it into a measuring cup ; when the cooking is
done, there should be 1 cup (25 cl) of liquid left.

Lift the rabbit and pork out of the pan. Use two forks to shred the meat
(discard the bones) by holding the meat with one fork and pulling at it with
the other fork. Place the shredded meat into a salad bowl. Season with salt
and pepper, add the strained cooking liquid, and refrigerate overnight
before serving.

**Serving suggestions :** Serve with bread and a Green Salad (p. 80), or Vinegar Pickles (p. 51).

# HARE OR VENISON IN MUSTARD SAUCE
*Râble de lièvre, ou selle de chevreuil, à la moutarde*

PREPARATION TIME : 30 to 50 minutes

INGREDIENTS FOR 4 TO 6 SERVINGS :
2 saddle of hare weighing about 14 ounces (400 g) each, *or* 1 saddle of
   venison weighing about 1 3/4 pound (800 g)
Salt, pepper
5 tablespoons (100 g) Dijon mustard
6 1/2 tablespoons (100 g) butter
*Bouquet garni,* made with thyme and bay leaf
2 cloves garlic, whole and unpeeled
1 cup (25 cl) dry white wine
Generous 3/4 cup (20 cl) *crème fraîche* or heavy cream

Salt and pepper the meat, then rub it on all sides with the mustard.
Heat the butter in a high-sided frying pan until it foams, then add the
meat, *bouquet garni,* and garlic. Cook hare for a total of 20 minutes, venison 40 minutes, over moderate heat, turning over once.
Lift the meat out of the pan and place on a hot platter. Stir in the wine
over high heat, scraping the bottom of the pan to dissolve any meat juices
stuck to it. Stir in the cream and lower the heat (the sauce should be very
hot, but the cream should not boil). Remove the *bouquet garni,* season
with salt and pepper if needed, spoon the sauce over the meat, and serve.

**Serving suggestions :** This is delicious with the Potato Crêpe (p. 269) or
Chanterelles (p. 241).

# CHAPTER 9

# MEAT

There is no substitute for quality. This is as true for meat as for fish, vegetables, or fruits. You may have to pay more, but good meat is worth the difference in price. Remember to leave any refrigerated meat at room temperature for an hour before cooking.

ROAST TENDERLOIN *(Filet de bœuf rôti)*

FRENCH BOILED DINNER *(Pot-au-feu)*

BOILED BEEF AU GRATIN *(Pot-au-feu au gratin)*

PEPPER STEAKS *(Steaks au poivre)*

STEAK WINE-GROWER'S-STYLE *(Entrecôte vigneronne)*

BEEF STEW BURGUNDY-STYLE *(Bœuf bourguignon)*

HUNGARIAN GOULASH *(Goulach hongrois)*

FAMILY-STYLE BRAISED BEEF *(Bœuf mode)*

VEAL CUTLETS WITH CREAM SAUCE *(Côtes de veau)*

VEAL AND OLIVES *(Rôti de veau)*

VEAL SHANK WITH BABY VEGETABLES *(Jarret de veau primeurs)*

VEAL BIRDS AND OLIVES *(Oiseaux sans tête)*

VEAL BLANQUETTE *(Blanquette de veau)*

LEG OF LAM ENGLISH-STYLE *(Gigot à l'anglaise)*

ROAST SHOULDER OF LAMB *(Épaule d'agneau à la broche)*

LAMB STEW *(Sauté d'agneau)*

ROAST PORK WITH MUSTARD *(Rôti de porc à la moutarde)*

SAUERKRAUT *(Choucroute fraîche)*

BOILED PORK DINNER *(Potée au chou)*

BOUDIN WITH APPLES *(Boudin aux pommes)*

BOUDIN WITH ONIONS *(Boudin)*

SAUSAGES WITH WHITE WINE *(Saucisses au vin blanc)*

TRIPE SAUSAGE *(Andouillettes)*

# ROAST TENDERLOIN
*Filet de bœuf rôti*

PREPARATION TIME : About 1 hour

INGREDIENTS FOR 5 TO 6 SERVINGS :
2 1/4 pounds (1 kg) beef tenderloin, all fat removed
About 7 ounces (200 g) leaf fat (barding fat)
Salt, pepper
3 1/2 tablespoons (50 g) softened butter, broken into 10 pieces
4 tablespoons (6 cl) hot water

Preheat the oven to 425°F (220°C).
Wrap the beef in the leaf fat and tie with kitchen string. Salt and pepper
the roast, then place it in a roasting pan and roast for about 40 to 45 minutes (allow 15 minutes per pound, including the weight of the leaf fat).
15 minutes before the time is up, remove the fat from around the meat so
the meat will brown. When the time is up, turn off the oven but leave the
meat inside for an additional 5 minutes ; this will make for more evenly
cooked and tender slices (the meat will be very rare, as it should be).
Lift the roast out of the pan, place on a cutting board, and slice, being
careful to keep any juices. Cover the meat and keep warm while making
the sauce.
Pour off any fat in the roasting pan and place the pan on top of the stove
over high heat. Add the juices that came from the meat while slicing it, the
butter, and the hot water. Salt and pepper, heat until the sauce foams up,
then immediately pour it into a sauceboat and serve.

**Serving suggestions :** Serve with Potatoes au Gratin (p. 275) and watercress, sprinkled with a little salt and vinegar.
If there is any meat left over, it is excellent served cold with Vinegar Pickles (p. 51), Black Olives (p. 52), and mustard.

# FRENCH BOILED DINNER
*Pot-au-feu*

PREPARATION TIME : 4 hours

INGREDIENTS FOR 6 TO 8 SERVINGS :

2 or 3 marrow bones
A small beef shank weighing
   about 6 pounds (2.8 kg) or an
   equal weight of oxtail and
   short ribs of beef
1 veal foresbank weighing about
   2 3/4 pounds (1.25 kg)
6 quarts (6 liters) water
4 teaspoons (30 g) coarse salt
*Bouquet garni* made with 1 sprig
   thyme, 1 bay leaf, 5 sprigs
   parsley tied together
1 onion, peeled and stuck with a
   clove

5 peppercorns
4 medium carrots, peeled
4 medium turnips, peeled
Heart of 1 head of celery, split
   lengthwise
4 leeks, cleaned and tied in a
   bunch
Toast (for the marrow)
Vinegar pickles (p. 51)
Dijon mustard
Coarse sea salt

Wrap the marrow bones in a piece of cheesecloth and tie the ends together to seal them inside. Reserve.

Place the beef and veal in a large pot, add the cold water (the meat should be covered) and the coarse salt, and bring to a boil. Skim off any foam that surfaces using a skimmer or slotted spoon.

When the water boils, add the *bouquet garni,* the onion stuck with a clove, and the peppercorns. Lower the heat and simmer uncovered for 3 hours, then add the vegetables and simmer 45 minutes more.

To serve, lift the beef and veal out of the pot and place on a hot serving platter with the vegetables and marrow bones around them. Serve with toast (to spread the marrow on), vinegar pickles, plain or flavored Dijon mustard, and a bowl of coarse sea salt all on the side.

COMMENT : On a cold winter's night, serve a bowl of the hot bouillon as a first course (salt and pepper to taste). Whether or not you serve the bouillon, save it, since it is invaluable in making various soups, sauces, and stews. To keep the bouillon, pour it into a large bowl to cool overnight, then use a spoon to remove the layer of fat that will have formed on the surface. You can keep the bouillon for several days in the refrigerator.

*(Continued p. 200)*

**Serving suggestions :** Serve the meat and vegetables with a Risotto (p. 294) made with the bouillon.

*Note : The veal and marrow bones don't really need to cook as long as the beef. The veal can be added after 2 hours, and the marrow bones can be added at the same time as the vegetables.*
*Save any leftover meat for making the Boiled Beef au Gratin p. 200, the Stuffed Cabbage, Tomatoes, or Zucchini (pp. 242, 246, and 249), or the French Shepherd's Pie p. 278. Ed.*

# BOILED BEEF AU GRATIN
*Pot-au-feu au gratin*

PREPARATION TIME : 1 hour 15 minutes

INGREDIENTS FOR 4 SERVINGS :
2 tablespoons (30 g) butter
2 medium onions, peeled and sliced
6 tablespoons (10 cl) red wine vinegar
1 tablespoon (10 g) flour
4 tablespoons tomato paste
4 1/4 cups (1 liter) bouillon (see French Boiled Dinner p. 198)
4 tablespoons chopped parsley
1 clove garlic, peeled
12 to 16 thin slices leftover boiled beef (see French Boiled Dinner
    p. 198)
1/2 cup (80 g) breadcrumbs

Preheat the oven to 425°F (225°C).
Melt the butter in a frying pan and cook the onions until soft but not brown. Add the vinegar and boil until it has evaporated completely, then add the flour, stir, add the tomato paste, bouillon, and parsley, and simmer uncovered for 25 minutes. Crush the garlic into the baking dish and rub energetically, spreading it around the dish. Lay the slices of leftover beef in the dish so that they overlap slightly, then add the sauce, spreading it over the meat. Sprinkle with the breadcrumbs (they should absorb most of the liquid), then place in the oven and bake for 45 minutes.

**Serving suggestions :** Serve with the Baked Vermicelli (p. 292).

# PEPPER STEAKS
*Steaks au poivre*

PREPARATION TIME : 20 minutes

INGREDIENTS FOR 4 SERVINGS :
2 tablespoons (15 g) whole peppercorns
2 steaks from the tenderloin, weighing 10 1/2 ounces (300 g) each
Salt
2 tablespoons (30 g) butter
1 teaspoon Dijon mustard
6 tablespoons (10 cl) *crème fraîche* or heavy cream

Place the peppercorns on a cutting board or table and coarsely crush them with a rolling pin. Lightly salt the steaks, then roll them in the peppercorns, pressing down on them as you do so. Leave for 15 minutes before cooking.
Heat the butter in a large frying pan until very hot, add the steaks, and cook over high heat 5 or 6 minutes on a side, then lift them out of the pan and keep warm on a serving platter while making the sauce.
Remove the pan from the heat, stir in the mustard and the cream, scraping the bottom of the pan to dissolve any meat juices, then place the pan back over the heat just long enough to heat the sauce (don't allow to boil). Add a little salt if needed, then pour over the meat and serve.

**Serving suggestions :** Serve with Sauteed Potatoes (p. 265).

# STEAK WINE-GROWER'S-STYLE
## *Entrecôte vigneronne*

PREPARATION TIME : 25 minutes

INGREDIENTS FOR 4 SERVINGS :
1 boneless rib steak weighing 1 3/4 pounds (800 g)
3 shallots
1 medium onion
2 anchovy filets in oil
3 1/2 tablespoons (50 g) butter
Salt, pepper
1/2 cup (12 cl) red wine

Cut off any excess fat from around the steak.
Finely chop the shallots, onion, and anchovies, either by hand or in a food processor. Place all together in a bowl and reserve for making the sauce.
Melt the butter in a large frying pan until very hot, salt and pepper the steak on both sides, then place it in the pan. Cook the steak for 6 minutes on a side over moderately high heat if you like it rare, 8 minutes on a side if you like it medium rare. When done, lift the meat out of the pan and keep warm while making the sauce.
Stir the chopped onion mixture into the pan and cook for about 5 minutes, or until the onions have softened and begun to brown. Stir in the wine, bring to a boil, and boil for 1 to 2 minutes, or until the sauce has thickened slightly ; add salt an pepper if needed.
To serve, either serve the steak as it is on a hot platter and slice it at the table with the sauce in a sauceboat on the side, or slice the meat, strain the sauce, spoon a little onto each dinner plate, place the slices of steak on top, and serve, with any extra sauce in a sauceboat (see photo).

# BEEF STEW BURGUNDY-STYLE
*Bœuf bourguignon*

PREPARATION TIME: 3 hours

INGREDIENTS FOR 4 SERVINGS:
2 1/3 pounds (1 kg) blade of beef
1/4 pound (125 g) salt pork or slab bacon
4 tablespoons (60 g) butter
12 baby onions, peeled
Salt, pepper
4 carrots, peeled, halved lengthwise, and quartered
*Bouquet garni* made with 2 stalks celery, 1 sprig thyme, 4 sprigs
  parsley, and 1 bay leaf tied together
1 1/2 tablespoons (15 g) flour
1 generous teaspoon tomato paste
1 bottle red wine
Salt, pepper
2 small cloves garlic, peeled and crushed

Cut the meat into egg-sized pieces and the bacon into 1/2-inch (1 cm) cubes.
Melt the butter in a large cast-iron pot, add the onions and bacon, and cook over moderate heat for 3 minutes, or until they begin to brown. Salt and pepper the meat, then add it to the pot and brown over high heat on all sides. Lower the heat, add the carrots and the *bouquet garni,* cover, and simmer for 20 minutes ; then lift the meat and bacon out of the pot with a slotted spoon. Stir the flour into the pot and heat until it starts to color. Stir in the tomato paste, then add the wine little by little, stirring constantly. Salt and pepper, add the garlic, and bring to a boil, stirring constantly. Return the meat and bacon back to the pot, cover, and simmer for 2 1/2 hours. Remove the *bouquet garni,* then serve the stew in the pot it cooked in.

**Serving suggestions:** serve with steamed potatoes or a Potato Crêpe (p. 269).

# HUNGARIAN GOULASH
*Goulasch hongrois*

PREPARATION TIME: 2 hours

INGREDIENTS FOR 4 SERVINGS:
1/2 pound (250 g) slab bacon
3 1/2 tablespoons (50 g) butter
2 medium onions, peeled and sliced
Salt, pepper
2 tablespoons Hungarian paprika
2 medium tomatoes, peeled and diced
*Bouquet garni,* made of thyme, bay leaf, and parsley
1/2 cup (12 cl) dry white wine
6 tablespoons (10 cl) *crème fraîche* or heavy cream
2 1/2 pounds (1 kg) potatoes, peeled
Country-style bread
Butter

Cut the bacon into cubes about 1/2 inch (1 cm) on a side.
Melt the butter in a large pot or high-sided frying pan, lightly brown the bacon, then add the onions, meat, salt, and pepper. Stir, then sprinkle in both kinds of paprika, stir again, and simmer uncovered for 10 to 15 minutes. Add the tomatoes, *bouquet garni,* and wine. Bring just to a boil, then immediately lower the heat, cover the pot, and cook at a very gentle boil for 1 hour and 15 minutes, stirring occasionally (add a little water if necessary so that the meat is always just barely covered by liquid).
Meanwhile, place the potatoes in a large pot, cover with cold water, salt lightly, bring to a boil, and boil gently for 30 minutes. Time it so that the meat and potatoes finish cooking at the same time.
Just before serving, remove the meat from the heat and stir in the cream. Return to the heat just long enough to warm the sauce, but don'allow it to boil. Season with salt and pepper.
Serve, with the potatoes, slices of country-style bread, and a dish of fresh butter all on the side.

# FAMILY-STYLE BRAISED BEEF
## *Bœuf mode*

PREPARATION TIME : 3 1/2 hours

INGREDIENTS FOR 4 SERVINGS :
2 1/4 pounds (1 kg) rump roast
About 1/4 pound (125 g) fatback (for larding)
1/2 calf's foot
Salt, pepper
1/2 pound (250 g) salt pork
6 small onions, peeled
6 carrots, peeled, halved lengthwise, and quartered
*Bouquet garni,* made of thyme, bay leaf, and parsley
2 cups (50 cl) dry white wine
Generous 3/4 cup (20 cl) water

Lard the beef with strips of fatback, using a larding pin (or ask your butcher to do it). Salt and pepper the meat and calf's foot. Cut the salt pork into 1/2-inch (1 cm) cubes.
In a large stew pot, melt the butter. When it starts to foam, add the onions and salt pork, and brown over high heat, stirring frequently. Add the beef and calf's foot, brown on all sides, then add the carrots, *bouquet garni,* and wine. Simmer uncovered for 1 hour, during which time some of the wine should evaporate. Add the water, salt, and pepper. Turn the meat over, bring to a boil, then cover the pot and simmer slowly for 2 hours (this dish must cook very slowly and for a long time).
To serve, discard the *bouquet garni,* then lift the meat and calf's foot out of the pot. Slice the meat and cut the foot into pieces, then place them on a hot platter, surrounded by the vegetables and salt pork. Use a spoon to skim off the fat on the surface of the cooking liquid, then pour the liquid over the meat and serve.

**Serving suggestions :** Serve with Mashed Potatoes (p. 268), Split Pea Purée (p. 261), or Rice Pilaf (p. 291).

VARIATION : *Leftovers are delicious eaten cold ; as a matter of fact, some people always eat this dish cold rather than hot. Place the meat in a deep dish or bowl, arrange the carrots and onions around it and on top of it, then strain the cooking liquid over it. Leave to cool, then refrigerate overnight before serving. Serve with a Green Salad (p. 80) (see photo).*

Family-style Braised Beef

# VEAL CUTLETS WITH CREAM SAUCE
*Côtes de veau*

PREPARATION TIME : 25 minutes

INGREDIENTS FOR 4 SERVINGS :
1 1/2 tablespoons (20 g) butter (for the mushrooms)
6 medium mushrooms, cleaned and sliced
3 tablespoons (40 g) butter (for the veal)
4 veal cutlets weighing about 7 to 8 ounces (200 to 250 g) each
Salt, pepper
1/2 cup (12 cl) dry white wine (preferably Pouilly-Fuissé)
6 tablespoons (10 cl) *crème fraîche* or heavy cream

Melt 1 1/2 tablespoons (20 g) of butter in a small frying pan, then add the mushrooms and cook slowly until they soften ; season with salt and pepper, and reserve.

In a large frying pan, melt 3 tablespoons (40 g) of butter. Salt and pepper the cutlets, then place them in the pan, when the butter starts to foam. Cook over moderately high heat for 7 to 8 minutes on a side, then remove from the pan and keep warm while making the sauce.

Pour the wine into the pan the veal cooked in, stirring over high heat to detach any meat juices stuck to it, then add the mushrooms, cream, and salt and pepper as needed. Heat the sauce to boiling, pour immediately over the veal, and serve.

**Serving suggestions :** Serve with Spinach (p. 254).

# VEAL AND OLIVES
*Rôti de veau*

PREPARATION TIME : About 1 hour

INGREDIENTS FOR 4 SERVINGS :
1 3/4 pounds (800 g) rump roast of veal
1/4 pound (125 g) veal breast or tail, cut into pieces
4 tablespoons (60 g) butter
1 onion, peeled and sliced
2 medium tomatoes, chopped
Salt
1 cup (125 g) pitted green olives

Cut off any large pieces of fat from the veal. In a pot just large enough for the meat, place the scraps of fat, along with the pieces of veal breast or tail, and brown lightly. Add the butter ; when it has melted, add the onions and the veal roast. Cook to brown the meat evenly over moderate heat for 5 to 10 minutes, then add the tomatoes and stir to detach any meat juices stuck to the bottom of the pot. Salt lightly, cover the pot, place over low heat, and simmer for 40 minutes, turning the meat several times as it cooks.
While the meat is cooking, desalt the olives in a bowl of cold water ; change the water once or twice.
After the 40 minutes is up, lift the meat out of the pot and place it on a plate. Strain the contents of the pot into a mixing bowl, pressing on the meat and vegetables in the strainer to extract all of their juices. Place the strained liquid back in the pot, add the meat, drain the olives, and add them as well, then cover and simmer 20 minutes longer.
To serve, lift the meat out of the pot and place on a warm platter surrounded by the olives. Serve the sauce in a sauceboat on the side.

**Serving suggestions :** Serve with Mashed Potatoes (p. 268).

# VEAL SHANK WITH BABY VEGETABLES
*Jarret de veau primeurs*

PREPARATION TIME : About 2 hours

INGREDIENTS FOR 4 SERVINGS :
1 veal shank, weighing about
 2 3/4 pounds (1.25 kg)
Salt, pepper
4 tablespoons (60 g) butter (for
 the meat)
1 clove garlic, whole and
 unpeeled (for the meat)
3 tomatoes, peeled and chopped
2 tablespoons (30 g) butter (for
 the vegetables)
1 tablespoon olive oil

1/2 pound (250 g) new baby
 carrots, peeled and cut in half
 lengthwise (larger carrots
 should be halved lengthwise
 and quartered)
1 pound (500 g) new baby
 potatoes, peeled and cut in
 half lengthwise
1 clove garlic, whole and
 unpeeled (for the vegetables)

Salt and pepper the shank before cooking.

Over moderate heat, melt 4 tablespoons (60 g) butter in a pot just large enough to hold the veal. When hot, add the veal and a clove of garlic, and brown for about 15 minutes, turning frequently. Add the tomatoes, cover the pot, lower the heat, and simmer for 1 1/2 hours, turning the meat occasionally. If the liquid from the tomatoes evaporates and the meat begins to stick, add a little warm water to the pot.

While the meat finishes cooking, heat 2 tablespoons (30 g) of butter and 1 tablespoon of oil in a large frying pan. Add the carrots and potatoes (they should all fit on the bottom of the pan, or almost), garlic, salt, and pepper. Cook the vegetables until lightly browned, then lower the heat and cook very slowly for 15 to 20 minutes or until done, shaking the pan frequently.

To serve, lift the veal out of the pot and slice on a cutting board. Season with salt and pepper. Place on a hot platter, surrounded with the vegetables, taste the cooking liquid for salt and pepper, and serve in a sauceboat on the side.

**Serving suggestions :** Serve with a Green Salad (p. 80).
*Note : Two whole tomatoes, peeled, placed in a roasting pan, seasoned with salt, pepper, and a few spoonfuls of olive oil, can be roasted in a hot oven for about 20 minutes and served as well (see photo). Ed.*

Veal Shank with Baby Vegetables.

# VEAL BIRDS AND OLIVES
*Oiseaux sans tête*

PREPARATION TIME : 1 hour

INGREDIENTS FOR 4 SERVINGS :
1 cup (125 g) pitted green olives
8 thin veal scallops weighing about 2 1/2 to 3 ounces (70 to 80 g) each
Salt, pepper
8 thin slices ham
1/4 cup (6 cl) olive oil
2 onions, peeled and chopped
1/2 pound (250 g) tomatoes, peeled and chopped
*Bouquet garni,* made of thyme, bay leaf, and parsley
1 clove garlic, whole and unpeeled

Soak the olives in lukewarm water for 30 minutes.
In the meantime, make the veal birds : place the veal scallops on the table, and season with salt and pepper. Place a piece of ham (it should be about the same size as the scallop) on top of each one, fold in the ends, then roll each one up like a sausage. Tie with kitchen string, with one piece going around the "bird" lengthwise and the other crosswise, like a little package.
Heat the oil in a large frying pan, add the onions, and cook to color lightly ; then add the veal birds and brown on all sides over moderate heat. Add the tomatoes, the *bouquet garni,* and the garlic. Raise the heat and boil for about 10 minutes, or until the water from the vegetables has all evaporated ; then lower the heat, cover the pan, and cook for 8 minutes. Add the olives and cook 7 minutes more, taste for salt and pepper, and serve.

**Serving suggestions :** These are delicious with Mashed Potatoes (p. 268) or Potato Soufflé (p. 276).
Veal birds are also very good cold, served with a Green Salad (p. 80).

# VEAL BLANQUETTE
*Blanquette de veau*

PREPARATION TIME : 1 1/2 hours

INGREDIENTS FOR 4 SERVINGS :

1 pound (500 g) veal shoulder
1 pound (500 g) breast of veal
About 3 cups (75 cl) water
*Bouquet garni,* made with 2
    stalks celery, 1 sprig thyme,
    and 1/4 bay leaf tied together
3 carrots, peeled and cut into
    thick sticks
12 baby onions, peeled
3 peppercorns

1 teaspoon (7 g) coarse salt
4 tablespoons (60 g) butter
3 tablespoons (30 g) flour
2 egg yolks
6 tablespoons (10 cl) heavy cream
1 tablespoon lemon juice
Pepper
1 tablespoon chopped parsley

Cut the veal into pieces about the size of an egg. Place in a pot, add the water (the meat should be almost, but not quite, covered by the water), and bring to a boil, skimming off any foam that rises. Add the *bouquet garni,* along with the carrots, onions, peppercorns, and salt as soon as the water comes to a boil. Cover the pot, lower the heat, and simmer slowly for 1 hour.

Lift the meat and vegetables out of the pot with a slotted spoon, place in a serving dish, and keep warm while making the sauce. Discard the *bouquet garni.*

In a saucepan, melt the butter, then stir in the flour. When the mixture is smooth (do not allow to color), add the cooking liquid from the veal, little by little, whisking constantly. Once all the liquid has been added, bring to a boil and boil rapidly for 2 to 3 minutes to thicken the sauce, then remove the pot from the heat.

In a mixing bowl, whisk together the egg yolks and cream. Ladle in a little of the hot sauce, whisking constantly. Add the lemon juice, then pour back into the pot, stirring constantly. The sauce should be very hot but not boiling. Add a little pepper, pour the sauce over the meat and vegetables, sprinkle with parsley, and serve immediately.

# LEG OF LAMB ENGLISH-STYLE
*Gigot à l'anglaise*

PREPARATION TIME : 50 minutes

INGREDIENTS FOR 5 TO 6 SERVINGS :
3 1/2 quarts (3 1/2 liters) water
4 teaspoons (30 g) coarse salt
2 onions, peeled and quartered
2 carrots, peeled and sliced
4 sprigs parsley
1 sprig thyme
1 bay leaf
2 stalks celery
3 peppercorns
3 1/2 pounds (1.6 kg) leg of lamb, excess fat removed

Bring the water to a boil in a pot large enough to hold the lamb comfortably. Add the salt, onions, carrots, parsley, thyme, bay leaf, celery, and peppercorns. When the liquid is boiling rapidly, add the lamb and cook 14 minutes per pound at a very slow, even boil. Skim off any foam that rises. When the cooking time is up, remove the pot from the heat, but leave the lamb in the liquid an additional 10 minutes, then lift it out and carve into thick slices (they will be nice and rare). Sprinkle with salt and pepper, place on a hot platter, and serve.

**Serving suggestions :** Serve with Baked Potatoes with Tomatoes (p. 272) and a Green Salad (p. 80). Any leftovers are delicious served cold with Vinegar Pickles (p. 51) and mustard.

*Note : This plain dish can be livened up, if you like, with a Garlic Mayonnaise (p. 110) or Gribiche Sauce (p. 116) served in a sauceboat on the side. Ed.*

# ROAST SHOULDER OF LAMB
*Epaule d'agneau à la broche*

PREPARATION TIME : 1 hour

INGREDIENTS FOR 6 SERVINGS :
2 cloves garlic
A 2 3/4-pound (1.25 kg) boned shoulder of lamb (weight without bone)
Salt, pepper
1/2 cup (12 cl) water (for the roasting pan)
6 tablespoons (10 cl) water (for the sauce)
2 tablespoons (30 g) softened butter, broken into 5 pieces

Peel the garlic and cut each clove into three wedges. Use a small knife to make six incisions in the meat and slide a wedge of garlic into each one. Salt and pepper the meat generously. Roll and tie into a sausage-like shape if the butcher hasn't already done so.
Roast the lamb on a spit if possible (see *Note*). Use a stove-top rotisserie or the spit attachment to your oven if it comes with one. Preheat for about 15 minutes, then spit the lamb, set it into place, pour 1/2 cup (12 cl) of warm water into the drippings pan under the meat, and roast for 15 minutes per pound. Turn off the heating unit and leave the lamb turning on the spit 5 to 7 minutes more before making the sauce and serving (the meat will be very rare, as it should be).
To serve, remove the meat from the spit, place on a cutting board, and slice, being careful not to lose any of the juices that come out of the meat. Place the meat on a warm platter. Add the meat juices as well as 6 tablespoons (10 cl) of water to the roasting pan dans bring to a boil, scraping the bottom of the pan to dissolve anything stuck to it. Stir in the butter, salt and pepper lightly, then pour the sauce into a sauceboat to serve on the side.
Serve immediately.

**Serving suggestions :** Serve with White Beans Provençale (p. 256) or Green Beans (p. 255).

*Note : If you don't have a rotisserie, cook the lamb in the oven. Preheat the oven to 425°F (220°C), place the lamb in a roasting pan, and roast for 15 minutes per pound. Turn off the oven but leave the lamb inside for 7 minutes, then carve and make the sauce as described above, but in this case, add 1/2 cup (12 cl) water to the roasting pan before adding the butter. Ed.*

# LAMB STEW
*Sauté d'agneau*

PREPARATION TIME : 1 hour

INGREDIENTS FOR 4 SERVINGS :
1 pound (450 g) neck of lamb, cut into 5 or 6 pieces
1 1/4 pounds (600 g) shoulder of lamb, cut into 5 or 6 pieces
Salt, pepper
5 tablespoons (80 g) butter
4 carrots, peeled and cut into thick sticks
12 baby onions, peeled
*Bouquet garni,* made with 2 stalks celery, 1 spring thyme, and 1/4 bay
  leaf tied together
1 tablespoon (10 g) flour
1/2 cup (12 cl) dry white wine
3 medium tomatoes, peeled and chopped
1 pound (500 g) new baby potatoes, peeled

Generously salt and pepper the lamb.
Melt the butter in a large, high-sided frying pan or stew pot. When it starts
to foam, add the meat and brown, turning frequently, over high heat. Add
the carrots, onions, and *bouquet garni,* cook for 5 to 10 minutes to brown
the vegetables, then stir in the flour, the wine, and the tomatoes. Bring to a
boil, stirring constantly, then immediately lower the heat, cover the pot,
and simmer for 10 minutes. Add the potatoes, cover, and finish cooking
30 minutes more, stirring from time to time. Salt and pepper when the
potatoes are done.
Serve immediately, either in the pot the lamb cooked in or in a serving
dish.

**Serving suggestions :** Serve with a Green Salad (p. 80) on the side.

# PORK ROAST WITH MUSTARD
*Rôti de porc à la moutarde*

PREPARATION TIME : About 2 hours

INGREDIENTS FOR 4 SERVINGS :
1/3 cup (100 g) Dijon mustard
2 pounds (900 g) boneless blade or pork loin roast
About 6 ounces (175 g) pig's caul (lace fat) or thinly sliced fatty bacon
8 baby onions, peeled
Salt, pepper
1/2 cup (12 cl) dry white wine
1/4 cup (6 cl) hot water

Preheat the oven to 425°F (220°C).
Use a small spoon to spread the mustard all over the pork roast, then spread out the lace fat and completely wrap the pork up in it (if using slices of bacon, tie them around the roast from end to end). Tie off both ends of the lace fat, then tie two strings around the roast to hold the fat in place. Place the meat in a roasting pan, surround with the onions, season with salt and pepper, add the white wine, and place in the oven. Once the roast begins to brown, baste it every 10 or 15 minutes. Cook for a total of 1 1/2 hours, then turn off the oven but leave the roast inside for an additional 10 minutes.
Lift the roast out and place on a warm serving platter ; place the roasting pan on top of the stove and boil the pan juices over high heat, add the hot water and a little pepper, boil rapidly for about 10 seconds, then pour into a sauceboat and serve with the meat.

**Serving suggestions :** Serve with Potatoes Au Gratin (p. 275) or Split Pea Puree (p. 261). Roast pork is also excellent cold with a green salad, so don't be afraid of making too much (if using a larger roast, remember to increase the cooking time proportionally).

# SAUERKRAUT
## *Choucroûte fraîche*

PREPARATION TIME : 2 hours (plus desalting the pork)

INGREDIENTS FOR 6 TO 8 SERVINGS :
2 3/4 pounds (1.25 kg) fresh, raw sauerkraut
1 lightly salted (cured) shoulder hock or loin of pork, weighing about
   2 1/4 pounds (1 kg)
1/2 pound (250 g) salt pork (belly)
About 5 ounces (150 g) pork rind
1 clove garlic, peeled
5 juniper berries
5 peppercorns
1 teaspoon caraway seeds
2 sprigs thyme
1/4 bay leaf
6 tablespoons (100 g) goose fat or lard (total)
2 carrots, peeled ans sliced
2 onions, peeled and sliced
2 cups (50 cl) dry white wine (preferably from Alsace)
A 3/4-pound (350-g) pure pork poaching sausage
6 to 8 pure pork frankfurters
6 to 8 small new potatoes, peeled
Dijon mustard (for serving)

Buy only fresh, raw (uncooked) sauerkraut ; the whiter it is the better.
Soak the salt pork (shoulder, belly, and rind) to desalt, in a large pot or
bowl of cold water for 1 1/2 hours if it is very lightly salted, otherwise
overnight — ask how long to soak it when you purchase it.
Place the sauerkraut in a colander and rinse it under cold running water,
lifting and spreading it out to wash it thoroughly ; then drain it and
squeeze out all the water with your hands.
Tie the garlic, juniper berries, pepper, caraway, thyme, and bay leaf inside
a little piece of thin cloth and reserve.
Melt half the goose fat or lard in a large pot, add the carrots and onions,
cook to color lightly, then pour in the wine and add the sauerkraut. It
should be barely covered with liquid to cook properly, so add water to the
pot if necessary. Spread the remaining goose fat or lard over the surface,
bring just to a boil, then immediately lower the heat, cover the pot, and
cook over very low heat for 1 1/2 to 2 hours, stirring from time to time.

*(Continued p. 220).*

Meanwhile, cook the meat separately. Place the rind, fat side down, in the bottom of a large pot, then add the shoulder, belly, the little bag of spices, and enough water or bouillon to cover by about 2 inches (5 cm). Bring to a boil, then lower the heat and simmer slowly for 1 1/2 to 2 hours. Thirty minutes before the meat has finished cooking, add the sausages and potatoes to it.

To serve, place the sauerkraut in the center of a large, hot platter and surround it with the meat, rind, sausages, and potatoes. Serve accompanied by various flavored Dijon mustards.

# BOILED PORK DINNER
*Potée au chou*

PREPARATION TIME : About 2 hours (plus time to desalt)

INGREDIENTS FOR 4 TO 6 SERVINGS :
1/2 pound (250 g) salt pork (belly)
1 salted shoulder hock of pork weighing about 2 1/4 pounds (1 kg)
1/2 pound (250 g) salted pork rind
4 quarts (4 liters) cold water (for the meat)
1 onion, peeled and stuck with a clove
*Bouquet garni,* made with 1 sprig thyme and 1 bay leaf tied together
4 peppercorns
1 small green cabbage
2 quarts (2 l) water (for the cabbage)
4 stalks celery
4 leeks, cleaned and split lengthwise
4 turnips, peeled
1 pound (500 g) small potatoes, peeled

Salt pork must be desalted, generally 6 hours to overnight, before cooking. Place it in a large bowl or pot, cover with cold water, and leave for the required time, changing the water at least two or three times (when you buy the pork, ask how long to desalt it).

Place the pork (belly, shank, and rind) in a large pot, add 4 quarts (4 liters) cold water, the onion, *bouquet garni,* and peppercorns. Bring the water to a boil, skimming off any foam, then lower the heat and simmer for 1 hour and 15 minutes.

While the pork is cooking, prepare the vegetables. Cut the cabbage into 4 pieces. Bring 2 quarts (2 liters) of unsalted water to a boil in a large pot, add the cabbage, and boil for 10 minutes, then drain in a colander. Tie the celery and leeks together with kitchen string, and prepare the turnips and potatoes.

Add the vegetables to the pot with the pork, cover, and cook for 30 minutes more.

To serve, lift the vegetables out with a slotted spoon and place them on a hot platter. Lift out the pork, slice it on a cutting board, place it on the platter with the vegetables, and serve, with plain or flavored Dijon mustards, black olives, and country-style bread on the side.

# BOUDIN WITH APPLES
*Boudin aux pommes*

PREPARATION TIME : 45 minutes

INGREDIENTS FOR 4 SERVINGS :
1 3/4 pound (800 g) apples
1 pound (500 g) *boudin* (see *Note)*
2 tablespoons (30 g) butter (for the *boudin)*
Salt, pepper
1 1/2 tablespoons (20 g) softened butter (for the applesauce)
Dijon mustard, for serving

Peel, core, and slice the apples. Place them in a saucepan with enough water to half cover, bring to a boil, then lower the heat and cook uncovered until the apples are soft enough to mash with a fork and virtually all of the water has evaporated. When done, whisk them to make applesauce.
While the apples are cooking, cook the *boudin*. Cut it into pieces about 6 inches (15 cm) long, and prick each piece in several places with a pin to keep them from bursting open while they cook. Melt 2 tablespoons (30 g) of butter in a frying pan ; when it starts to foam, fry the *boudin* over moderate heat, turning frequently for about 15 minutes. Season with salt and pepper.
Once the apples and *boudin* are cooked, add 1 1/2 tablespoons (20 g) of softened butter to the applesauce, season it with salt and pepper, place on a hot platter, and arrange the *boudin* around it. Serve with Dijon mustard.

VARIATION : If preferred, wedges of apple and small pieces of bacon can simply be fried in the pan with the *boudin* as in the photo.

*Note : Boudin is a French black pudding (blood sausage) ; although not quite the same, blutwurst, when available, could be used instead. Ed.*

Boudin with Apples.

# BOUDIN WITH ONIONS
*Boudin aux oignons*

PREPARATION TIME : 30 minutes

INGREDIENTS FOR 4 SERVINGS :
1 pound (500 g) *boudin* (see *Note* to Boudin with Apples, p. 222)
2 tablespoons (30 g) butter
2 onions, peeled and sliced
Salt, pepper

Cut the *boudin* into pieces about 6 inches (15 cm) long, then prick each one in several places with a pin so they won't burst open while cooking. Heat the butter in a frying pan until it starts to foam, then add the onions and brown over moderate heat for 10 to 15 minutes. Remove them from the pan with a slotted spoon and keep warm while cooking the *boudin*.
Place the *boudin* in the same pan and cook over moderate heat 15 minutes, turning frequently. Season with a little salt and pepper.
Place the onions on a hot platter, place the pieces of *boudin* on top, and serve immediately.

**Serving suggestions :** Serve with Mashed Potatoes (p. 268).

# SAUSAGES WITH WHITE WINE
*Saucisses au vin blanc*

PREPARATION TIME : 20 minutes

INGREDIENTS FOR 4 SERVINGS :
8 fresh pure pork sausages
3 tablespoons (40 g) butter
1 onion, peeled and finely chopped
1 clove garlic, peeled and finely chopped
1/2 cup (12 cl) dry white wine
Salt, pepper

Prick the sausages in several places to keep them from bursting open while cooking.

Melt the butter in a frying pan. When hot, add the sausages and onion, and brown over moderate heat for about 10 minutes. Add the garlic and white wine, stirring to detach any juices stuck to the bottom of the pan. Cook 5 to 8 minutes more, then lift the sausages out of the pan and keep warm on a platter.

Add a little warm water to the cooking liquids in the pan if there isn't enough left to make a light sauce. Bring to a boil, season with freshly ground pepper and a little salt, stir, then pour over the sausages and serve.

**Serving suggestions :** Serve with Mashed Potatoes (p. 268) or Split Pea Purée (p. 261).

# TRIPE SAUSAGES
## *Andouillettes*

PREPARATION TIME: About 1 hour 15 minutes

INGREDIENTS FOR 4 SERVINGS:
3 1/2 tablespoons butter
4 *andouillettes* (French tripe sausages)
2 shallots, peeled and coarsely chopped
2 tablespoons breadcrumbs (preferably white — see *Note)*
Salt, pepper
1 cup (25 cl) dry white wine
6 tablespoons (10 cl) hot water
2 tablespoons coarsely chopped parsley

Preheat the oven to 400°F (200°C).
Melt the butter in a small roasting pan, add the sausages, and place in the oven for at least 45 minutes (the longer the better), turning over every 10 to 15 minutes.
Lift the sausages out of the pan and set them aside on a plate. Add the shallots, breadcrumbs, salt, and pepper to the pan, stir in the white wine, heat to simmering on top of the stove, then place the sausages back in the pan and cook in the oven 15 minutes more. Turn off the oven but leave the sausages inside for another 10 minutes.
To serve, remove the sausages from the pan and either slice them on a cutting board or leave them whole. Keep warm on a hot serving platter while making the sauce.
Place the roasting pan on top of the stove over high heat. Add the hot water, and boil, whisking, until the sauce is nice and creamy (see photo), then pour over the sausages, sprinkle with the parsley, and serve.

*Note : White breadcrumb can be made by pulverizing stale white bread in a mortar or heavy-duty blender, but ordinary breadcrumbs may be used instead. The sauce will simply be brown instead of white. Ed.*

# CHAPTER 10

# VEGETABLES

Some of the recipes in this chapter could be served as lunches or light meals, especially the stuffed vegetables — tomatoes, zucchini, etc.
Vary the vegetables you serve, and always buy them fresh. Buy what is in season, and everything you make will taste better. Wash vegetables under cold running water ; never leave them to soak, as they lose both vitamins and taste this way.

BABY ARTICHOKES "BARIGOULE" *(Artichauts "barigoule")*

CARDOONS AU GRATIN *(Gratin de cardons)*

CARROTS AND PEAS *(Carottes et petits pois)*

CARROTS IN CREAM *(Carottes à la crème)*

GLAZED CARROTS AND TURNIPS *(Carottes et navets glacés)*

CREAMED CELERIAC *(Celeri-rave à la crème)*

MIXED VEGETABLES *(Jardinière de légumes)*

MUSHROOMS AND CREAM AU GRATIN *(Champignons à la crème)*

CHANTERELLES *(Girolles ou chanterelles)*

STUFFED CABBAGE *(Chou farci)*

CAULIFLOWER AU GRATIN *(Gratin de chou-fleur)*

BROCCOLI *(Brocolis)*

STUFFED TOMATOES *(Tomates farcies)*

TOMATOES PROVENÇALE-STYLE *(Tomates provençales)*

STUFFED ZUCCHINI *(Courgettes farcies)*

ZUCCHINI FRITTERS *(Beignets de courgettes)*

ENDIVES WITH HAM *(Endives au jambon)*

SPINACH *(Epinards)*

GREEN BEANS *(Haricots verts)*

WHITE BEANS PROVENÇALE *(Haricots blancs à la provençale)*

BRAISED LETTUCE *(Laitues braisées)*

LEEKS AU GRATIN *(Gratin de poireaux)*

GLAZED ONIONS *(Oignons glacés)*

SPLIT PEA PURÉE *(Purée de pois cassés)*

SNOW PEAS *(Pois gourmands)*

POTATOES WITH CHIVE SAUCE *(Pommes de terre en robe des champs)*

SAUTEED POTATOES *(Pommes de terre sautées)*

BAKED POTATOES *(Pommes de terre en papillotes)*

MASHED POTATOES *(Purée de pommes de terre)*

POTATO CRÊPE *(Crique)*

POTATO BARBOTON *(Barboton de pommes de terre)*

BAKED POTATOES WITH TOMATOES *(Pommes boulangères)*

MASHED POTATO PANCAKES *(Galettes de pommes de terre)*

POTATOES AU GRATIN *(Gratin de pommes de terre au lait)*

POTATO SOUFFLÉ *(Soufflé de pommes de terre)*

FRENCH SHEPHERD'S PIE *(Hachis parmentier)*

BAKED PUMPKIN FLAN *(Flan au potiron)*

BAYALDI

RATATOUILLE

# BABY ARTICHOKES "BARIGOULE"
*Artichauts "barigoule"*

PREPARATION TIME : About 1 hour

INGREDIENTS FOR 4 SERVINGS :
2 1/2 quarts (2 1/2 liters) water
8 baby artichokes weighing about 1 1/4 pounds (600 g) total
3 tablespoons olive oil
4 large tomatoes, peeled and chopped
4 medium mushrooms, cleaned and quartered
8 baby onions, peeled
2 cloves garlic, whole and unpeeled
1 sprig thyme
1/4 bay leaf
1/4 pound (125 g) salt pork or bacon, diced
Salt, pepper

Bring the water to a boil in a large pot.
Cut off the leaves of each artichoke about a third of the way down from
the top. Cut off the stems, then remove the tough outer leaves around the
base and cut each artichoke into four pieces. Use a little spoon to scoop
out the choke in the centrer of each piece. Quickly rinse the artichokes in
warm water, then drop them into the boiling water, cook for 15 minutes,
and drain.
Heat the oil in a high-sided frying pan or cast-iron pot. Add the tomatoes,
mushrooms, onions, garlic, thyme, bay leaf, and salt pork. Cook for 10 to
20 minutes, or until half of the moisture from the vegetables has evaporated, then add the artichokes, salt, and pepper. Cover the pan and simmer
for 25 minutes.
Serve immediately, either in the pan the artichockes cooked in or in a
serving dish.

*Note : Artichokes cooked this way are excellent cold as well as hot. Ed.*

# CARDOONS AU GRATIN
*Gratin de cardons*

PREPARATION TIME : 1 hour

INGREDIENTS FOR 4 SERVINGS :

2 small cardoons
2 cups (50 cl) milk
2 1/2 quarts (2 1/2 l) water (for the cardoons)
2 marrow bones
2 cups (50 cl) water (for the marrow bones)
Salt

1 1/2 tablespoons (20 g) butter (for the dish)
1 2/3 cups (125 g) grated Swiss cheese
2 tablespoons (30 g) butter (for the sauce)
1 tablespoon (10 g) flour

The cardoon is a relative of the artichoke that looks rather like a large head of celery ; unfortunately it isn't found everywhere, nor at all seasons. A winter vegetable, it is best from November to February. When you buy them, pick those which are small an dull white in color — they are generally the most tender.

Peeling the cardoons is a time-consuming process that requires great care. Cut off the hollow ends of the stalks and remove all the strings, as you would with celery. Cut the remaining (solid) part of the stalks into pieces about 2 1/4 inches (3 cm) long ; the base, where all the stalks are joined together, can simply be sliced — this is the best part in my mind. Wash under cold running water and drain.

Heat the milk and water in a large pot until boiling, add the salt and the cardoons, partially cover the pot, and cook for 15 to 20 minutes. Lower the heat if it looks as if the milk is rising and will overflow.

Preheat the oven to 400°F (200°C).

While the cardoons are cooking, poach the marrow bones. Place them in a small saucepan, add the cold water, salt lightly, and heat almost to boiling. Simmer for 10 minutes. Lift the bones out of the pot with a slotted spoon and take out the marrow ; cut it into thick slices and reserve. Save 1 cup (25 cl) of the water the bones cooked in for later use.

Butter a small baking dish. Drain the cardoons, then put them in the dish and sprinkle them with the grated cheese.

Melt the butter in a saucepan, stir in the flour, and cook until it starts to change color, then, little by little, stir in the reserved marrow-bone water. Boil until the sauce is just thick enough to coat a spoon.

Place the slices of marrow on the cardoons, pour over the sauce, bake for 25 minutes or until beginning to brown, and serve.

**Serving suggestions :** The cardoons can be kept in the turned-off oven up to 15 minutes after being baked. They are excellent with any red meat.

---

# CARROTS AND PEAS
*Carottes et petits pois*

---

PREPARATION TIME : 1 hour

INGREDIENTS FOR 4 SERVINGS :
3 tablespoons (40 g) butter
4 large carrots, peeled and cut into thick stick 2 inches (5 cm) long
8 baby onions, peeled
*Bouquet garni,* made with thyme and bay leaf
3 1/3 cups (500 g) shelled fresh peas — purchase 3 1/4 pounds (1.25 kg)
Salt, pepper
1 teaspoon granulated sugar

Melt the butter in a high-sided frying pan, add the carrots and onions, and simmer for about 5 minutes, stirring occasionally. Pour in enough water to barely cover, add the *bouquet garni,* and cook for 20 minutes. Add the peas, salt, pepper, and sugar (add more water if necessary so that the peas will be barely covered). Bring to a boil, cover the pan, lower the heat, and simmer for 20 minutes more, stirring from time to time. Remove the *bouquet garni,* then serve in a dish or as a garnish on a platter with meat.

---

# CARROTS IN CREAM
*Carottes à la crème*

PREPARATION TIME : 50 minutes

INGREDIENTS FOR 4 SERVINGS :
5 tablespoons (75 g) butter
2 pounds (900 g) carrots, peeled and cut into thick sticks 2 inches (5 cm)
    long
5 baby onions, peeled
Salt
5 baby onions, peeled
Salt
1 teaspoon granulated sugar
2 tablespoons finely chopped parsley
6 tablespoons (10 cl) heavy cream

Melt the butter in a frying pan, add the carrots and onions, salt lightly, and sprinkle with sugar. Cover the pan and simmer for 40 minutes, stirring from time to time.

When the carrots have finished cooking, mix the parsley with the cream, pour onto the carrots, and cook 5 minutes more, or until very hot (the cream should not boil). Serve immediately in a hot dish.

**Serving suggestions :** Carrots cooked this way are very good with roast veal.

Carrots in Cream.

# GLAZED CARROTS AND TURNIPS
*Carottes et navets glacés*

PREPARATION TIME : 30 minutes

INGREDIENTS FOR 4 SERVINGS :
1 pound (450 g) baby carrots, peeled and halved
1 pound (450 g) baby turnips, peeled and halved
4 tablespoons (60 g) butter
1 tablespoon (15 g) granulated sugar
Salt, pepper

Boil the carrots and turnips in a large pot of lightly salted water for 8 to 10 minutes, then drain.
Melt the butter in a high-sided frying pan, add the vegetables, and cook over moderate heat for 10 to 15 minutes to dry out and coat with butter ; shake the pan frequently while the vegetables are cooking.
Lower the heat, sprinkle in the sugar, and cook, shaking the pan, until the sugar coats the vegetables and begins to brown. Season with salt and pepper, and serve.

**Serving suggestions :** Serve as garnish with meat.

# CREAMED CELERIAC
*Céleri-rave à la crème*

PREPARATION TIME : 45 minutes

INGREDIENTS FOR 4 SERVINGS :
1 celeriac (celery root) weighing about 1 pound (500 g), peeled and
    diced
2 medium potatoes, peeled and diced
Salt
6 tablespoons (10 cl) *crème fraîche* or heavy cream
Pepper
2 tablespoons (30 g) butter

Rinse the diced vegetables under cold running water. Place in a saucepan, pour in enough cold water to cover, add salt, bring to a boil, and cook for 30 minutes.
Drain, then immediately purée the vegetables in a food mill with a medium grill or use a potato masher. Place in a hot serving dish. Whisk in the cream, pepper, and salt if necessary. Stir in the butter and serve.

**Serving suggestions :** Serve with either meat or fish.

# MIXED VEGETABLES
## *Jardinière de légumes*

PREPARATION TIME : About 1 hour

INGREDIENTS FOR 6 to 8 SERVINGS :
6 to 8 baby onions, peeled
1 1/2 pound (700 g) potatoes, peeled an diced
5 medium carrots, peeled and cut into thick sticks
*Bouquet garni,* made with thyme and bay leaf
1/4 pound (125 g) salt pork or bacon, diced
2 2/3 cups (400 g) shelled fresh peas — purchase 2 pounds (900 g)
8 lettuce leaves
Salt, pepper
3 1/2 tablespoons (50 g) butter

Bring a large saucepan of salted water to a boil and add the onions, potatoes, carrots, and *bouquet garni.* Cover and boil gently for about 20 minutes, then add the salt pork, peas, and lettuce, and cook 15 minutes uncovered.

To serve, drain the vegetables, discard the *bouquet garni,* and place in a hot serving dish. Season with salt and pepper, stir in the butter, and serve immediately.

Mixed Vegetables.

# MUSHROOMS AND CREAM AU GRATIN
*Champignons à la crème*

PREPARATION TIME : 40 minutes

INGREDIENTS FOR 4 SERVINGS :
1 pound 10 ounces (750 g) fresh mushrooms
3 1/2 tablespoons (50 g) butter
Butter (for the dish)
3 eggs yolks
6 tablespoons (10 cl) heavy cream
Salt, pepper
Nutmeg
1 cup (60 g) grated Swiss cheese

When buying the mushrooms, choose tan ones if possible ; in any case, whether tan or white, they should not be bruised, but uniformly colored. Cut off any dirt on the stems, wash rapidly under cold running water, then either slice or quarter depending on their size.
Preheat the oven to 400°F (200°C).
Melt the butter in a saucepan, add the mushrooms, and cook slowly, stirring frequently, for 15 minutes or until all the water they give out has evaporated and only butter is left in the pan.
Lightly butter a small baking dish, then pour in the mushrooms. Whisk the egg yolks and cream together, season with salt, pepper, and a little nutmeg, then pour over the mushrooms. Sprinkle with the grated cheese, then bake for 15 to 20 minutes or until beginning to brown. Serve the mushrooms hot from the oven in the dish they cooked in.

# CHANTERELLES
*Girolles ou chanterelles*

PREPARATION TIME : 30 minutes

INGREDIENTS FOR 4 SERVINGS :
1 3/4 pound (800 g) fresh chanterelles (see *Note* to Creamy Scrambled
    Eggs with Chanterelles, p. 98)
3 1/2 tablespoons (50 g) butter
Salt, pepper
1 clove garlic, peeled and coarsely crushed (optional)
1 shallot, peeled and finely chopped (optional)
2 tablespoons coarsely chopped parsley (optional)

Cut off the dirt from the base of each mushroom, then wash them quickly under cold running water and drain.

Melt the butter in a frying pan, add the mushrooms, and cook over moderate heat for approximately 20 minutes, or until all the water they give out has evaporated completely. Continue cooking until the mushrooms begin to brown. At this point, they are done (this method of cooking is good for almost all mushrooms).

Salt and pepper the mushrooms, and serve as they are. If you prefer, stir in garlic, shallots, or both, and sprinkle with parsley just before serving.

**Serving suggestions :** Chanterelles are marvelous served with Veal and Olives (p. 209).

# STUFFED CABBAGE
*Chou farci*

PREPARATION TIME: About 3 hours (plus soaking the pork)

INGREDIENTS FOR 6 SERVINGS:
1/2 pound (250 g) salt pork
1 green cabbage weighing about 2 1/4 pounds (1 kg), tough outer leaves
   removed
3 1/2 quarts (3 1/2 liters) water
Salt
1 cup (25 cl) milk
1 large onion, peeled and sliced
1/2 cup (20 g) crumbled dry toast or melba toast
3 tablespoons chopped parsley
Generous 2 3/4 cups (400 g) chopped leftover boiled beef (see French
   Boiled Dinner p. 198)
1 egg
Pepper
3 1/2 tablespoons (50 g) butter
3 medium carrots, peeled and cut into thick strips
6 tablespoons (10 cl) water

Desalt the salt pork by soaking it 7 to 8 hours in cold water with ice cubes, before cooking. Change the water once or twice.

Drain the pork and pat dry in a clean cloth, then cut off one slice and reserve. Place the rest of the pork in a saucepan, cover with cold water, bring to a boil, then lower the heat and simmer for 1 hour. Drain, cool, then chop it coarsely and reserve.

Once the salt pork has started cooking, cook the cabbage. Bring 3 1/2 quarts (3 1/2 liters) of water to a boil in a large pot and add a little salt. Turn the cabbage upside down and cut out the hard central core. Detach all the leaves and drop them into the boiling water, lower the heat, and simmer for 7 minutes. Drain and cool under cold running water, then place on a towel to drain and dry.

In a small saucepan, bring the milk to a boil, add the onions, and simmer for 8 minutes. Lift out the onions with a slotted spoon, chop coarsely, and reserve. Keep the milk.

Place the crumbled toast in a large bowl, pour in enough of the milk left from cooking the onions to barely cover, stir, and allow to soak for about 10 to 15 minutes. Crush the toast using the prongs of a fork, then pour off

242

any excess milk. Add the onions, parsley, garlic, chopped salt pork, and beef (see Comment). Stir in the egg, salt, and pepper, and knead the stuffing with your hands to mix the ingredients perfectly together.

Preheat the oven to 400°F (200°C).

Melt the butter in a cast iron pot only slightly larger than the cabbage when it was whole. Add the carrots and the slice of uncooked salt pork reserved earlier. Cook until both begin to brown, then remove from the heat and leave to cool. When the pot is cool enough to touch, line the bottom (on top of the carrots and pork) and sides with about 2/3 of the cabbage leaves, allowing the ends of the leaves to drape over the sides of the pot a little. Pour the stuffing into the center, cover with the remaining leaves, then fold in the cabbage leaves that drape over the sides to completely enclose the stuffing. Add the water, heat for 1 minute on top of the stove, then cover the pot and bake in the oven for 1 hour. Serve the cabbage hot from the oven in the pot it cooked in.

COMMENT : All the ingredients for the stuffing can be worked through a meat grinder rather than chopped by hand, if preferred. In this case, the beef and salt pork can simply be cut into cubes, and the onion left in slices, before grinding. Use a large grill, since the stuffing shouldn't be chopped too fine.

# CAULIFLOWER AU GRATIN
*Gratin de chou-fleur*

PREPARATION TIME : 1 hour

INGREDIENTS FOR 4 SERVINGS :
1 cauliflower weighing about 2 pounds (900 g)
3 quarts (3 liters) water
Salt
1 tablespoon olive oil
A stale breadcrust (optional)
1 cup (25 cl) milk
1 tablespoon (10 g) cornstarch
1 tablespoon water
6 tablespoons (10 cl) heavy cream
Salt, pepper
Nutmeg
1 scant cup (50 g) grated Swiss cheese

Cut the central core from the cauliflower and separate the flowerlets. Wash carefully in cold water.
Bring lightly salted water to a boil and add the oil ; you can also add a stale breadcrust to the water (it will absorb some of the odor of the cauliflower as it cooks). Add the cauliflower, boil for 5 minutes from the time the water comes back to a boil, then drain. Butter a baking dish, place the cauliflower in it, and reserve.
Preheat the oven to 400°F (200°C).
Heat the milk in a saucepan ; while it's heating, mix the cornstarch and cold water together. Once the milk boils, remove the pot from the heat and stir in the cornstarch mixture. Return to the heat and bring to a boil, stirring constantly. Cook until the sauce is thick enough to coat the spoon. Stir in the cream, salt, pepper, nutmeg, and grated cheese, then pour the sauce over the cauliflower and bake in the oven for 20 minutes, or until golden brown on top.
Serve in the dish it cooked in.

# BROCCOLI
*Brocolis*

PREPARATION TIME : 15 minutes

INGREDIENTS FOR 3 TO 4 SERVINGS :
2 1/4 pounds (1 kg) broccoli
3 1/2 tablespoons (50 g) butter, *or* generous 3/4 cup (20 cl) *crème
    fraîche* or heavy cream
Salt, pepper

If necessary, separate the broccoli into flowerlets.
Bring a large pot of lightly salted water to a boil, then drop in the broccoli
and boil for 7 to 10 minutes, or until tender but not soft. Lift the broccoli
out and leave to drain for a few seconds on a clean cloth (be careful not to
damage the flowerlets which are quite fragile when cooked).
Place the broccoli in a hot serving dish and sprinkle with salt and pepper.
Then you can either pour a little melted butter over it, or cream that has
been boiled until thick, or simply the juices from the meat it's being served
with.

VARIATION : The broccoli can be boiled for only 2 or 3 minutes, to finish
cooking in either the butter, cream, or meat juices. In this case, simmer
slowly for 10 to 15 minutes more, gently shaking the pan frequently so as
not to damage the broccoli (don't stir with a spoon). Add salt and pepper,
and serve.

**Serving suggestions :** Broccoli is delicious with the Fricassee of Scallops in
Cream Sauce (p. 148). It is also excellent with meat or poultry.

# STUFFED TOMATOES
*Tomates farcies*

PREPARATION TIME: About 3 hours (plus soaking time)

INGREDIENTS FOR 6 SERVINGS:

7 ounces (200 g) salt pork
12 large tomatoes
1 sprig thyme
1/4 bay leaf
Salt, pepper
4 small onions, peeled and sliced
1 cup (25 cl) milk
3/4 cup (30 g) crumbled dry toast
  or melba toast
1 clove garlic, peeled and
  chopped

1 generous cup (300 g) chopped
  leftover boiled beef or veal (see
  French Boiled Dinner p. 198,
  or Veal with Olives p. 209)
2 tablespoons chopped parsley
1 egg
Salt, pepper
Nutmeg
4 tablespoons (60 g) butter (for
  the dish)

Soak the salt pork overnight in cold water before cooking. To cook, rinse it in cold water, place in a saucepan, cover with cold water, bring to a boil, then lower the heat and simmer for about 1 hour. Drain and leave to cool before using to stuff the tomatoes.

Wash the tomatoes, then use a small knife to cut off the top third of each one. Reserve the tops. Use a spoon to carefully scoop out the seeds and pulp from the center of each tomato, being careful not to puncture the skins. Save the scooped-out pulp and seeds for making the sauce. Lightly salt the inside of each tomato and reserve.

Preheat the oven to 400°F (200°C).

Place the seeds and pulp in a small saucepan with a little thyme, bay leaf, salt, and pepper, and simmer for 15 to 20 minutes or until the consistency of a thin tomato sauce, stirring frequently. Reserve.

While the sauce is cooking, place the onions in a saucepan with the milk, bring to a boil, then lower the heat and simmer for 7 to 8 minutes. Lift the onions out of the milk with a slotted spoon and chop them coarseley. Save the milk.

Place the toast in a mixing bowl and add the milk used in cooking the onions. Allow to soak for about 10 minutes, then crush the toast with a fork; pour off any excess milk. Chop the salt pork, and add it to the toast along with the onion, garlic, leftover meat, and parsley (see Comment to

Stuffed Tomatoes. Stuffed Zucchini *(recipe p. 249)*.

the recipe for Stuffed Cabbage, p. 242). Mix well, then add the egg, salt, pepper, and nutmeg, and knead with your hands to mix thoroughly.

Butter a baking dish just large enough to hold all the tomatoes. Fill each tomato with stuffing, then put the top sections back in place and arrange them in the baking dish. Pour the tomato sauce made earlier into the dish around the tomatoes, then place in the oven and bake for 1 hour. Serve hot from the oven in the baking dish.

**Serving suggestions :** Large tomatoes should be used. Since stuffed tomatoes are excellent reheated, don't be afraid of making more than you need.

# TOMATOES PROVENÇALE-STYLE
*Tomates provençales*

PREPARATION TIME : 35 minutes

INGREDIENTS FOR 4 SERVINGS :
4 large, ripe tomatoes
Salt
2 1/2 teaspoons finely chopped celantro (Chinese parsley)
2 1/2 teaspoons finely chopped basil
4 teaspoons breadcrumbs
Pepper
2 cloves garlic, peeled and finely chopped
5 tablespoons (7.5 cl) olive oil

Preheat the oven to 450°F (240°C).

Wash the tomatoes, dry with a towel, then cut out the stems. Cut each tomato in half, then place them in a baking dish, cut side up. Sprinkle generously with salt, then with celantro, basil, and breadcrumbs.

Pepper lightly, then place a little freshly chopped garlic on top of each tomato half, pour over the oil, and bake for 25 minutes. Serve hot from the oven in the baking dish.

**Serving suggestions :** Serve with either meat or fish.

# STUFFED ZUCCHINI
*Courgettes farcies*

PREPARATION TIME : 2 1/2 hours (plus soaking time)

INGREDIENTS FOR 4 SERVINGS :
1/2 pound (250 g) salt pork
4 large zucchini
1/2 cup (20 g) crumbled dry toast or melba toast
2/3 cup (15 cl) milk
1 cup (250 g) leftover cooked veal (see French Boiled Dinner p. 198, or
    Veal with Olives p. 209)
1 clove garlic, peeled and chopped
4 small onions, peeled and chopped
2 tablespoons chopped parsley
1 egg
Nutmeg
1/2 cup (12 cl) Tomato Sauce (p. 120)
1 teaspoon thyme leaves
1/4 bay leaf, crumbled
Salt, pepper
1 scant cup (50 g) grated Swiss cheese
3 1/2 tablespoons (50 g) butter
6 tablespoons (10 cl) water

Soak the salt pork in a large bowl of cold water overnight before cooking
(change the water several times). To cook, place it in a saucepan, add cold
water to cover, bring to a boil, then lower the heat and simmer for 1 hour.
Drain and cool before using to make the stuffing (the pork may be cooked
ahead of time and kept in the refrigerator until ready to use).
Remove the stems from the zucchini, then wash them and wipe them dry,
but do not peel. Cut each one in half lengthwise, then scoop out all the
seeds, being careful not to puncture the skins. Reserve.
Preheat the oven to 400°F (200°C).
Place the toast in a mixing bowl, add the milk, and allow to soak for about
10 minutes, then crush it with a fork and pour off any excess milk. Chop
the salt pork and add it to the bread along with the veal, garlic, onions,
and parsley (see Comment to the recipe for Stuffed Cabbage p. 242). Stir
in the egg, nutmeg, tomato sauce, thyme, bay leaf, salt, and pepper. Mix
well, then fill each half zucchini with stuffing.

Place the zucchini in a large roasting pan, sprinkle with the cheese, add the water, dot with the butter, and bake in the oven for 45 minutes.
Serve on a hot serving platter.

**Serving suggestions :** Stuffed zucchini can make a whole meal, especially if you serve them with Rice (p. 290).

## ZUCCHINI FRITTERS
*Beignets de courgettes*

PREPARATION TIME : 45 minutes (plus 1 1/2 hours resting time for the batter)

INGREDIENTS FOR 4 SERVINGS :
2 tablespoons (30 g) butter
1 scant cup (125 cl) flour
1 cup (25 cl) beer
1 teaspoon (7 g) salt
1 egg white
1 pound (500 g) zucchini (see Variations)
Oil for deep frying

To make the batter, melt the butter over very low heat or in a double boiler. Place the flour in a large mixing bowl, add the salt, then stir in the beer and melted butter. Beat to make a smooth batter ; if lumps remain after beating, work the batter through a sieve to remove them. Place the batter in the refrigerator for 1 1/2 hours. Just before using, beat the egg white until stiff and fold it into the batter.
Preheat the oven to 350°F (180°C).
Peel the zucchini and cut them into thin slices. Pat dry with a clean cloth. Heat the oil in a deep fryer ; it should be no more than a third full. When a drop of water dropped into the oil evaporates, making a sharp, quick, pop, the oil is ready.

*(Continued p. 252).*

Zucchini Fritters.

Coat 6 or 7 slices of zucchini with the batter and drop them, one by one, into the hot oil. Cook until golden brown and floating on the surface of the oil. When done, lift them out of the oil with a slotted spoon, drain on paper towels, and place on a serving platter in the oven to keep warm (leave the oven door ajar so it doesn't become too hot). Cook the remaining batches of 6 or 7 slices each in the same way (when the oil has cooled completely, it can be strained, stored, and used again).
Serve as soon as the last batch is done.

**Serving suggestions :** Serve with leg of lamb.

VARIATIONS : If you grow your own zucchini, deep fry the flowers exactly as described here — they are delicious.
Eggplant or oyster plant (salsify) can also be cooked as described above (oyster plant should be cut into 2-inch (5-cm) pieces, boiled, and cooled before being dipped into the batter and fried).

# ENDIVES WITH HAM
*Endives au jambon*

PREPARATION TIME : 1 hour

INGREDIENTS FOR 4 SERVINGS :
2 1/4 pounds (1 kg) Belgian endives
1 1/2 quarts (1 1/2 liters) water
1 1/2 teaspoons (10 g) salt
Juice of 1/2 lemon
1 1/2 tablespoons (20 g) butter (for the baking dish)
4 slices ham, cut into thin strips
Generous 3/4 cup (20 cl) *crème fraîche* or heavy cream
1 1/3 cups (100 g) grated Swiss cheese
Pepper

Preheat the oven to 400°F (200°C).
Use a small knife to hollow out the base of each endive, then rinse them off under hot water.
Bring the water, salt, and lemon juice to a boil, add the endives, cook for 20 minutes, and drain.
Place the endives in a buttered baking dish and sprinkle the strips of ham over them. Pour in the cream and spread it out evenly. Sprinkle with the grated cheese and a little pepper, then bake for 25 to 30 minutes, or until golden brown.
Serve the endives in the baking dish.

# SPINACH
*Épinards*

PREPARATION TIME : 30 minutes

INGREDIENTS FOR 4 SERVINGS :
3 1/2 quarts (3 1/2 liters) water
1 generous tablespoon (30 g) coarse salt
3 1/4 pounds (1.5 kg) fresh spinach
3 1/2 tablespoons (50 g) butter
1 medium onion, peeled and sliced
Salt, pepper
6 tablespoons (10 cl) *crème fraîche* or heavy cream

Bring the water and salt to a boil in a large pot.
While the water is heating up, carefully clean the spinach : remove the stem and thick rib from each leaf, then wash in several changes of cold water. Carefully drain after washing, then drop the spinach little by little into the boiling water, pushing each addition into the water with a slotted spoon before adding more. Boil for 5 minutes from the time the water comes back to a boil (if you don't have a pot large enough to cook all the spinach at once, cook only as much as you can, remove from the pot with a slotted spoon, drain, cool under running water, and leave in the colander while cooking the rest). When all the spinach is cooked, drain in a colander, cool immediately under cold running water, then squeeze out the water with your hands, and reserve the spinach in a bowl.
Melt the butter in a high-sided frying pan, brown the onion lightly, then add the spinach, salt, and pepper, and stir over moderate heat to heat thoroughly. Add the cream, cook 5 minutes more, and serve immediately on a hot platter.

**Serving suggestions :** You can serve the spinach garnished with hard-boiled eggs cut in half and squares or triangles of bread fried in butter (croûtons), for a nice effect.

VARIATIONS : Fresh sorrel can be cooked in the same way.

# GREEN BEANS
*Haricots verts*

PREPARATION TIME : 30 minutes

INGREDIENTS FOR 4 SERVINGS :
3 quarts (3 liters) water
1 tablespoon (25 g) salt
2 pounds (900 g) very thin green beans
3 1/2 tablespoons (50 g) butter
Salt, pepper
Lemon juice (optional)

Bring the water and salt to a boil in a large pot.
In the meantime, string the beans and break off the ends of each one.
Drop the beans into the boiling water and boil rapidly, uncovered, for 8 to
12 minutes, depending on size and how you like them. Use a slotted spoon
to push down any beans that stick out of the water.
Fill a large basin or bowl with cold water and a tray of ice cubes. When the
beans are done (taste one — you may want to cook them longer), drain
them and drop them immediately into the ice water. Leave for 3 minutes,
then lift out and drain completely.
Just before serving, melt the butter in a large frying pan, add the beans,
season with salt and pepper, and warm over low heat, shaking the pan frequently. Serve as soon as the beans are good and hot (if you like, you can
sprinkle them with a little lemon juice just before serving).

# WHITE BEANS PROVENÇALE
*Haricots blancs à la provençale*

PREPARATION TIME : 1 1/2 hours (plus soaking time, if needed)

INGREDIENTS FOR 3 TO 4 SERVINGS :
2 3/4 cups (500 g) shelled fresh white beans — purchase 2 1/2 pounds
   (1.15 kg) — *or* 1 1/3 cups (250 g) dried white beans
2 1/2 quarts (2 1/2 liters) water
1 tablespoon (25 g) coarse salt
4 peppercorns
1 large onion, peeled and stuck with a clove
1 large carrot, peeled and cut in half lengthwise
2 *bouquets garnis,* made of thyme, bay leaf, and parsley tied together
4 large tomatoes, peeled and chopped
Salt, pepper
3 tablespoons (40 g) butter

If using dried beans, they will have to be soaked overnight in cold water before cooking. To cook them, place them in fresh cold water, bring to a boil, then add the peppercorns, onion, carrot, and 1 *bouquet garni* (the cooking time will be longer than for fresh beans).
If using fresh beans, bring the water and salt to a boil, then add the peppercorns and white beans. Bring back to a boil and add the onion, carrot, and 1 *bouquet garni.* In either case, simmer for 1 hour, or until the beans are soft. When done, drain, and discard the *bouquet garni,* onion and carrot.
While the beans are cooking, make a tomato sauce. Place the tomatoes (without any butter or oil) in a saucepan. Add salt, pepper, and the second *bouquet garni,* and cook until the water from the tomatoes has evaporated and a thick sauce is formed (about 30 minutes). Discard the *bouquet garni.*
When both the beans and the tomato sauce are done, melt the butter in a large frying pan. Add the beans and tomato sauce, shake the pan (or stir gently) to combine, then serve in a hot dish.

# BRAISED LETTUCE
*Laitues braisées*

PREPARATION TIME : 25 minutes

INGREDIENTS FOR 4 SERVINGS :
4 small butterhead (Boston) lettuces
3 1/2 tablespoons (50 g) butter
12 baby onions, peeled
2 egg yolks
6 tablespoons (10 cl) heavy cream
Salt, pepper

Remove any tough outer leaves from the lettuces and cut off the base of the stem. Leave the lettuces whole and gently wash them in cold water.
Melt the butter in a high-sided frying pan, add the onions, and brown lightly. Add the lettuce, salt, and pepper. Lower the heat, cover, and cook slowly for 15 to 20 minutes, or until tender, turning the lettuces occasionally.
While the lettuce is cooking, beat the egg yolks and cream together in a small mixing bowl. Season with salt and pepper.
When the lettuces are done, lift them out of the pan with a slotted spoon and place them on a hot platter. Keep warm. Remove the pan from the heat and pour the pan juices into the bowl with the egg-cream mixture, stirring constantly. Pour the sauce back into the pan and place over low heat, stirring constantly, just long enough for the sauce to heat and thicken (do not allow to boil), then pour over the lettuces and serve.

**Serving suggestions :** Serve with any game bird.

# LEEKS AU GRATIN
*Gratin de poireaux*

PREPARATION TIME : About 1 hour

INGREDIENTS FOR 4 SERVINGS :
2 1/4 pounds (1 kg) large leeks
2 1/2 quarts (2 1/2 liters) water
1 tablespoon (7 g) salt
1 tablespoon (10 g) cornstarch
1 tablespoon water
1 cup (25 cl) milk
Salt, pepper
Nutmeg
2 tablespoons (30 g) butter (for the dish)
6 tablespoons (10 cl) *crème fraîche* or heavy cream
1 2/3 cup (125 g) grated Swiss cheese
2 tablespoons (30 g) softened butter

Cut the roots from each leek, then cut off about the top third of the green and discard. Slit open each leek lengthwise starting about an inch into the white and drawing the tip of the knife through to the end of the green. Wash each leek carefully, separating the leaves to remove any dirt, then cut each one in half, separating the green from the white. Tie the green together with a kitchen string.
Preheat the oven to 450°F (240°C).
Bring the water and salt to a boil in a large pot and add the leeks ; cook for 20 minutes, or until tender, from the time the water returns to a boil. Drain and remove the string.
Dissolve the cornstarch with the cold water. Bring the milk to a boil in a saucepan and add the cornstarch, stirring constantly. Cook for a minute or two, or until thick enough to coat the spoon. Remove from the heat, whisk in the cream, and season with salt, pepper, and nutmeg.
Butter a baking dish, then place the leeks in it, alternating the white and green. Pour over the sauce, sprinkle with the grated cheese, and dot with softened butter. Bake for 25 minutes, or until golden brown on top. Serve in the baking dish.

**Serving suggestions :** Serve with roast pork.

Leeks au Gratin.

## GLAZED ONIONS
*Oignons glacés*

PREPARATION TIME : 30 minutes

INGREDIENTS FOR 4 SERVINGS :
1 pound (500 g) new baby onions (weight without greens)
3 1/2 tablespoons (50 g) butter (total), broken into pea-sized pieces
1 tablespoon (15 g) granulated sugar
Salt, pepper

Peel the onions, leave them whole, wash in cold water, and dry.
Place them in a frying pan large enough to hold them all on the bottom, and add half the butter, the sugar, salt, and pepper. Cook over low heat until the onions start to brown, then pour in just enough water to barely cover them (they should not float). Cover the pan and raise the heat ; boil rapidly for about 10 to 15 minutes over moderate heat, or until all the water has evaporated. When the onions are done, there should be a thick syrup remaining in the pan ; shake the pan to glaze the onions by rolling them in the syrup. Add the remaining butter, salt and pepper again if necessary and serve.

**Serving suggestions :** Serve with meat or poultry.

# SPLIT PEA PURÉE
*Purée de pois cassés*

PREPARATION TIME : About 2 hours (plus soaking time)

INGREDIENTS FOR 4 SERVINGS :
1 3/4 cups (350 g) split peas
*Bouquet garni,* made of thyme, bay leaf and parsley tied together
3 baby onions, peeled
Salt, pepper
2 tablespoons *crème fraîche* or heavy cream

Soak the split peas overnight in a large bowl of cold water before cooking. To cook, drain the peas, place them in a pot, and add enough new cold water to barely cover. Add the *bouquet garni,* onions, salt, and pepper. Bring to a boil, then lower the heat and simmer for about 2 hours. Heat extra water and add it to the pot whenever necessary to keep the peas moist. Stir the peas frequently as they cook to make sure they don't stick to the bottom of the pot. By the time they are done, they should have formed a thick smooth puree, rather like mashed potatoes. Just before serving, stir in the cream and season generously with pepper. Serve in a hot dish.

**Serving suggestions :** Split peas are the perfect accompaniment to roast pork or sausages (stir the pan juices into the purée before serving).

# SNOW PEAS
*Pois gourmands*

PREPARATION TIME : 40 minutes

INGREDIENTS FOR 4 SERVINGS :
1 3/4 pounds (800 g) snow peas
1/4 pound (125 g) slab bacon, cut into 1/2-inch (1-cm) cubes
4 tablespoons (60 g) butter
8 baby onions
1 sprig thyme
Salt, pepper

String the snow peas and rinse quickly in cold water.
Fry the bacon in a frying pan (no fat is needed) until it begins to brown.
In a separate frying pan, melt the butter and lightly brown the onions,
then add the bacon, thyme, and peas. Cover and cook for 30 minutes over
very low heat, stirring ocasionally. Taste for salt and pepper, then serve in
a warm vegetable dish.

**Serving suggestions :** Serve with Calf's Liver (p. 158).

# POTATOES WITH CHIVE SAUCE
*Pommes de terre en robe des champs*

PREPARATION TIME : 45 minutes

INGREDIENTS FOR 5 TO 6 SERVINGS :
5 or 6 large potatoes
Salt
7 ounces (200 g) farmer's cheese
6 tablespoons (10 cl) *crème fraîche* or heavy cream
3 tablespoons finely chopped chives
Pepper
Toasted country-style or whole wheat bread (optional)

Before cooking, prick each potato in several places with a needle to keep the skin from breaking open. Place them in a large saucepan, cover with lots of cold water, add a little salt, and bring to a boil. Cook for 30 minutes.

Meanwhile, make a sauce by beating together the farmer's cheese and cream. Gently stir in the chives, salt, and pepper ; chill.

Once the potatoes are done, drain them and place them on a serving platter lined with a clean napkin. Serve the sauce in a sauceboat and slices of toasted country-style or whole wheat bread on the side.

# SAUTEED POTATOES
*Pommes de terre sautées*

PREPARATION TIME : 25 minutes

INGREDIENTS FOR 4 TO 5 SERVINGS :
1 3/4 pounds (800 g) new potatoes, *or* 2 1/4 pounds (1 kg) old potatoes
1 tablespoon olive oil
3 tablespoons (40 g) butter
1/4 teaspoon thyme leaves (or more, to taste)
1 clove garlic, whole and unpeeled
Salt, pepper

It is preferable to use new potatoes for this recipe ; their skins can be scraped off with a knife rather than peeled off with a vegetable peeler. If they are very small, they can be left whole or cut in half lengthwise. If you are using old potatoes, peel them, cut them in half, then cut them into slices 1/2 inch (1 cm) thick. In either case, wash the potatoes in cold water after peeling them and dry in a towel before cooking.
Heat the oil and butter in a large frying pan. When it starts to foam, add the potatoes, thyme, and garlic. Cook over moderate heat for about 15 to 20 minutes, or until tender, shaking the pan frequently to brown the potatoes evenly and avoid sticking. When the potatoes are done, season with salt and pepper, and serve immediately.

# BAKED POTATOES
*Pommes de terre en papillotes*

PREPARATION TIME : 1 hour

INGREDIENTS FOR 4 SERVINGS :
4 large old potatoes
Butter
Cream
Coarse salt
Pepper
Finely chopped fresh chives (optional)

Preheat the oven to 500°F (260°C).
Carefully wash the potatoes and dry them, but don't peel. Use a knife to cut a deep *X* into each one, then place it, *X* side up, in the center of a piece of aluminum foil. Wrap the potato up, pressing the foil closed above the *X*.
Bake the potatoes for 1 hour (test to see if they are done by sticking them with a needle ; if it goes in with no resistance, the potatoes are done).
To serve, open the aluminum foil and spread it out to form a sort of collar around the potato. Press the ends of each potato gently toward each other to open the *X*. Serve, with fresh butter, cream, coarse salt, pepper, and fresh chives (if you have any) all on the side.

**Serving suggestions :** Baked potatoes can be served with any grilled fish or meat.

Baked Potatoes.

# MASHED POTATOES
*Purée de pommes de terre*

PREPARATION TIME : 40 minutes

INGREDIENTS FOR 4 SERVINGS :
2 1/4 pounds (1 kg) old potatoes
1 to 1 1/2 cups (25 to 35 cl) hot milk
2 tablespoons *crème fraîche* or heavy cream
3 1/2 tablespoons (50 g) butter
Salt
Nutmeg

Peel the potatoes and rinse them off quickly under cold running water. Boil them in a large pot of lightly salted water for 20 to 30 minutes (a needle should pierce them easily when done). While the potatoes are cooking, heat the milk.
Drain the potatoes and purée them in a vegetable mill or use a potato masher. Put them in a clean saucepan and whisk in the milk little by little (the amount of milk you use will vary depending on the type of potato you use and how stiff or creamy you like them). Whisk to make a thick, smooth purée. Just before serving, stir in the cream if using, the butter, salt, and nutmeg. Serve immediately.

**Serving suggestions :** Mashed potatoes should never be prepared ahead of time and reheated but mashed and seasoned just before serving. Use any leftovers to make other dishes such as Mashed Potato Pancakes (p. 274), French Shepherd's Pie (p. 278), Potato Soufflé (p. 276), etc.

# POTATO CRÊPE
*Crique*

PREPARATION TIME : 30 minutes

INGREDIENTS FOR 2 TO 3 SERVINGS :
1 pound (500 g) old potatoes
1 egg
Salt, pepper
3 tablespoons olive oil (total)

Wash the potatoes, wipe them dry, and peel them (do *not* wash after peeling but wipe them off with a dry cloth if necessary). Grate the potatoes coarsely, place them in a bowl with the egg, salt, and pepper, and mix well. All this should be done just before cooking them.
Heat 2 tablespoons of the oil in a large frying pan (preferably cast iron). When very hot, add all the grated potatoes and spread them out with the prongs of a fork, pressing down on them lightly to make a large crêpe, or pancake, of even thickness. Cook over moderately high heat for 6 to 8 minutes, or until the underside has browned, then slide the crêpe out into a large plate.
Place 1 more tablespoon of oil in the pan, then place a second plate on top of the crêpe and turn it upside down. Lift off the first plate and slide the crêpe back into the pan to finish cooking 6 to 8 minutes on the second side. Serve immediately.

**Serving suggestions :** Serve as a garnish with meat or as a light lunch, accompanied by a Green Salad (p. 80) flavored with a little garlic, if you like it, and an Oil and Vinegar Dressing (p. 122) made with olive oil and seasoned with finely chopped fresh herbs (parsley, chervil, chives, tarragon, etc.), depending on what's in season.

# POTATOES BARBOTON
*Barboton de pommes de terre*

PREPARATION TIME : About 1 hour

INGREDIENTS FOR 4 SERVINGS :
10 1/2 ounces (300 g) salt pork or slab bacon cut into large cubes
1/2 pound (250 g) medium onions, peeled and sliced *or* baby onions,
    peeled
About 2 cups (50 cl) bouillon (see French Boiled Dinner p. 198), or
    water
2 1/4 pounds (1 kg) potatoes, peeled and cut into large cubes *or* baby
    potatoes, halved
*Bouquet garni* made of thyme, bay leaf, and parsley tied together
1 clove garlic, peeled and chopped
Salt, pepper
Nutmeg
5 tablespoons (80 g) softened butter, broken into pieces

Over low heat, cook the salt pork or bacon in a large cast iron pot until it
has given out some of its fat and begun to brown. Add the onions and
cook for about 5 minutes, being careful not to burn. Add the bouillon or
water, the potatoes, *bouquet garni,* and garlic (the liquid should come
about 2/3 of the way up the potatoes). Bring to a boil, season with salt,
pepper, and nutmeg, cover the pot, and lower the heat. Cook at a gentle
boil for 15 minutes, then stir so that the potatoes on top are pushed to the
bottom of the pot. Cover and cook 15 minutes more or until the potatoes
are tender. Check the level of the liquid — it should come about 1/3 of the
way up the potatoes. If there is more, boil rapidly uncovered to reduce to
this amount, then remove the pot from the heat and add the butter. Cover
again and leave for 10 minutes off of the heat, then shake the pot to combine the butter with the liquid and serve in the pot or in a serving dish.

**Serving suggestions :** The potatoes can be cooked ahead of time and
reheated — they are even better (in any case, don't add the butter until
10 minutes before serving, as described).
This is excellent with Roast Shoulder of Lamb (p. 215).

# BAKED POTATOES WITH TOMATOES
## *Pommes boulangères*

PREPARATION TIME : 1 1/2 hour

INGREDIENTS FOR 4 SERVINGS :
2 1/4 pounds (1 kg) old potatoes
Butter, for the dish
1 pound (500 g) tomatoes, peeled and chopped
1/4 pound (125 g) salt pork or bacon, cut into 1/2-inch (1 cm) cubes
1 teaspoon thyme leaves
1/4 bay leaf, crushed or crumbled
Salt, pepper
3 1/2 tablespoons (50 g) butter, broken into little pieces
About 1 cup (25 cl) water

Preheat the oven to 425°F (220°C).
Brown the salt pork or bacon in a frying pan, then drain on paper towels and reserve.
Peel the potatoes, wash them, and cut them into thin slices. Lightly butter a baking dish just large enough to hold the potatoes, then cover the bottom with a thin layer of potatoes. Sprinkle over some of the tomato, bacon, thyme, bay leaf, salt, pepper, and a little butter. Cover this with a second layer of potatoes, and season them in the same way as the first. Fill the dish in this manner, layer after layer, then pour in enough water to comme about halfway up the potatoes. Heat the dish on top of the stove until the water boils, then place in the oven and bake 45 minutes to 1 hour, or until the potatoes are tender and the top layer has begun to brown. Serve in the baking dish.

# MASHED POTATO PANCAKES
*Galettes de pommes de terre*

PREPARATION TIME : 30 minutes

INGREDIENTS FOR 4 SERVINGS :
1 1/3 cups (300 g) leftover Mashed Potatoes (p. 268)
1 tablespoon (10 g) flour
2 tablespoons milk
1 egg
2 tablespoons (30 g) butter (total)
Salt and pepper, or sugar

It is preferable to use 4 little blini pans 5 inches (12 cm) wide for cooking the pancakes (see *Note*).
Place the cold mashed potatoes in a mixing bowl, and whisk in the flour, milk and egg.
Place a quarter of the butter in each blini pan and heat until it starts to foam, then spoon a quarter of the potato mixture into it, spreading it out evenly. Cook over moderate heat for 7 minutes, then turn over and finish cooking 7 minutes (use two plates to turn the pancakes over, as described in the recipe for Potato Crêpe, p. 269). Add a little more butter to the pans if needed when you turn the pancakes over.
Serve the pancakes as soon as they are done. Sprinkle with salt and pepper, or with sugar, if you want to use them as a dessert (children like them that way).

COMMENT : You can make one large potato pancake instead of 4 small ones, but it's much harder to turn over.

*Note : if you don't have blini pans, form 4 potato pancakes with your hands and cook them in a large pan. In this case, turn them over with a spatula. Ed.*

# POTATOES AU GRATIN
*Gratin de pommes de terre au lait*

PREPARATION TIME : 1 hour

INGREDIENTS FOR 4 SERVINGS :
2 1/4 pounds (1 kg) potatoes
2 1/2 cups (60 cl) milk
Nutmeg
Salt, pepper
1 clove garlic, peeled and split lengthwise
1 2/3 cups (125 g) grated Swiss cheese
3 tablespoons (5 cl) heavy cream
2 tablespoons (30 g) butter, broken into small pieces

Preheat the oven to 400°F (200°C).
Peel the potatoes and wash quickly in cold running water, then wipe dry. Cut them into slices about 1/4 inch (5 mm) thick and reserve.
Bring the milk to a boil in a large saucepan, add the potatoes, a little nutmeg, and salt and pepper generously. Shake the pan gently to make the potatoes settle into the milk (they should be barely covered by the milk ; if not, add a little warm water). Lower the heat and simmer, uncovered, over very low heat for 20 to 25 minutes, or until tender.
Rub a baking dish (preferably porcelain or earthenware) with the garlic.
When the potatoes are done, lift some out of the milk with a slotted spoon and place them on the bottom of the baking dish. Sprinkle with a little grated cheese, add another layer of potatoes, sprinkle with cheese, and continue filling the dish, layer by layer, ending with cheese.
Measure the milk remaining from cooking the potatoes ; there should be about 2/3 cup (15 cl) left. If there is more than that, boil it to reduce to this amount, then pour it over the potatoes. Spoon in the cream, dot the surface with butter, then place the dish in the oven and bake for 20 minutes, or until the surface is golden brown.

# POTATO SOUFFLÉ
*Soufflé de pommes de terre*

PREPARATION TIME : 1 1/2 hours

INGREDIENTS FOR 4 SERVINGS :
1 3/4 pounds (800 g) old potatoes, peeled
3/4 cup (20 cl) cold milk
1 tablespoon *crème fraîche* or heavy cream
2 tablespoons (30 g) butter
4 egg yolks
Salt, pepper
1 2/3 cups (125 g) grated Swiss cheese (optional)
5 tablespoons (75 g) butter (for the mold)
4 egg whites

Preheat the oven to 400°F (200°C).
Boil the potatoes in a large pot of lightly salted water for 30 minutes, then drain and puree in a food mill or mash them until smooth. Place them in a large bowl, then stir in the milk, cream, 2 tablespoons (30 g) butter, egg yolks, salt, pepper, and cheese (if using).
Put 5 tablespoons (75 g) butter in a 7 inch (18 cm) soufflé mold or a 6 1/4 inch (16 cm) charlotte mold and place in the oven until the butter has melted. Remove from the oven and turn to coat the sides with butter.
In a large mixing bowl, beat the egg whites until stiff, then fold them into the potatoes (see Dictionary p. 345). Pour the mixture into the mold and place immediately in the oven to bake for 40 minutes. Do not open the oven door while the soufflé is baking, but check to see if it has browned by looking through the window in the oven door. Serve immediately when done.

# FRENCH SHEPHERD'S PIE
*Hachis parmentier*

PREPARATION TIME : 1 1/2 hour

INGREDIENTS FOR 4 SERVINGS :
2 1/4 pounds (1 kg) old potatoes, peeled
1 1/2 cups (35 cl) milk
1 egg
1 scant cup (50 g) grated Swiss cheese
Salt, pepper
Nutmeg
1 generous cup (300 g) leftover cooked meat or poultry, or a mixture of
    both, chopped
2 medium onions, peeled and chopped
1 tablespoon tomato paste
Butter (for the dish)
3 1/2 tablespoons (50 g) softened butter, broken into pieces

Boil the potatoes in lightly salted water for 30 minutes, then drain and
puree in a food mill or mash until smooth. Add the milk, then beat in the
egg, cheese, and a little salt, pepper, and nutmeg. Reserve.
Preheat the oven to 400°F (200°C).
Place the chopped meat, onions, tomato paste, salt, and pepper in a
mixing bowl. Beat together with a wooden spoon and reserve.
Butter a baking dish (preferably porcelain or enamelled cast iron). Spread
half of the mashed potatoes evenly over the bottom in a thick layer, then
pour in the meat mixture and spread it out evenly over the potatoes. Pour
in the remaining potatoes and use a fork to spread them over the meat and
to decorate the surface by making lines and patterns over it. Dot the surface with the softened butter (see Variations), then place in the oven and
bake for 45 minutes or until brown on top. Serve hot from the oven in the
baking dish.

**Serving suggestions :** This dish is a meal itself ; serve it with a Green Salad
(p. 80).

VARIATIONS : If you like, homemade Tomato Sauce (p. 120) or grated
Swiss cheese can be spread over the surface of the potatoes instead of butter before baking.

# BAKED PUMPKIN FLAN
*Flan au potiron*

PREPARATION TIME : 1 hour 45 minutes

INGREDIENTS FOR 3 TO 4 SERVINGS :
2 1/4 pounds (1 kg) fresh pumpkin
1 tablespoon (10 g) cornstarch
1 tablespoon water
1 cup (25 cl) milk
6 tablespoons (10 cl) heavy cream
2 eggs
Salt, pepper
Nutmeg

Peel the pumpkin and remove the seeds. Cut it into large cubes, then drop them into a pot of boiling salted water and cook at a moderate boil for 20 minutes. Drain in a colander (leave it in the colander for 5 to 10 minutes so that the maximum amount of water will drain off).
Puree the pumpkin in a food mill, blender, or food processor, and reserve. Preheat the oven to 425°F (220°C).
Mix the cornstarch. Remove from the heat and add first the cream, then the eggs, beating constantly. Stir in the pumpkin, then season with salt pepper, and a little nutmeg.
Lightly butter a small baking dish and pour in the pumpkin mixture, spreading it evenly around the dish. Place in the oven and bake for about 35 minutes or until golden brown on top. Serve hot from the oven in the baking dish.

VARIATIONS : You can make a pumpkin dessert by adding 1/4 cup (50 g) of granulated sugar and a little vanilla extract to flavor the pumpkin instead of salt, pepper, and nutmeg.

# BAYALDI

PREPARATION TIME : 1 1/2 hours

INGREDIENTS FOR 4 TO 6 SERVINGS :
4 medium zucchini weighing about 1 1/2 pounds (700 g) total
2 small eggplants, weighing about 1 1/4 pounds (600 g) total
1 1/4 pounds (600 g) tomatoes
1/2 pound (250 g) onions
1 clove garlic, peeled and crushed
1 teaspoon thyme leaves
1/2 bay leaf, crushed
Salt, pepper
Butter (for the dish)
1 1/3 cup (100 g) grated Swiss cheese (see *Note)*
5 tablespoons (80 g) butter (total) broken into small pieces

Preheat the oven to 425°F (220°C).
Wash the vegetables and wipe them dry, then cut them into slices about
1/2 inch (1 cm) thick (if using a large eggplant rather than 2 smaller ones,
cut it in half lengthwise before slicing). Keep all the vegetables separate
from each other.
Butter a large baking dish (preferably earthenware or enamelled cast iron).
Cover the bottom of the dish with the onions, then make a layer of zucchini and sprinkle with a little of the garlic, thyme, and bay leaf, salt, and
pepper. Next, make a layer of eggplant, and lastly a layer of tomato, seasoning each layer as you did the zucchini. Dot the surface with half of the
butter, then place in the oven for 30 minutes. At the end of this time,
sprinkle with the cheese, dot with the remaining butter, and bake 20 to
30 minutes more or until golden brown on top. (If the vegetables dry out
during the first 30 minutes' baking, cover them with aluminum foil;
remove the foil for only the last 10 minutes of the baking time).

**Serving suggestions :** Serve with roast or boiled meat.

*Note : If preferred, the cheese can be omitted and 1/3 cup (8 cl) of olive oil
used instead of butter. In this case, pour all of the oil over the surface of
the vegetables before putting them in the oven.*
*Instead of making layers as described here, you can simply make parallel
lines of overlapping vegetables as shown in the photo, and bake them in
individual baking dishes rather than in one large one. Ed.*

# RATATOUILLE

PREPARATION TIME : 2 hours

INGREDIENTS FOR 4 SERVINGS :
1 pound (500 g) eggplant, peeled and diced
Salt
1 3/4 pounds (800 g) tomatoes, peeled and chopped
*Bouquet garni,* made with thyme and bay leaf tied together
1 or 2 cloves garlic, peeled
3 tablespoons olive oil
1 pound (500 g) onions, peeled and sliced
1/2 pound (250 g) carrots, peeled and cut into thin sticks
1 3/4 pound (800 g) zucchini, diced
Pepper

Place the eggplant in a mixing bowl and sprinkle generously with salt;
leave for 30 minutes before cooking. When the time is up, press them between the palms of your hands to squeeze out all their water before mixing
them with the other vegetables.
Place the tomatoes in a saucepan with the *bouquet garni* and garlic (no oil
or butter), and simmer uncovered for at least 30 minutes to make a thick
sauce.
Meanwhile, heat the oil in a large pot, add the onions and carrots, and
brown lightly. Add the zucchini, cover, and simmer for 15 minutes, stirring occasionally ; then add the eggplant and the tomato sauce, which
should be cooked by then. Season with salt and pepper, cover once more,
and simmer for 1 hour, stirring from time to time.
Serve on a hot platter or in the pot it cooked in (especially if you used an
earthenware one).

*Note : Ratatouille is also excellent cold. Ed.*

# CHAPTER 11

# PASTA AND RICE

Pasta and rice can be served with many main dishes, and are excellent accompaniments to either fish or meat when well prepared.

PASTA WITH CREAM AND BASIL SAUCE
   *(Pâtes à la crème et au basilic)*

PASTA PROVENÇALE-STYLE *(Pâtes à la provençale)*

PASTA CRÊPE *(Galette de nouilles)*

MACARONI AU GRATIN *(Gratin de macaroni)*

PASTA PANCAKE *(Pain de nouilles)*

RICE *(Riz créole)*

RICE PILAF *(Riz pilaf)*

BAKED VERMICELLI *(Paillasson de vermicelle)*

RISOTTO WITH TOMATOES *(Risotto à la tomate)*

# PASTA WITH CREAM AND BASIL SAUCE
*Pâtes à la crème et au basilic*

PREPARATION TIME : About 30 minutes

INGREDIENTS FOR 4 SERVINGS :
3/4 cup (150 g) shelled fresh peas — purchase 3/4 pound (350 g)
About 1 1/4 pounds (600 g) fresh pasta (see Comment and Variation)
5 1/4 ounces (150 g) prosciutto or bacon, diced
2 tablespoons (30 g) butter
6 tablespoons (10 cl) *crème fraîche* or heavy cream
Salt, pepper
1 tablespoon coarsely chopped fresh basil

Boil the peas in a pot of lightly salted boiling water for 5 to 10 minutes, drain, and reserve.
In a pot large enough to comfortably hold the pasta, but not too large nevertheless, bring lightly salted water to a boil. Add the pasta and cook at a rapid boil for 2 to 7 minutes. Cooking times will vary depending on the pasta used ; generally speaking, when all of the pasta floats, it's done. In any case, taste one : the pasta should be cooked *al dente,* that is, somewhat firm inside but *never* overcooked and mushy.
When the pasta is cooked, drain in a colander and return to the pot over moderate heat. Add the peas and ham, and stir in the cream, salt, pepper, and basil. Heat to warm through, stirring gently, but do not allow the cream to boil. Serve immediately.

COMMENT : If freshly made pasta is unavailable, buy 12 to 14 ounces (350 to 400 g) of egg-enriched pasta. Cooking times vary, so consult instructions given on the package.

VARIATION : You can use spinach noodles as well as plain ones, as shown in the photo. I suggest cooking them separately but mixing the two together.

# PASTA PROVENÇALE-STYLE
*Pâtes à la provençale*

PREPARATION TIME : 45 minutes

INGREDIENTS FOR 4 SERVINGS :
1 pound (500 g) tomatoes, peeled and chopped
1 clove garlic, peeled
*Bouquet garni,* made with thyme and bay leaf
2 tablespoons (30 g) butter
1 tablespoon olive oil
1 medium onion, peeled and sliced
1/4 pound (125 g) bacon, diced
Salt, pepper
About 1 1/4 pound (600 g) fresh pasta (see Comment and Variation, p. 284)
Freshly grated Parmesan

First make the sauce. Place the tomatoes, garlic, and *bouquet garni* in a saucepan and bring to a boil. Lower the heat and simmer for 15 minutes, stirring frequently.

Meanwhile, heat the butter and oil in a frying pan, add the onion and bacon, and cook to brown lightly. When the tomatoes are cooked, stir them into the pan, season with salt and pepper, and simmer 15 minutes more, stirring occasionally. When the sauce is done, remove the *bouquet garni* and discard.

Cook the pasta in rapidly boiling salted water for 2 to 7 minutes (see Pasta with Cream and Basil Sauce, p. 284). Drain, put the pasta in a large, hot serving dish, stir in the sauce, and serve, with a bowl of freshly grated Parmesan on the side.

# PASTA CRÊPE
*Galette de nouilles*

PREPARATION TIME : 25 minutes

INGREDIENTS FOR 2 SERVINGS :
2 2/3 cups (200 g) leftover cooked pasta (*tagliatelli*)
1 egg
1 tablespoon *crème fraîche* or heavy cream
Salt, pepper
2 tablespoons (30 g) butter (total)

Place the leftover pasta in a mixing bowl ; separate the pieces with your fingers if they are stuck together. Add the egg, cream, salt, and pepper. Stir gently to mix, being careful to break the pasta as little as possible.
Melt half the butter in a frying pan. When it starts to foam, pour in the pasta, spread it out, and flatten it into a sort of pancake or crêpe, using a fork, and cook for about 7 minutes. When brown on the first side, turn the crêpe over using two plates as described in the recipe for Potato Crêpe (p. 269). Add the remaining butter to the pan and slide the crêpe back in. Cook 7 minutes on the second side, then slide onto a serving platter and serve immediately.

# MACARONI AU GRATIN
*Gratin de macaroni*

PREPARATION TIME : 1 hour 15 minutes

INGREDIENTS FOR 6 SERVINGS :
16 to 17.6 ounces (450 to 500 g) long macaroni
1 clove garlic, peeled and split lengthwise
Butter, for the dish
5 1/4 cups (1 1/4 liters) milk
Salt, pepper
Nutmeg
Generous 3/4 cup (20 cl) cream
1 2/3 cups (125 g) grated Swiss cheese
3 1/2 tablespoons (50 g) butter, broken into small pieces

Preheat the oven to 350°F (180°C).
Cook the macaroni in rapidly boiling salted water for 7 minutes, then drain in a colander (do not cool).
Rub a large baking dish with the pieces of garlic and butter generously.
Heat the milk in a large saucepan and season generously with salt, pepper, and nutmeg. Stir in the cream and the macaroni, then pour into the baking dish. Sprinkle with the grated cheese, dot with butter, and bake for 1 hour (the macaroni should bake for a long time ; it will finish cooking in the milk and become beautifully browned on top).

Macaroni au Gratin.

## PASTA PANCAKE
*Pain de nouilles*

PREPARATION TIME : 15 minutes

INGREDIENTS FOR 4 SERVINGS :
5 1/4 cups (400 g) leftover cooked pasta (preferably *tagliatelli*)
Salt, pepper
2 eggs
3 tablespoons chopped chives, basil, or parsley
3 1/2 tablespoons (50 g) butter

Place the noodles in a bowl and separate them with your fingers. Season with salt and pepper, then stir in the eggs and the herb of your choice. Melt the butter in a large frying pan ; when very hot, pour in the noodle mixture and spread it out into a large pancake using a fork. Cook 5 minutes or until brown, then turn over using two plates, as described in the recipe for Potato Crêpe, p. 269. Cook about 5 minutes on the second side, then slide out of the pan and onto a hot serving platter. Serve immediately.

## RICE
*Riz créole*

PREPARATION TIME : 20 minutes

INGREDIENTS FOR 4 SERVINGS :
6 1/3 cups (1 1/2 liters) water
Salt
1 1/4 cups (250 g) rice

Bring the water to a boil in a saucepan, add the salt, and stir in the rice. Boil gently, uncovered, for 15 minutes, stirring occasionally ; then drain and serve.

**Serving suggestions :** Serve with butter, salt, and pepper, with a Tomato Sauce (p. 120), or with the meat juices or sauce that goes with the dish it is used to garnish.

# RICE PILAF
*Riz pilaf*

PREPARATION TIME : About 25 minutes

INGREDIENTS FOR 4 SERVINGS :
3 1/4 cup (75 cl) bouillon (see French Boiled Dinner p. 198), or water
4 tablespoons (60 g) butter
1 onion, peeled and sliced
1 1/4 cups (250 g) rice
Salt, pepper
1 1/3 cups (100 g) grated Swiss cheese

Heat the bouillon or water in a saucepan.
Melt the butter in a second saucepan and brown the onion, then stir in the rice. Use a ladle to add enough of the bouillon or water to barely cover the rice, salt lightly, stir, and boil gently uncovered until the liquid has been absorbed (about 5 minutes). Add half of the remaining liquid ; when this has been absorbed, add the rest. Cook the rice a total of about 20 minutes ; when done, all the liquid should have evaporated.
Salt and pepper to taste, then serve, with a bowl of freshly grated cheese on the side.

**Serving suggestions :** Rice pilaf can be served with many meat and fish dishes.

# BAKED VERMICELLI
*Paillasson de vermicelle*

PREPARATION TIME : 30 minutes

INGREDIENTS FOR 4 SERVINGS :
2 tablespoons (30 g) butter
2 tablespoons olive oil
8 ounces (250 g) vermicelli
1 clove garlic, whole and unpeeled
2 cups (50 cl) bouillon (see French Boiled Dinner, p. 198)
Salt, pepper

Preheat the oven to 425°F (220°C).
On top of the stove, heat the butter and olive oil in a medium sized, enamelled cast iron baking dish. Add the vermicelli and garlic, and cook for 6 to 7 minutes, stirring and tossing the vermicelli almost constantly to brown them lightly.
Lower the heat and add the bouillon ; simmer for 5 to 6 minutes or until it has completely evaporated. Remove the pan from the heat, sprinkle with salt and pepper, then place in the oven to finish cooking for 10 minutes. Either serve in the baking dish or turn out by running the tip of a knife all around the edge, placing a large flat platter on top of the dish, and flipping everything upside down so the cake of vermicelli is sitting on the platter. Serve immediately.

**Serving suggestions :** This is an excellent accompaniment to the Boiled Beef au Gratin p. 200.

Baked Vermicelli.

# RISOTTO WITH TOMATOES
*Risotto à la tomate*

PREPARATION TIME : About 1 hour

INGREDIENTS FOR 4 SERVINGS :
1 1/2 pound (700 g) tomatoes, peeled and chopped
2 tablespoons olive oil (for the tomatoes)
4 medium onions, peeled and chopped
3 tablespoons (5 cl) olive oil (for the rice)
2 cups (50 cl) bouillon (see French Boiled Dinner p. 198)
1 1/4 cups (250 g) rice
Salt, pepper
1 pinch saffron (optional)
Generous 3/4 cup (75 g) freshly grated Parmesan

First cook the tomatoes. Heat 2 tablespoons of oil in a saucepan, add the onion, and cook to brown lightly, then add the tomatoes, stir, and simmer uncovered for 15 to 20 minutes.

When the tomatoes are done, cook the rice. Heat the remaining olive oil in a large saucepan. Heat the bouillon in another saucepan.

When the olive oil is very hot, add the rice. Stir for a few seconds or until translucent, then add the tomato sauce and the hot bouillon. Salt and pepper, add the saffron (if using), stir, then cover the pan and simmer slowly for 25 to 30 minutes. When the rice is done, all the liquid should have been absorbed.

Gently stir in the Parmesan, taste for salt and pepper, and serve immediately.

**Serving suggestions :** Risotto is an excellent accompaniment to the French Boiled Dinner p. 198.

# CHAPTER 12

# DESSERTS

Most of these desserts are traditional family fare in France — everyone's favorites.

CHERRY CLAFOUTIS *(Clafoutis)*

FARMER'S CHEESE LYONS-STYLE *(Cervelle des canuts)*

APPLESAUCE *(Compote de pommes)*

STEWED DRIED FRUITS *(Compote de fruits secs)*

VANILLA CUSTARD SAUCE *(Crème anglaise)*

CRÊPES

CHOCOLATE MARBLE CAKE *(Marbré au chocolat)*

APPLE PANCAKE LYONS-STYLE *(Matefaim lyonnais)*

CHOCOLATE MOUSSE *(Mousse au chocolat)*

PEARS IN RED WINE *(Poires au vin)*

MY CHESTNUT PUDDING *(Pudding de chez nous)*

RICE CUSTARD *(Riz au lait)*

BAKED APPLES *(Pommes au four)*

DRIED APRICOT SOUFFLÉ *(Soufflé aux abricots)*

PLAIN SOUFFLÉ *(Soufflé bonne femme)*

FRUIT SALAD *(Salade de fruits)*

YOGURT ICE CREAM *(Glace au yaourt)*

# CHERRY CLAFOUTIS
*Clafoutis*

PREPARATION TIME : 1 hour 15 minutes

INGREDIENTS FOR 6 SERVINGS :
1 pound (500 g) dark, ripe cherries
1 1/2 teaspoons (5 g) baking powder
1 3/4 cups (250 g) flour
3 eggs
1/4 cup (50 g) granulated sugar
1/2 cup (12 cl) milk
1 pinch salt
2 tablespoons (30 g) butter (for the pan)
Sugar (to finish)

Preheat the oven to 400°F (200°C).
Wash the cherries, dry them in a clean cloth and remove the stems, but do not pit them. Reserve.
Mix the baking powder and flour together in a mixing bowl, then push it up against the sides of the bowl to form a well in the center. Break the eggs into the well, add the sugar, milk, and salt, and stir, mixing the flour in as it falls from the sides. The finished batter should be smooth ; if there are any lumps, work the batter through a sieve to eliminate them.
Butter a 10-inch (25-cm) pie or cake pan (preferably porcelain). Stir the cherries into the batter, then pour it into the pan and bake for 45 minutes to 1 hour. When golden brown, remove the clafoutis from the oven and sprinkle with sugar. Serve either hot or cold in the pan.

Cherry Clafoutis.

# FARMER'S CHEESE LYONS-STYLE
## Cervelle des canuts

PREPARATION TIME : 10 minutes (plus 2 hours refrigeration)

INGREDIENTS FOR 4 SERVINGS :
3/4 cup — about 7 ounces (200 g) — fresh farmer's cheese
6 tablespoons (10 cl) *crème fraîche* or heavy cream
2 tablespoons olive oil
1 1/2 teaspoons red wine vinegar
1 clove garlic, peeled and finely chopped
1 shallot, peeled and finely chopped
Salt, pepper
1 tablespoon finely chopped chervil
1 tablespoon finely chopped chives
1 tablespoon finely chopped parsley
1/2 tablespoon finely chopped tarragon
Radishes

This is not a dessert, but I didn't really know where else to put it in the book. It's a speciality of Lyons which we eat either as a starter before dinner or after the main dish (before dessert), or simply as a snack. It can also be served with drinks or as part of the Lyons-style brunch (*mâchon*). To make it, simply beat together the farmer's cheese and the cream until smooth, then beat or whisk in the oil, vinegar, garlic, and shallot. Season with salt and pepper, then stir in the fresh herbs (if you want, you can add more herbs, to taste). Refrigerate for at least 2 hours before serving. Serve cold with pieces of toast and radishes.

# APPLESAUCE
*Compote de pommes*

PREPARATION TIME : 30 minutes

INGREDIENTS FOR 4 SERVINGS :
2 1/4 pounds (1 kg) apples
4 tablespoons (6 cl) water
1/4 cup (50 g) granulated sugar
Either 1 pinch cinnamon, and lemon juice to taste, *or*
   1/2 cup (70 cl) light brown sugar and 2 tablespoons water

Peel, quarter, and seed the apples, then cut into thin slices. Place in a saucepan with the water and sugar, and simmer uncovered for 20 minutes, stirring occasionally. Beat vigorously (preferably with a wire whisk) to make applesauce.

You can either flavor the applesauce with cinnamon and lemon juice, or with caramel. In the second case, make a caramel by cooking the brown sugar and water together until the mixture darkens and caramelizes. Stir the hot applesauce into the caramel and serve warm.

# STEWED DRIED FRUITS
*Compote de fruits secs*

PREPARATION TIME : 20 minutes (plus cooling)

INGREDIENTS FOR 4 SERVINGS :
7 ounces (200 g) dried apricots
5 1/4 ounces (150 g) dried figs
1/4 pound (125 g) prunes
1/4 pound (125 g) dried bananas
3 cups (75 cl) water
10 hazelnuts
10 almonds

Place the fruit in a large saucepan and add the cold water. Bring just to a boil, then immediately lower the heat, cover, and simmer slowly for 20 to 30 minutes or until very tender. Pour into a salad bowl and leave to cool completely, then chill for at least an hour in the refrigerator.
Just before serving, stir in the nuts.

**Serving suggestions :** Serve with Madeleines (p. 322).

# VANILLA CUSTARD SAUCE
*Crème anglaise*

PREPARATION TIME : About 30 minutes (plus cooling time)

INGREDIENTS FOR 6 SERVINGS :
1 vanilla bean
2 cups (50 cl) milk
3 eggs
1/2 cup (100 g) granulated sugar
1 pinch salt

Split open the vanilla bean lengthwise, place in a medium saucepan with the milk and bring just to a boil. Remove the pan from the heat and leave to infuse for 7 to 8 minutes, then remove the vanilla bean.
Away from the heat, in the top of a double boiler, whisk together the eggs, sugar, and salt, then whisk in the hot milk. Set the top of the double boiler in place and heat, stirring the mixture constantly for about 8 minutes or until it thickens (it should not boil). Immediately pour the sauce into a serving bowl and allow to cool, stirring occasionally before refrigerating. Serve cold.

**Serving suggestions :** Serve with Chocolate Marble Cake, p. 303 (also, see *Note*).

VARIATION : Instead of vanilla, various other flavors can be given to the sauce : for example, stir a little chocolate, coffee, caramel, or rum into the sauce after it thickens but before it cools.

*Note : Vanilla custard sauce is also excellent with fresh fruit such as strawberries, raspberries, pears, etc. Ed.*

# CRÊPES

PREPARATION TIME : About 40 minutes (plus 1 hour resting time)

INGREDIENTS FOR 6 SERVINGS :
3 1/2 tablespoons (50 g) butter
1 3/4 cups (250 g) flour
3 eggs
1 tablespoon granulated sugar
1 pinch salt
2 cups (50 cl) cold milk
Butter or oil (for the pan)

Melt the butter in a small saucepan and reserve.
Place the flour, sugar, and salt in a mixing bowl ; stir in the eggs, then pour in the cold milk little by little, stirring at first, then whisking to make a smooth liquid batter. Finally whisk in the melted butter. Leave the batter at room temperature for about 1 hour before making the crêpes.
Lightly butter or oil a frying pan (preferably cast iron or nonstick). When very hot, spoon about 1/4 cup (6 cl) of the batter into the center of it, and tip and turn the frying pan to cover the bottom with the batter and make a very thin pancake (crêpe). Cook the crêpe for about 2 minutes over moderate heat, turn it over using a flexible-blade spatula, and finish cooking about 3 minutes on the second side. Remove the crêpe and lightly butter the pan before cooking the next one. To keep the crêpes warm after cooking, heat a little water to simmering in a saucepan. Set a large plate on top of the saucepan. As the crêpes finish cooking, put them on the plate and cover with a second plate turned upside down.

**Serving suggestions :** Serve the crêpes hot with honey, walnuts, jam, or chestnut cream.

*Note : Crêpes are also delicious simply spread with a little butter and sprinkled with granulated sugar. Ed.*

# CHOCOLATE MARBLE CAKE
*Marbré au chocolat*

PREPARATION TIME : 1 hour

INGREDIENTS FOR 6 SERVINGS :
2 Large eggs
2/3 cup (120 g) granulated sugar
1 scant cup (125 g) flour
1 stick (120 g) softened butter
1 pinch salt
1 3/4 ounces (50 g) semi-sweet chocolate
Butter (for the mold)

Preheat the oven to 400°F (200°C).
Beat the eggs and sugar in a mixing bowl until smooth and a pale yellow color, then sift in the flour, whisking as it is being added. Whisk in the softened butter and the salt ; the finished batter should be smooth.
Melt the chocolate in a double boiler.
Lightly butter a 9 1/2-inch (24-cm) poundcake or loaf pan, line it with parchment paper, then lightly butter the paper as well. Pour the melted chocolate over the batter, then barely stir it in, so that there will be light and dark patches. Pour the batter into the mold, smooth the surface, and bake for 45 minutes. Test to see if the cake is done by sticking a needle or knife blade into the center ; it should come out clean and dry. If not, bake the cake a little longer.
Turn the mold upside down on a cake rack to cool as soon as you take the cake from the oven, but don't lift it off of the cake until it has cooled completely.
When cool, lift off the mold, peel off the paper, turn right side up and serve on a serving platter.
This cake will stay fresh up to a week wrapped in aluminium foil.

**Serving suggestions :** Serve with a Vanilla Custard sauce (p. 301) or a Chocolate Mousse (p. 305) on the side.

# APPLE PANCAKE LYONS-STYLE
## *Matefaim lyonnais*

PREPARATION TIME : 45 minutes (plus 3 hours resting time)

INGREDIENTS FOR 4 TO 5 SERVINGS :
1 1/2 cups (200 g) flour
2 eggs
6 tablespoons (80 g) granulated sugar
1/2 tablespoon cooking oil
1/2 teaspoon salt
1 cup (25 cl) milk
1 tablespoon cognac, or 1 teaspoon orange flower water or vanilla
    extract (or more, to taste)
3/4 pound (350 g) apples
3 tablespoons (40 g) granulated sugar
Oil (for the pan)


The batter must be made 3 hours before cooking. Place the flour and eggs in a mixing bowl, beat with a spoon, and add 6 tablespoons (80 g) of sugar, the oil, and the salt. Continue beating as you pour in the cold milk little by little to make a smooth batter. Add the flavoring of your choice. If there are any lumps in the batter, work it through a fine sieve into another mixing bowl. Leave at room temperature for 3 hours.

Just before cooking, peel the apples and core them. Chop them coarsely, then stir them into the batter as well as the remaining 3 tablespoons (40 g) of sugar. Lightly oil a large frying pan (preferably cast iron or nonstick) ; when very hot, pour in the batter and spread it out to make a thick pancake. Cook over moderate heat for 30 to 45 minutes, turning over every 6 to 8 minutes (see the Potato Crêpe (p. 269) for instructions on turning over). When the pancake is done, a knife or needle stuck into it should come out clean and almost dry.

Serve warm with sugar and cream on the side.

# CHOCOLATE MOUSSE
*Mousse au chocolat*

PREPARATION TIME : 30 minutes (plus 2 hours refrigeration)

INGREDIENTS FOR 4 SERVINGS :
4 1/2 ounces (125 g) semi-sweet chocolate
2 tablespoons (30 g) softened butter
4 tablespoons (50 g) granulated sugar
4 eggs yolks
4 egg whites

Chocolate mousse should be prepared at least 2 hours before serving; ideally, it should be made 24 hours ahead of time.

Melt the chocolate and butter in a double boiler over low heat, stirring gently as they begin to melt. Stir in the sugar little by little. When thick and creamy, pour the chocolate mixture into a large mixing bowl and stir until it has cooled to lukewarm, then stir in the egg yolks.

Beat the egg whites until stiff in another mixing bowl, then slide them into the bowl with the chocolate and fold them in, using a wooden spatula or spoon (see Dictionary p. 345).

When the egg whites have been completely incorporated into the chocolate, place the mousse in the refrigerator for 2 hours or more before serving.

**Serving suggestions :** Serve with warm Almond Cookies (p. 328).

# PEARS IN RED WINE
## *Poires au vin*

PREPARATION TIME : 45 minutes (plus time to cool)

INGREDIENTS FOR 4 SERVINGS :
8 very small or 4 medium pears weighing a total of about 2 pounds
   (900 g)
Juice of 1/2 lemon
1/2 cup (100 g) granulated sugar
1 cup (25 cl) red wine
1/2 vanilla bean, split in half lengthwise
1 sprig thyme
2 peppercorns
1 clove
4 tablespoons (6 cl) *crème de cassis* (black currant liqueur)

Preferably use a smooth-skinned variety of pear. Small ones need not be peeled (simply rinse them off and dry with a cloth) ; large ones can be peeled, cored, then halved or quartered (see *Note*).
Place the pears in a saucepan just large enough to hold them (stand small pears upright). Add the lemon juice, sugar, red wine, vanilla, thyme, peppercorns, clove, and *crème de cassis*. Bring just to a boil, then cover and simmer very slowly for 30 minutes. Lift the pears out of the pan and stand them upright in a serving bowl. Pour the contents of the saucepan over them and leave to cool before serving (several hours will do, but overnight is best). Baste the pears periodically with the wine as they cool, and before serving.

**Serving suggestions :** Serve with Lyons-style Fritters (p. 318).

*Note : Whole pears (even large ones) make for a nicer presentation. Peel them, then place them on their sides in the wine and turn over halfway through the cooking time. When done, stand them upright and baste as described for small pears. Ed.*

Pears in Red Wine.

# MY CHESTNUT PUDDING
*Pudding de chez nous*

PREPARATION TIME : 1 1/2 hours

INGREDIENTS FOR 4 SERVINGS :
2 teaspoons (10 g) softened butter (for the mold)
1 tablespoon (15 g) granulated sugar
1/2 pound (250 g) candied chestnuts (see *Note*)
3 tablespoons (40 g) softened butter
3 tablespoons (5 cl) *crème fraîche* or heavy cream
4 egg yolks
3 egg whites

Bring a large saucepan of water to a boil.
Preheat the oven to 425°F (220°C).
Generously butter a 6 1/4-inch (16-cm) charlotte mold or a 7-inch (18-cm) souffle mold. Sprinkle in the sugar and turn the mold to coat the sides with it. Place the mold in the refrigerator while making the pudding.
Place the chestnuts in a mortar with the butter and pound to a paste, then stir in the cream. Pour the chestnut mixture into a fine sieve and use a wooden spoon to work it through and make a fine, smooth paste. Stir in the egg yolks.
Beat the egg whites until stiff, then fold them into the chestnut cream (see Dictionary p. 345). When all the egg whites have been added and the mixture is smooth, remove the mold from the refrigerator and pour in the chestnut mixture. Place the mold in a roasting pan and pour in enough boiling water to come about 1/3 of the way up the sides of the mold, then place in the oven and bake for 45 minutes. Test to see if the pudding is done by sticking the tip of a knife or a trussing needle into it ; if it comes out clean and dry, the pudding is done. If not, it needs to cook longer.
Either turn out the pudding when it comes from the oven and sprinkle with confectioner's sugar, or serve in the mold (in which case it's preferable to bake it in a porcelain soufflé mold). Serve warm, but not hot.

**Serving suggestions :** Serve with Apricot Jam (p. 330) and macaroons.

*Note : Candied chestnuts are sold at Christmastime in France ; in the course of being candied, many of them break, and they are sold at much lower prices than the whole ones. It is these broken ones that Paul Bocuse uses in making this dessert, but whole ones can of course be used instead. Ed.*

# RICE CUSTARD
*Riz au lait*

PREPARATION TIME : 1 hour 15 minutes (plus cooling time)

INGREDIENTS FOR 4 SERVINGS :
4 1/4 cups (1 liter) milk
1 cup (200 g) granulated sugar
1/2 teaspoon salt
1 vanilla bean, split in half lengthwise
1 cup (200 g) rice

Place the milk, sugar, salt, and vanilla bean in a large saucepan and bring
to a boil. Sprinkle in the rice, stirring. Lower the heat (use a heat diffuser
for very low, even heat) and cook the rice 45 minutes to 1 hour or until it is
tender and has absorbed practically all of the milk (the milk left over will
be absorbed as the rice cools).
Remove the vanilla bean, pour the rice into a bowl, and leave to cool ; it
can be served either warm or cold.

**Serving suggestions :** Serve with a homemade jam (Chapter 14), poached
fruits, or candied fruits.

# BAKED APPLES
*Pommes au four*

PREPARATION TIME : 1 hour 15 minutes

INGREDIENTS FOR 4 SERVINGS :
4 large apples
Butter (for the dish)
2 tablespoons (30 g) butter (for the apples)
1/2 cup (12 cl) water
1/3 cup (60 g) granulated sugar
4 tablespoons raspberry or red currant jelly

Preheat the oven to 400°F (200°C).
Wash the apples and wipe them dry ; cut out the stems, but I wouldn't core them since the seeds give a nice taste to them (if you prefer, you can core them, of course).
Place the apples in a lightly buttered baking dish, put a little butter on top of each one, add the water, and place in the oven. After 15 minutes, sprinkle each apple with sugar, then place back in the oven and bake for 30 minutes more or until tender.
Remove the apples from the oven and allow to cool for 10 to 15 minutes ; they should be served warm but not hot. Just before serving spoon a little jelly into each one, and serve in the baking dish.

Baked Apples.

# DRIED APRICOT SOUFFLÉ
*Soufflé aux abricots*

PREPARATION TIME : 45 minutes

INGREDIENTS FOR 4 SERVINGS :
Softened butter (for the molds)
Granulated sugar (for the molds)
1/4 pound (125 g) dried apricots (see *Note*)
2 tablespoons water
2 tablespoons granulated sugar
2 egg yolks
4 egg whites

Preheat the oven to 350°F (180°C).
Butter 4 individual soufflé molds about 4 inches (10 cm) wide. Sprinkle sugar into each one and turn to coat the sides with it. Pour out any excess sugar, then place the molds upside down on a plate in the refrigerator while making the soufflé batter.
Chop the apricots to a fine paste. Place the water and sugar in a small saucepan and bring just to a boil. Remove from the heat and stir in first the apricots, then the egg yolks ; pour into a large mixing bowl and reserve.
Whisk the egg whites until stiff, then fold them into the apricot mixture (see Dictionary, p. 345). Pour the soufflé batter into the molds and bake for about 25 minutes or until golden brown on top (don't open the oven door, but check by looking through the window in it).
Serve immediately.

**Serving suggestions :** Serve with black currant jelly and cookies.

*Note : Be sure to use very soft apricots when making this dish. Ed.*

# PLAIN SOUFFLÉ
*Soufflé bonne femme*

PREPARATION TIME : 45 minutes

INGREDIENTS FOR 6 SERVINGS :
Softened butter (for the molds)
Granulated sugar (for the molds)
3/4 cup (20 cl) milk
Scant 1/2 cup (90 g) granulated sugar
6 tablespoons (10 cl) milk
3 tablespoons (30 g) flour
3 tablespoons (40 g) softened butter
6 egg yolks
9 egg whites
Confectioner's sugar (to sprinkle on top).

Preheat the oven to 400°F (200°C).
Lightly butter 6 individual soufflé molds about 4 inches (10 cm) wide.
Sprinkle in some sugar and turn to coat the sides of the molds with it. Pour
out any excess sugar, then place the molds upside down on a large platter
in the refrigerator while making the soufflé batter.
Place 3/4 cup (20 cl) of milk in a saucepan with the sugar and bring to a
boil. Meanwhile, stir the remaining 6 tablespoons (10 cl) of milk into the
flour. Pour the flour mixture into the boiling milk, stirring, then simmer
very slowly for 3 minutes, stirring occasionally. Allow to cool for 2 minutes, then place in a mixing bowl and stir in the butter and the egg yolks.
Beat the egg whites until stiff, then fold them into the other ingredients
(see Dictionary p. 345). Pour the soufflé batter into the molds and bake
for about 20 minutes. Sprinkle with a little confectioner's sugar as soon as
they come from the oven, and serve immediately.

VARIATIONS : When adding the egg yolks, you can add 2 tablespoons (or
more to taste) of rum, cognac, Grand Marnier, or any other alcohol to the
batter to flavor it.

*Note : This soufflé batter can be made and poured into the molds up to
1/2 hour before baking. Ed.*

# FRUIT SALAD
*Salade de fruits*

PREPARATION TIME : 30 minutes (plus refrigeration)

INGREDIENTS FOR 4 SERVINGS :
2 apples, peeled, cored, and quartered
2 pears (not too ripe), peeled, cored, and quartered
1 orange
1/2 grapefruit
1/2 pineapple
Juice of 1 lemon
1 cup (100 g) walnut meats
1/4 cup (50 g) granulated sugar
2 bananas
6 mint leaves, finely sliced

Place the apples and pears in a large salad bowl. Use a knife to cut off the peel (including the white inner skin) of the orange and grapefruit, then cut out the wedges and add them to the bowl, along with any juice they gave out. Cut the skin off of the pineapple, cut out the central core, then cut it into wedges and add to the salad. Add the lemon juice, walnut meats, and sugar. Stir gently, then refrigerate for about 1 hour before serving.
Just before serving, peel and slice the bananas and add them, sprinkle with the slices of mint, and serve.

**Serving suggestions :** Serve with Almond Cookies (p. 328).

VARIATION : All kinds of fruits other than the ones used here can be used in fruit salads ; for example tropical fruits such as kiwis or lichees, or fresh grapes are all excellent additions to a fruit salad.
Il you like, 3 tablespoons (5 cl) of brandy or a fruit brandy can be added to the salad at the same time as the lemon juice.

Fruit Salad.

# YOGURT ICE CREAM
*Glace au yaourt*

PREPARATION TIME : 45 minutes

INGREDIENTS FOR 6 SERVINGS :
8 egg yolks
2/3 cup (125 g) granulated sugar
1 pint (50 cl) plain yogurt
6 tablespoons (10 cl) *crème fraîche* or heavy cream
1/4 cup (50 g) chopped mixed candied fruit

Place the egg yolks in a bowl with the sugar and whisk until the mixture becomes smooth and pale in color. Stir in the yogurt, then the cream, and finally the candied fruit. Pour into an ice cream freezer and churn for 30 minutes or until stiff. You can serve the ice cream directly from the freezer (it's best this way), or put it in containers and keep in a deep freezer for later use.

**Serving suggestions :** Serve with cookies, and a sauce made with fresh raspberries and a little sugar blended until smooth in a blender or food processor.

# CHAPTER 13

# PASTRIES

French pastries can be very elaborate, but here are a few that are easy to make and very good.

LYONS-STYLE FRITTERS *(Bugnes)*

PLAIN CAKE *(Gâteau manqué)*

ALSATIAN-STYLE CAKE *(Gâteau alsacien)*

MADELEINES

LEMON PIE *(Tarte au citron)*

CHEESE CAKE *(Tarte au fromage blanc)*

RHUBARB PIE *(Tarte à la rhubarbe)*

APPLE TART *(Tarte aux pommes)*

ALMOND COOKIES *(Tuiles)*

# LYONS-STYLE FRITTERS
## *Bugnes*

PREPARATION TIME : About 3 hours

INGREDIENTS FOR ABOUT 8 SERVINGS :
Scant 3 3/4 cups (500 g) flour
3 eggs
1/4 cup (50 g) granulated sugar
1/2 teaspoon (4 g) salt
Generous 1/4 teaspoon (2 g) baking powder
1 stick (125 g) softened butter, broken into about 20 pieces
2 tablespoons dark rum (optional)
2 quarts (2 liters) oil (for frying)
Confectioner's sugar

These fritters, similar to doughnuts, are a speciality of Lyons. We make them particularly around Mardi Gras — they keep very well, so we always make plenty of them.

Place the flour in a large bowl and push it up against the sides to make a well in the center. Put the eggs, sugar, salt, baking powder, butter, and rum into the well. Use a spoon to beat the flour in as it falls from the sides of the bowl. Once the dough becomes thick and difficult to stir, use your hands to knead it like bread dough. When the dough is smooth, place it on a lightly floured cutting board or plate, cover, and leave for 2 hours before making the fritters.

When ready to cook, heat the oil in a deep fryer.

Spread out some paper towels for draining the fritters.

Line a large basket or bowl with a clean cloth.

On a lightly floured table, roll out about 1/3 of the dough at a time into a thin sheet. Use a cookie cutter, knife, or pastry wheel to cut the dough into squares, triangles, or any shape you like.

Test the oil to see if it's hot enough by dropping in a little piece of the dough ; if it comes back to the surface almost immediately and begins to brown quickly, the oil is ready.

Fry about 6 to 8 fritters at a time, depending on the size of your deep fryer. Fry about 2 minutes on a side or until golden brown, then lift them out and drain on the paper towels and begin cooking more fritters. When the first batch has drained sufficiently, put them in the basket prepared ear-

lier, sprinkle them with confectioner's sugar, and fold the towel over them to keep them warm.

The fritters can be served either warm, as soon as the last batch has been fried, or cold, in which case they can be made ahead of time.

**Serving suggestions :** Serve with jams, jellies, or stewed fruits.

# PLAIN CAKE
*Gâteau manqué*

PREPARATION TIME : 50 minutes

INGREDIENTS FOR 4 SERVINGS :
3/4 cup (100 g) flour
Generous 2/3 cup (150 g) granulated sugar
2 eggs
1/2 cup (12 cl) milk
Butter (for the cake pan)
2 tablespoons (30 g) butter, broken into pieces
2 tablespoons (30 g) granulated sugar

Preheat the oven to 450°F (240°C).
Place the flour, sugar, eggs, and milk in a bowl and beat to make a smooth batter.
Generously butter an 8-inch (20-cm) cake pan (preferably porcelain), pour in the batter, and place immediately in the hot oven. Bake for 20 minutes, then lower the heat to 400°F (200°C), dot with the butter, sprinkle with the remaining sugar, and bake for 20 minutes more.
Serve hot or cold, either alone or with Vanilla Custard Sauce (p. 301).

# ALSATIAN-STYLE CAKE
*Gâteau alsacien*

PREPARATION TIME: About 1 1/2 hour

INGREDIENTS FOR 6 SERVINGS:
5 1/2 cups (250 g) white bread or soft dinner rolls, cut into 1/2-inch
(1-cm) cubes
3/4 cups (20 cl) milk
1 vanilla bean, cut in half lengthwise
6 tablespoons (75 g) granulated sugar
2 egg yolks
1 pound (450 g) apples, peeled, cored, and sliced
1 tablespoon cherry brandy (Kirsch)
2 egg whites
Butter (for the mold)
2 tablespoons cinnamon
2 tablespoons breadcrumbs
1 1/2 tablespoons (20 g) butter, broken into little pieces

Leave the bread out overnight in a mixing bowl so that it will become stale
using it to make the cake.
Place the milk in a saucepan with the vanilla bean and bring to a boil, then
pour onto the bread and leave for 30 minutes.
Preheat the oven to 400°F (200°C).
Remove the vanilla bean from the bowl with the bread and crush the bread
to a paste with a fork. Stir in the sugar, then the egg yolks, and finally the
apples and the cherry brandy.
Beat the egg whites until stiff and fold them into the other ingredients (see
Dictionary p. 345). Butter an 8-inch (20-cm) square or 9-inch (22-cm) cake
pan and pour in the batter. Mix the cinnamon and breadcrumbs together,
then sprinkle over the batter. Dot with the butter, then bake for 40 to
45 minutes, or until a knife stuck into the center comes out clean.
Serve cold.

# MADELEINES

PREPARATION TIME : 30 minutes

INGREDIENTS FOR 24 LARGE MADELEINES :
1 1/4 sticks (150 g) butter
Generous 2/3 cup (150 g) granulated sugar
1 tablespoon orange flower water (see *Note)*
3 eggs
1 generous cup (150 g) flour

Preheat the oven to 400°F (200°C).
Melt the butter in a small saucepan and reserve. Place the sugar, orange flower water, and eggs in a mixing bowl and beat with a whisk. Whisk in the melted butter, then add the flour little by little, whisking constantly to make a smooth batter.
Lightly butter the madeleine molds, then fill them by about 3/4 with the batter. Bake for 20 minutes, or until a rich golden brown, then turn out onto a cake rack and allow to cool before serving.

*Note : Madeleines are always baked in elongated, shell-shaped molds, but any shallow cupcake or cookie mold could be used for baking them.*
*Orange flower water can be replaced by a tablespoon of finely grated orange peel or lemon peel if preferred. Ed.*

# LEMON PIE
*Tarte au citron*

PREPARATION TIME: 2 hours (plus 3 hours refrigeration)

INGREDIENTS FOR 6 TO 8 SERVINGS:
> *For the dough:*
1 3/4 cup (250 g) flour
1 stick (125 g) softened butter, broken into pieces
6 tablespoons (75 g) granulated sugar
1 egg
> *For the filling:*
6 1/2 tablespoons (100 g) softened butter, broken into pieces
2/3 cup (125 g) granulated sugar
3 eggs
4 tablespoons (6 cl) *crème fraîche* or heavy cream
Juice of 3 lemons
Finely grated zest of 3 lemons

First make the dough : place the flour, butter, sugar, and egg in a large mixing bowl. Use your fingers to "pinch" the ingredients together, working quickly, until a ball of dough is formed. Place it on a lightly floured table or plate, cover, and leave for 1 hour before baking.
Preheat the oven to 400°F (200°C).
Lightly butter and flour a 9 1/2-inch (24-cm) pie pan, then roll the dough out into a thin sheet and line the pan. Cut off any excess dough from around the edges (see *Note),* then prick the bottom in several places with the prongs of a fork. Place a piece of parchment paper on top of the dough ; it should be large enough to cover the bottom and sides of the dough and stick up above the edges of the pan. Press the paper well against the dough lining the sides of the pan, then fill the pan with uncooked rice, beans, or lentils. Place in the oven and bake for 15 minutes, then remove from the oven and lower the oven temperature to 325°F (160°C). Carefully lift out the paper containing the rice or beans (save the rice or beans for baking other pie doughs in the same way).
Make the filling by beating together first the butter and sugar, beat in the eggs and cream, then add the lemon juice and zest. Pour the filling into the pie pan, place back in the oven and bake for 40 to 45 minutes or until the filling and crust have begun to brown. Allow to cool completely, then chill in the refrigerator for 3 hours before serving.

*Note : Use any leftover pie dough to make cookies : pack it into a ball, roll it out, and cut into any shape you like. Bake about 20 minutes or until golden brown. Ed.*

# CHEESE CAKE
*Tarte au fromage blanc*

PREPARATION TIME : About 2 hours

INGREDIENTS FOR 5 TO 6 SERVINGS :
*For the dough :*
1 generous cup (150 g) flour
5 tablespoons (75 g) softened butter, broken into pieces
1 pinch salt
2 tablespoons water
*For the filling :*
8 ounces (250 g) cream cheese
6 tablespoons (10 cl) *crème fraîche* or heavy cream
2 eggs
1 egg yolk
1/2 cup (100 g) granulated sugar
1 tablespoon (10 g) flour
1/4 teaspoon vanilla extract (or more, to taste).

Make the dough by placing the flour, butter, and salt in a bowl and "pinching" them together until a crumbly mixture is formed. Add the water and knead lightly to make a smooth dough. Place on a lightly floured plate, cover, and place in the refrigerator for 1 hour before baking.
Preheat the oven to 400°F (200°C).
Place the cheese in a strainer and drain if necessary, then work it through the strainer into a clean bowl to eliminate any lumps if there are any. Add the cream and beat until smooth. Beat in the whole eggs, one by one, then the egg yolk. Mix the sugar and flour together, then beat them into the cheese little by little ; add the vanilla extract.
Roll out the dough on a lightly floured table into a thin sheet. Lightly butter an 8-inch (20-cm) pie pan, line it with the dough, and prick the bottom all over with a fork. Pour in the cheese filling, bake for 20 to 25 minutes ; then lower the oven temperature to 350°F (180°C) and bake 25 minutes more.
Serve warm.

# RHUBARB PIE
*Tarte à la rubarbe*

PREPARATION TIME : 2 hours 45 minutes

INGREDIENTS FOR 5 TO 6 SERVINGS :
Pie dough from Cheese Cake recipe (p. 324)
2 1/4 pounds (1 kg) rhubarb with partial leaves
Generous 2/3 cup (150 g) granulated sugar
Butter (for the pie pan)
1 egg yolk
Generous 1/2 cup (50 g) slivered almonds
2 tablespoons (20 g) confectioner's sugar.

Make a pie dough exactly as described in the recipe for Cheese Cake, using the same measurements.
Remove the rhubarb leaves and discard, peel the rhubarb, then cut each stalk into pieces about 1/2 inch (1 cm) long. Place them in a saucepan with the sugar and leave for 15 minutes or until the rhubarb has given out water and the sugar has dissolved (stir to help dissolve the sugar). Place the saucepan over moderate heat, bring just to a boil, then lower the heat and simmer for 30 minutes, stirring occasionally (the mixture will thicken and darken in color). Remove from the heat and reserve.
Preheat the oven to 400°F (200°C).
Roll the dough out into a thin sheet on a lightly floured table. Butter an 8-inch (20-cm) pie pan and line with the dough. Place a large sheet of parchment paper on top of the dough — it should be large enough to cover the bottom and sides of the dough and stick up above the edges of the pan. Press the paper well against the dough lining the sides of the pan, then fill the pan with uncooked rice, beans, or lentils. Brush the edge of the dough with egg yolk (this will make it brown nicely as it bakes), then place it in the oven and bake for 40 to 45 minutes.
Remove the pie pan from the oven ; carefully lift out the paper containing the rice or beans (save the rice or beans for baking other pie doughs in the same way).
Pour the stewed rhubarb into the pie pan, sprinkle with the slivered almonds, and place back in the oven for 8 to 10 minutes. Remove from the oven and sprinkle with confectioner's sugar.
Serve warm.

# APPLE TART
*Tarte aux pommes*

PREPARATION TIME : 2 hours

INGREDIENTS FOR 6 TO 8 SERVINGS :
1 3/4 cups (250 g) flour
1 stick (125 g) softened butter, broken into pieces
1 pinch salt
3 tablespoons (5 cl) water
Butter (for the pan)
Flour (for the pan)
1 3/4 pounds (800 g) apples, peeled, cored, halved, and sliced
1/4 cup (50 g), granulated sugar
Black currant jelly, or raspberry or apricot jam (optional).

Make the dough by placing the flour, butter, and salt in a large mixing bowl and "pinching" them together until a crumbly mixture is formed. Add the water and knead lightly to make a smooth dough. Form it into a ball, wrap in a clean, lightly floured towel, and leave for 1 hour before baking.
Preheat the oven to 400°F (200°C).
Roll the dough out into a thin sheet on a lightly floured table. Butter and flour a 10-inch (25-cm) pie pan, then line it with the dough. Prick the bottom in several places with a fork. Lay in the slices of apple so that they slightly overlap each other ; you can arrange them in concentric circles to make a flower pattern, for example (see photo). Sprinkle the apples with the sugar and bake for 35 to 40 minutes.
When the tart comes from the oven, you can spread a little jelly over the apples if you like.
Serve warm or cold.

*Note : This tart can also be made without a pie pan, as in the picture. Simply roll out the dough, place it on a buttered and floured baking sheet, and crimp the edges a bit with your fingers to make a slight border before arranging the apples on it. Ed.*

Apple Tart.

# ALMOND COOKIES
*Tuiles*

PREPARATION TIME : 45 minutes

INGREDIENTS FOR ABOUT 24 COOKIES :
1 egg yolk
Generous 2/3 cup (150 g) granulated sugar
1/3 cup (50 g) flour
1 pinch salt
1 1/2 cup (120 g) slivered almonds
3 egg whites
Butter (for the baking sheet).

Preheat the oven to 400°F (200°C).
In a mixing bowl, beat the egg yolk and sugar until smooth and pale, then stir in the flour, salt, and almonds.
In a separate bowl, beat the egg whites until thick and foamy, but not stiff, then pour them into the bowl with the almond mixture. Cut and fold them into the other ingredients (see Dictionary, p. 345).
Generously butter a baking sheet. Place a generous teaspoon of the batter on the sheet and flatten it out completely, spreading out the almonds with the back of the spoon to make a thin disc about 2 inches (5 cm) wide. When the baking sheet is full — leave lots of space between the cookies — place in the oven and bake for 6 to 8 minutes. When done, the edge of each cookie will be golden brown, but the center will remain pale. Remove the cookies three or four at a time and lay them on a lightly floured rolling pin (leave the baking sheet with the remaining cookies in the oven with the door ajar). Press the cookies against the rolling pin and hold them in place for about 15 seconds so that when they cool they will be arched rather than flat.

*Note : You will have to bake the cookies in several batches. Don't make them more than a few hours before you intend to serve them, because they don't keep well. In any case, as soon as they are completely cool, place them in a tightly closed cookie box. Ed.*

# CHAPTER 14

# JAMS AND JELLIES

The best jams and jellies are homemade. Only perfectly ripe, unbruised fruit should be used in making them.

I think the best thing to cook jam in is a large, unlined copper preserving pan. Clean it before using, each time, by putting a handful of coarse salt and a few spoonfuls of vinegar into it, scouring it with this mixture, then rinsing it out with running water (no soap). Aluminium or stainless steel preserving pans may also be used, but they tend to stick more than copper ones.

APRICOT JAM *(Confiture d'abricots)*

STRAWBERRY JAM *(Confiture de fraises)*

RASPBERRY JAM *(Confiture de framboises)*

RHUBARB JAM *(Confiture de rhubarbes)*

TOMATO JAM *(Confiture de tomates)*

QUINCE JELLIES *(Pâte de coings)*

APPLE JELLIES *(Pâte de pommes)*

# APRICOT JAM
*Confiture d'abricots*

PREPARATION TIME : About 1 hour

INGREDIENTS FOR 8 ONE-POUND (450 G) JARS :
5 pounds (2.25 kg) ripe fresh apricots
10 cups (2 kg) granulated sugar
2 cups (50 cl) water.

Wash the fruit in cold water, drain, and pat dry in a towel. Cut open each apricot and remove the pit ; you need 4 quarts (2 kg) apricot halves for making the jam. Place half of the apricots in a preserving pan, add the sugar and water, and bring to a boil, stirring frequently. Once the water boils, add the remaining apricots and boil for 20 minutes or until the jam is bubbling thickly and coats a spoon. The jam has cooked enough when a drop or two allowed to cool on a clean plate will stick to the plate even when turned upside down. When the jam is done, remove it from the heat and ladle into clean jars. Allow to cool completely, then cover the jars with cellophane for storing.

*Note : Cooking times for jam vary depending on the ripeness of the fruit used. You can use a candy thermometer to test it : generally when it reaches about 220°F (104°C) it is done. When cooked enough, most jams will bead, i.e., dropped onto a clean plate, a drop will hold its shape and not collapse. Ed.*

1. Black Currant Jelly. — 2. Apricot Jam.
3. Red Currant Jelly. — 4. Raspberry Jam.
5. Quince Jelly. — 6. Plum Jam.
7. Strawberry Jam.

# STRAWBERRY JAM
*Confiture de fraises*

PREPARATION TIME : About 40 minutes (plus macerating overnight)

INGREDIENTS FOR 8 ONE-POUND (450 G) JARS :
4 1/2 quarts (2.2 kg) fresh ripe strawberries
10 cups (2 kg) granulated sugar

Wash the strawberries and stem them ; you need 3 1/2 quarts (2 kg) for making the jam. Place them in a preserving pan, add the sugar, and leave overnight before cooking.
Place the pan over high heat and bring to a boil, then boil for about 15 minutes or until it coats a spoon and a drop or two allowed to cool on a clean plate will stick to the plate when turned upside down (see *Note* to Apricot Jam, p. 330).
When the jam is cooked, remove from the heat and ladle it into clean jars. Allow to cool completely, then cover the jars with cellophane for storing.

# RASPBERRY JAM
*Confiture de framboises*

PREPARATION TIME : About 1 hour

INGREDIENTS FOR 8 ONE-POUND (450 G) JARS :
4 quarts (2 kg) fresh ripe raspberries
2 cups (50 cl) water
10 cups (2 kg) granulated sugar

Wash the raspberries. Place them in a preserving pan with the water and sugar and bring to a boil, stirring gently. Boil for 30 minutes or until the jam coats a spoon and a drop or two allowed to cool on a clean plate will stick to it when turned upside down (see *Note* to Apricot Jam, p. 330). When done, remove the jam from the heat and ladle into clean jars. Allow to cool completely before covering the jars with cellophane for storing.

## RHUBARB JAM
*Confiture de rhubarbe*

PREPARATION TIME: about 2 hours

INGREDIENTS FOR 8 ONE-POUND (450 G) JARS:
8 3/4 pounds (4 kg) rhubarb with partial leaves
Water
Granulated sugar
Juice of 1 lemon.

Cut the leaves from the rhubarb and discard. Peel the rhubarb and cut into pieces about 2 inches (5 cm) long.

Bring about 2 quarts (2 liters) of water to a boil in a large pot. Add the rhubarb — it's important that the water *just* cover the rhubarb, so if there is too much, ladle it out, and if there is not enough, add hot water as needed. Bring back to a boil and boil the rhubarb for 5 to 7 minutes, then drain it in a colander set over a large bowl to catch the water used for cooking.

Quickly rinse the rhubarb off under cold running water and drain.

Measure the water used for cooking the rhubarb and place it in a preserving pan. For every quart (liter) of water, add 5 cups (1 kg) of sugar to the pan. Boil the water and sugar for about 30 minutes or until it makes a "thread" when a spoon is dipped into it and lifted out (or use a candy thermometer and cook to 223°F (106°C). Add the rhubarb and lemon juice (it keeps the jam a nice green color when cooked), and boil for about 40 minutes or until it coats a spoon and a drop or two allowed to cool on a plate will stick to it even turned upside down (see *Note* to Apricot Jam, p. 330).

When done, remove the pan from the heat, and ladle the jam into clean jars. Allow to cool completely before covering the jars with cellophane for storing.

# TOMATO JAM
*Confiture de tomates*

PREPARATION TIME : 1 1/2 hour (plus overnight)

INGREDIENTS FOR MAKING 6 ONE-POUND (500 G) JARS :
9 pounds (4 kg) red or green tomatoes
4 quarts (4 liters) water
About 4 1/2 pounds (2 kg) granulated sugar
Juice of 2 lemons.

Either red or green tomatoes, or a mixture of the two may be used in making this jam.

Wash the tomatoes and wipe them dry. Cut out the stems, then dice the tomatoes and reserve.

Bring the water to a boil in a large saucepan or pot, add the tomatoes, bring back to a boil, then drain in a colander. Measure the tomatoes, then place them in a preserving pan and add 2 1/3 cups (475 g) of sugar for every 2 cups (475 g) of tomatoes. Bring the tomatoes and sugar to a rolling boil, skim, then remove from the heat. Pour into a large mixing bowl and leave overnight before making the jam.

The next day, pour the tomato mixture back into the preserving pan and add the lemon juice. Boil gently for 30 to 40 minutes, stirring frequently ; watch carefully, because this jam sticks to the pan very easily. The jam is done when it is very thick and a drop or two left to cool on a plate sticks to it without running when tipped, or even when turned upside down.

Remove the jam from the heat and ladle it into clean jars. Allow to cool completely before covering the jars with cellophane and storing.

## QUINCE JELLIES
*Pâte de coings*

PREPARATION TIME : 2 1/2 hours

INGREDIENTS FOR 10 SERVINGS :
2 1/4 pounds (1 kg) quinces
About 1 1/2 pounds (700 g) granulated sugar
Granulated sugar (to sprinkle over and to serve).

Use only perfectly ripe, unbruised quinces. Peel them and cut the pulp off of the hard, central core. Place in a preserving pan with just enough water to barely cover, bring to a boil and boil rapidly for about 20 minutes or until the quinces are very soft and the water has evaporated. Puree the quinces in a food mill, using a fine grill, or in a blender or food processor. Measure the puree and place it back in the preserving pan. For every cup (250 g) of puree, add 1 1/4 cups (250 g) of granulated sugar. Bring to a boil and boil for 40 minutes, or until the jelly is extremely thick, stirring almost constantly ; if the jelly splatters while cooking, lower the heat.
Pour the jelly into a shallow porcelain pie dish or earthenware platter — it should be no more than 1 inch (2.5 cm) thick.
Preheat the oven to 300°F (150°C).
Sprinkle the surface of the jelly with a little sugar, then place in the oven for 20 minutes to dry out. Remove from the oven and allow to cool completely, then cut the jelly into long bands. Wrap each band in parchment paper or waxed paper and store in a cool, dry place (do not refrigerate), or serve immediately.
To serve, cut the bands into squares, roll them in granulated sugar, and arrange on a plate or platter.

# APPLE JELLIES
*Pâte de pommes*

PREPARATION TIME : 5 hours

INGREDIENTS FOR 10 SERVINGS :
2 1/4 pounds (1 kg) tart cooking apples
Juice of 1 lemon
About 1 1/2 pounds (700 g) granulated sugar
Granulated sugar (to sprinkle on top, and to serve).

Make sure the apples you use are perfectly ripe and not bruised. Peel and core them, then cut them into 6 to 8 wedges each. Place them in a preserving pan with the lemon juice and just enough water to barely cover. Bring to a boil and boil rapidly for about 20 minutes, or until the apples are very soft and somewhat translucent  and the water has evaporated. Puree the apples in a food mill, using a fine grill, or in a blender or food processor. Measure the puree and place it in a large mixing bowl. For every cup (250 g) of puree, add 1 1/4 cup (250 g) of granulated sugar. Stir the apples and sugar together, then leave for 2 to 3 hours before cooking. Pour the apples and sugar into a preserving pan and boil for about 40 minutes or until the puree has become very thick, stirring almost constantly (if it splatters while cooking, lower the heat). Pour the jelly into a shallow porcelain pie dish or earthenware platter — it should be no more than 1 inch (2.5 cm) thick.
Preheat the oven to 300°F (150°C).
Sprinkle the jelly with a little sugar, then place in the oven for 20 minutes to dry out. Remove from the oven, allow to cool completely, then cut into long bands about 1 inch (2.5 cm) wide. Wrap each band in parchment paper or waxed paper and store in a cool, dry place (do not refrigerate), or serve immediately.
To serve, cut the bands into squares, roll in granulated sugar, and arrange on a plate or platter.

# CHAPTER 15

# HOT DRINKS

These are the perfect thing to warm you up on a cold winter's night, or when you're coming down with a cold.

GROG

HOT SPICED WINE *(Vin chaud)*

FRENCH EGGNOG *(Lait de poule)*

# GROG

PREPARATION TIME : 10 minutes

INGREDIENTS FOR 2 SERVINGS :
1 lemon
4 lumps light brown sugar
6 tablespoons (10 cl) rum ou cognac
1 1/3 cup (30 cl) water.

Wash the lemon in warm water and wipe dry. Rub the sugar lumps against the peel to flavor them, then place 2 sugar lumps and 3 tablespoons (5 cl) of rum or cognac into each of two mugs or large, heat resistant glasses (you will be pouring boiling water into them).
Cut the lemon in half, cut a thin slice from each half, and reserve. Squeeze the remaining lemon and pour half the juice into each glass.
Bring the water to a boil in a small saucepan. Place a teaspoon in each glass, add the water, stir, place a slice of lemon in each one, and serve immediately.

# HOT SPICED WINE
*Vin chaud*

PREPARATION TIME : 10 minutes

INGREDIENTS FOR 4 SERVINGS :
3 1/4 cups (75 cl) good red wine
10 lumps light brown sugar
1 large pinch cinnamon
1 clove
1 lemon.

Place the wine, sugar, cinnamon, and clove in a saucepan and bring to a boil.
While the wine is heating up, wash the lemon, dry in a towel, and cut four thin slices from it. Place one slice of lemon in each glass. Squeeze the remaining lemon and add the juice to the pan with the wine. As soon as the wine boils, remove the clove, then pour the wine into the glasses and serve. Hot wine is excellent for you when you feel a cold coming on.

# FRENCH EGGNOG
*Lait de poule*

PREPARATION TIME : 15 minutes

INGREDIENTS FOR 4 SERVINGS :
4 egg yolks
4 tablespoons (50 g) granulated sugar
4 mugs or bowlfuls of milk.

Place the egg yolks and sugar in a mixing bowl and whisk lightly to combine. Bring the milk to a boil in a saucepan, then remove from the heat and wait for 5 minutes before adding it to the egg yolks. Whisk in the hot milk little by little, then pour into the mugs or bowls and serve immediately.

**Serving suggestions :** You can flavor the eggnog, if you like, with a little rum or cognac to taste just before serving ; for children, flavor it with a little coffee, chocolate, or orange flower water.

*Note : In France, eggnog ("hen's milk," if literally translated) is said to be very good for you if you have a bad cold or the flu.*

# DICTIONARY OF TERMS AND PROCEDURES

See also INGREDIENTS, p. 15.

BEAT : When the term "beat" is used, either a wire whisk or electric mixer may be used, unless a specific utensil is mentioned. The term is used most often in connection with egg whites, which are usually beaten until "firm" or "stiff". This means that the egg whites peak and will not slide out of the mixing bowl, even if it is turned upside down. Stiffly beaten egg whites are "folded," not stirred, into other ingredients (see FOLD); they must be used immediately after being beaten or they will separate and become watery.

BROWN or COLOR : These two terms are used interchangeably. They generally refer to cooking a food in fat until the surface takes on a golden or brownish color. Instructions can vary, depending on the degree of color to be attained ("until it begins to color," "until lightly browned," or simply "brown...").
A food should be browned in a pan large enough for it to all sit on the bottom without piling up ; if this is impossible, the food will have to be browned in several batches. Browning is a preliminary operation, so even if the food is divided into batches to brown, it should all be placed in the pot together to finish cooking.
These terms can also be used in connection with roasting and baking ; the meaning is the same, referring to the color the surface should attain.

DICE : To cut meat, vegetables, etc., into small cubes between 1/4 and 1/2 inch (5 to 1 cm) on a side.

DOUBLE BOILER : A double boiler consists of two parts: a bottom, in which a little water is placed and brought just below the boiling point to simmer, and a top, in which the ingredients to be cooked over the simmering water are placed. It is important that the water should simmer, not boil, and that it never touch the bottom of the top section.
A double boiler can be improvised by heating the water in a saucepan and setting a mixing bowl (preferably stainless steel) in it (make sure the bowl does not touch the water).

FOLD : Stiffly beaten egg whites (and whipped cream) are folded into other ingredients rather than stirred, to keep them from collapsing. To do this, spoon about a third of the beaten egg whites onto the ingredients they are to be mixed with. Using a flat, wooden spatula (a wooden spoon may be used, but it's not as efficient), cut down through the egg whites to the bottom of the bowl, then lift or scoop the other ingredients up onto the egg whites, giving the bowl a quarter-turn as you do so. Repeat this motion over and over until the two are mixed together, then add the remaining egg whites and continue in the same manner. The final mixture should be perfectly homogenous, with no unmixed particles in it.

HALVE AND QUARTER : This expression is used for often vegetables, and sometimes for fruits. For long vegetables, such as carrots, it means to cut in half lengthwise, then in half again crosswise, forming 4 pieces. For round fruits and vegetables, it means to cut in half from top to bottom, then to cut in half again from top to bottom, making the second cut perpendicular to the first.

JULIENNE STRIPS : These are very thin strips about 2 inches (5 cm) long. The easiest way to make them is to cut the vegetable into 2-inch (5-cm) lengths, then into slices about 1/16 inch (2 mm) thick. Pile the slices up 2 or 3 at a time, and cut them into strips 1/16 inch (2 mm) wide.

PEEL : Most vegetables can simply be peeled with a vegetable peeler, but tomatoes are peeled in the following way : Drop them into boiling water, leave for just 10 seconds, drain, and cool immediately under cold running water. The skin will peel off easily. Cut out the stem. *Do not seed the tomatoes unless the recipe includes this instruction* (when this is called for, cut the tomato in half crosswise, press each half very gently and give a flick of the wrist to shake the seeds out).

Most vegetables, including tomatoes, can be peeled and chopped up to an hour or two before being used in a recipe, but potatoes should be peeled right before being cooked, because they tend to discolor when exposed to air. Peeled potatoes should not be left in a basin of water — they lose their taste and vitamins.

PREHEAT : An oven must be preheated before placing food in it to roast or bake. Allow 15 to 20 minutes for the oven to heat to the correct temperature. *Never* put food into a cold oven and simply set the thermostat to the required temperature : not only will the cooking time be way off, but generally speaking, the food will dry out (especially when roasting), and cakes, etc. will not rise properly.

PUREE : To crush or blend to a cream or paste, generally in a blender, but a food processor or food mill will often work as well.

Starchy vegetables (potatoes, split peas, etc.) should never be pureed in a blender or food processor : use a food mill, potato masher, or wire whisk.

REFRIGERATE : The term "refrigerate" simply means to put in the refrigerator. It should be kept in mind that many meats and vegetables are stored in the refrigerator. All refrigerated foods (meat, eggs, butter, etc.) should be left at room temperature for at least 1 hour before being used in a recipe.

STICKS, TO CUT : Whenever the expression "cut into sticks" is used, it means to cut into rectangular pieces about 2 to 2 3/4 inches (5 to 7 cm) long and about 1/2 inch (1 cm) wide.

WARM (for serving dishes and foods) : Any hot food should preferably be served on hot plates or serving platters. To warm them, simply place them in a moderately hot oven for 5 to 10 minutes, leaving the oven door ajar so they don't heat too much. If the oven is being used, you can either place the plates or platters in the drawer under the oven to warm for at least 20 minutes, or set them over a large pot of boiling water and cover them with a large lid or another plate turned upside down. All these methods can be used for keeping foods warm as well ; this is generally required when sauces using the pan juices are made at the last minute.

WHISK : Whenever the term "whisk" is used, it always means to beat with a wire whisk, *never* with an electric mixer (see BEAT). It is employed especially in connection with sauces, many of which require the use of a wire whisk if they are to be made successfully.

ZEST : This is the thin, colored, outer layer of citrus fruit peels. It can either be removed in strips with a vegetable peeler or grated off with a fine-holed grater, depending on how it is being used. When the zest is called for, first wash off the fruit in warm water and wipe it dry. If grating the zest, be careful to grate off only the colored part of the peel ; the white, spongy part of the peel, just under the zest, has a very strong, bitter taste.

Whenever possible, use fruits what have not been sprayed with chemicals. These are generally available in health food shops.

346

# LIST OF ILLUSTRATIONS